Reading of Qín Bamboo Slips

秦簡中英讀本

趙 岩
Zhao Yan

［美］
陳光宇
Kuang Yu Chen

［美］
詹富國
Dietrich Tschanz

—— 編著

上海人民出版社
SHANGHAI PEOPLE'S PUBLISHING HOUSE

前　言

20 世紀以来，大量的簡帛文獻出土並被公佈，簡帛文獻也因此成爲當代中外學者研究的熱點。其中，秦簡牘是最爲重要的内容之一。迄今出土的秦簡牘多達十幾批，内容涵蓋 100 多年間的秦社會文化的方方面面，對於秦文明的研究已産生了巨大的影響。雖然專家學者的研究成果可謂車載斗量，但是目前仍缺乏全面介紹秦簡的入門書籍，更缺少可以面向廣大英語讀者的普及性著述，所以我們不揣淺陋，編寫此書。

如何定位本書，本書應該包含哪些内容，這是我們一直在思考的問題。這裏談談本書努力的幾個方向，也是本書的幾個特點。

一是兼顧入門性、普及性與學術性。近些年來，古文字與出土文獻對於傳承中華文明的重要性越來越凸顯，國内很多高校建立了古文字强基班、專長班等，甚至建立了古文字學專業，培養古文字方向的學生。這就需要一些入門性的讀本，來引導初學者熟悉出土文獻、文字面貌，掌握一定數量的字形、詞彙，以滿足他們將來進行專業研究的需要。然而，到目前爲止，還没有一種秦簡讀本可供參考。此外，還有很多人對於秦簡及它所記録的秦文明感興趣，卻苦於没有普及性著作可供參考。本書主要面對這兩部分人群，力圖使讀者能夠通過閲讀本書窺見秦簡面貌，使有進一步學習需求的讀者初步掌握讀懂秦簡的方法和知識，可以用於古文字與出土文獻研究人才的培養，也可以滿足大衆的閲讀需要。

爲此，我們在選篇方面，盡可能選擇篇幅較短、容易讀懂的篇章，對於一些篇幅較長的篇章則截取部分内容。在字詞釋讀方面，盡量避免争議，或者選擇我們同意的意見，或者選擇有代表性的意見，避免大量羅列不同意見，使讀者無所適從。寫作體例方面，在原文部分對簡文做較爲嚴格的隸定，以方便讀者對讀圖版與釋文，寬式隸定部分則採用寬式隸定釋文，以方便讀者做一般性閲讀；不僅在注釋部分解釋疑難字詞，還在白話文部分通釋選篇内容；還在每組選篇最後設置了練習，供讀者檢驗學習成果。

在追求入門性、普及性的同時，本書並未放鬆對學術性的追求。在文獻定名、性質判定、簡牘綴合、字詞釋讀、歷史知識介紹等方面，都努力吸收學術界的前沿成果，盡可能做到前沿、科學、可靠。

二是集成中文讀本與英文讀本。秦簡文獻及其所記録的秦文明是人類文明的構成部分。然而，秦簡文獻在中國外的世界其他地區還缺乏廣泛的介紹與傳播。爲此，本書不僅有中文部分面對熟悉漢語的讀者，還有英文部分供英文讀者瞭解秦簡及相關的中國古代歷史、文化，是中文讀本與英文讀本的集合體。必須强調的是，本書的英文部分，絶不僅僅是中文部分的翻譯，而是有很多再創造的内容。爲了使英文讀者流暢閲讀本書，閲讀體驗更佳，英文部分有時會删掉一些不易讀懂或容易引起誤解的注解及譯文。

三是緊密結合秦簡釋讀。作爲讀本，每一篇選文都緊密圍繞一個目標設計内容，即讓讀者能夠初步掌握秦簡常見字形、詞語及釋讀方法。

本書盡量選取有代表性的選文内容，覆蓋大部分秦簡文獻類型。秦簡所涉及的内容類型是非常豐富的，陌生的文獻類型往往成爲釋讀秦簡的障礙。因此，本書共收録秦簡牘 16 組，前 15 組每一組是一種文獻類型，最後一組則收録不好歸類的兩種文獻，涵蓋目前公佈的大部分秦簡文獻類型。在每一組文獻開篇部分都簡介該類文獻的性質及基本内容等，力争使讀者能夠通過本書概覽不同類型的秦簡文獻。

本書不僅釋讀簡文，還在注釋部分、附録部分拓展相關知識，以保證讀者閲讀其他秦簡文獻的需要。如在第 1 篇《喜》的注釋①中，我們介紹了秦武王至秦二世的世系情況，這涵蓋了目前所公佈的秦簡的年代範圍，可使讀者對秦簡的年代區間有基本認知。我們還在該篇注釋③中介紹了秦時閏月的設置情況，在第 2 篇《三十四年質日》的注釋①及附録一中介紹了干支紀日、紀年情況，以使讀者掌握秦簡所涉日期的解釋方法。再如我們在附録一中系統介紹了秦爵位名稱、行政層級、度量衡、官吏身份名稱、刑罰名稱等，以使讀者瞭解秦簡常見的術語系統，滿足閲讀相關文獻的需要。

作爲第一本秦簡中英讀本，這些嘗試是否成功，還有待讀者的檢驗。我們希望本書能夠對讀者有所幫助，能夠在中華文明的傳播上作些貢獻，也歡迎大家的批評。

Foreword

Large quantities of ancient texts of pre-Qín, Qín and Hàn Dynasties written with brush on bamboo slips and silk have been unearthed since the twentieth century, these texts have become a hot research topic for scholars from China and other countries. Thus far a total of over 10 batches of Qín bamboo slips, covering a period of about 100 years, have been discovered, and many of them have been compiled into a number of corpuses, a treasure trove for scholars to study almost every aspects of the Qín society during that time. Undoubtedly, these Qín bamboo slips have profoundly influenced our understanding of Qín civilization and history.

The discovery of Qín bamboo slips in such a large quantity is considered as no less significant than the astonishing discovery of Qín terra-cotta soldiers. However, this fact has not been widely appreciated even in China, not to mention the world outside China. So far, there is no book available introducing readers to this field, either in Chinese or in English. For this reason, one feature of this book *Reading of Qín Bamboo Slips* is to have both Chinese and English versions combined into one volume. For the Chinese-speaking readers, the English part may help them to become more familiar with the western literature on ancient China and Qín bamboo slips. For English-speaking readers, they may be amazed to find out, even with only limited knowledge on Chinese language, that they can delve into the ancient Qín world. Although the English version follows closely with the text of the Chinese version, it is not a direct word-by-word translation. In some cases, we have avoided a cumbersome annotation in our translation.

Reading of Qín Bamboo Slips aims at the general public and college and graduate students who are interested in ancient China, particularly the state of Qín, and who wish to become familiar with ancient writings of the state of Qín and later Qín Empire. The book contains a total of 44 pieces of reading materials (i.e. text) that we have selected from tens of thousands of Qín bamboo slips in various corpus collections. According to the nature of the texts, we have divided them into 16 text groups (組), covering various topics from administrative, legal, and military matters, personal letters, forensic reports, to the commands and orders from the emperor. For each text group, we start with an introduction of the background, followed with the information on the bamboo or wood slips, and relevant literature references. Whenever possible, we provide high quality photos of the selected bamboo slips accompanied with transcriptions in modern characters (*lìdìng* 隸定), so that the reader can match the modern character, word by word, with each Qín script on bamboo slips.

For each selected text, we introduce the Bamboo Script (原文) that presents the original bamboo scripts in modern Chinese. This is followed by the Annotation, where we provide detailed explanations to new characters and phrases. Regarding words that are still controversial or have different interpretations, we choose the one that we feel most comfortable with. Then we have the so-called Loose Transcription

(寬式隸定), which allows the readers to read the Qín bamboo slips like they read classical Chinese texts (文言文). The sections of Vernacular Chinese (白話文) and English Translation should give the reader a full understanding of the Qín text in modern Chinese and in English. We have included a section of Practice at the end of each text group, so that the readers can test their proficiency in reading the Qín scripts directly from the bamboo slips.

While trying to ensure that the book is accessible to readers who have little prior knowledge of Qín bamboo slips, we still strive to maintain a rigorous scholarly standard and keep abreast with the most recent developments in the field. In addition, whenever possible we also make an effort to relate the reading materials to the historical records and recent archaeological findings. Whenever appropriate we have also included useful information regarding Qín society and culture so that the readers can have a better appreciation of the text. For example, in the Annotation of Piece 1, *Xǐ*, we introduced the list of kings from King Wǔ of Qín to the Emperor II of Qín, spanning the time period covered in the Qín bamboo slips unearthed so far. We also explained how to determine the leap month in the Qín state in the Annotation. The *gānzhī* system for numbering days and years in ancient China is explained in the Annotation of Piece 2 and a table of *gānzhī* is shown in Appendix 1. In addition, we also include a detailed list of Qín orders of ranks and titles, Qín Administrative levels, and Qín Units of Measurement in the Appendix. A list of names of official titles and a list of different punishment methods are also included.

The ongoing archaeological work that is being conducted in contemporary China is generating huge quantities of excavated documents like oracle bones and bronzes of the Shāng and Zhōu Dynasties and bamboo and wood slips from multiple kindoms of the Warring States Period. This has created a great need for paleo-epigraphic education at the senior undergraduate and graduate level. This book, with detailed annotations and translations in modern Chinese and English, and the photos of original bamboo slips, is designed to meet this need. We hope that it will stimulate readers' interest to learn more about paleography and Qín civilization.

凡　例

一、本書收録秦簡牘共16組44篇，1—9組是典籍類文獻，10—15組大多是文書類文獻，有學者將第12組律令類文獻歸入典籍類文獻，但因爲它們與官府文書關係密切，我們暫將其歸入文書類文獻。第16組中的兩種文獻性質較爲特殊，暫獨立作爲一組。涉及睡虎地11號秦墓竹簡、睡虎地4號秦墓竹簡、周家臺30號秦墓竹簡、放馬灘1號秦墓竹簡、郝家坪木牘、里耶秦簡、嶽麓書院藏秦簡、北京大學藏秦簡等批次的秦簡。

二、每組篇數不固定，選取有代表的篇章收録。部分篇章篇幅較長，僅節選一部分。篇章的收録綜合考慮内容的代表性、圖版的清晰度等。

三、每一組包括“簡介”“篇目來源”“參考文獻”“照片、隸定本”“練習”等内容及对應的英文翻譯（參考文獻不譯）。每一篇包括“原文”“注釋”“寬式隸定”“白話文”“英文翻譯”等内容，“原文”對簡文做較爲嚴格的隸定，以方便讀者對讀圖版與釋文，“寬式隸定”部分則採用寬式隸定，以方便讀者做一般性閱讀。此外，本書還包含幾種附録，附録一以表格的形式羅列部分秦制術語；附録二是練習的參考答案；附録三名爲《西方學者秦簡研究論著目録》，羅列本書英文翻譯所參考的英文、法文、德文參考文獻。

四、篇名或沿用整理者的命名，或根據内容重新命名。如第1組葉書類的選篇源自睡虎地秦墓竹簡《葉書》，爲避免篇名與組名重複，我們將節選的睡虎地秦墓竹簡《葉書》命名爲《喜》。再如第25篇原無名稱，根據内容命名爲《新地吏勿廢制書》。

五、“原文”中篇幅相對較長而有必要保留編號的，保留編號，編號一般採用阿拉伯數字編號。里耶秦簡較爲特殊，如8-269號簡，8指簡牘在里耶古井中的層位，269是具體編號，K1/25/50中的K指簡牘出自護城壕，1、25、50是具體編號。有些簡牘兩面書寫，我們會在編號後標明正面、背面。簡文有多列時，用“Ⅰ、Ⅱ、Ⅲ”或“1、2、3”等標明列數，簡文分欄時，用“壹、貳、叁”或“A、B、C”等標明欄數。

六、“原文”部分，異體字、假借字用（ ）注出通行字；錯字隨文注出，對應的正確的字寫在〈 〉内；根據文義或文例補出的字置於【 】内；筆畫不清或殘去的字，用□標示，一個□對應一個字；字數無法確認時，用……標示；脱漏的字或多出的字，在釋文中照録，在注釋中説明；合文符、重文符照録，用（ ）補出合文、重文文字。

七、爲更好地呈現秦簡文字面貌並符合版面，本書所載圖版大小、色彩等都有所調整，有的還會截爲兩段。

Explanatory Notes

1. This book contains a total of 44 pieces of inscriptions selected from Qín bamboo and wood slips collected in the following sources: (i) Qín tomb No.4 and No.11 at Shuìhǔdì, Qín tomb No.30 at Zhōujiātái, Qín tomb No.1 at Fàngmǎtān and Qín tomb No.50 at Hǎojiāpíng; (ii) the well and moat site at Lǐyē; and (iii) Yuèlù Academy corpus of Qín slips and Peking University corpus of Qín slips. The 44 pieces are divided into 16 groups: groups 1-9 are of general types, related to various aspects of Qín society, including daily life, customs, medicine, divination etc. Groups 10-15 are mostly related to official activities, including royal documents, laws, and bureaucratic correspondence. The two pieces in Group 16 are unrelated and are thus put into their own unique group.

2. We tried to find the most representative pieces for each group. We also considered the quality of photo reproduction of the slips and the length of the texts. Thus, the number of pieces in each group may vary.

3. The sequence of sections in each group includes: (i) Introduction, (ii) Text Source, (iii) References, (iv) Photo and Transcription, and (v) Practice. The content of each piece includes (i) Bamboo Script, (ii) Annotation, (iii) Loose Transcription, (iv) Vernacular Chinese, and (v) English Translation. For the part of Bamboo Script, the transcription was made as close to the inscription as possible, so that the reader can see how the original inscription on the slip was written in brush. For the part of Loose Transcription Text, we adopted a loose transcription, so that the reader can read the text like reading classical Chinese articles. In addition to the main body of the book, we include the following appendices: Appendix 1 lists special Qín terminology; Appendix 2 lists answers to the Practice sections; Appendix 3 lists western scholarship on excavated texts of the pre-dynatic and dynatic Qín state.

4. Most of the time, we have assigned the title for each piece as given by the editors of various Qín bamboo slips corpuses. Occasionally we use different titles to avoid confusion. For example, Piece 1 is called *Xǐ*, instead of *Yèshū*, as *Yèshū* was used already as the title for Group 1. Or, in some cases, the original text has no title, so we add a new one according to the content.

5. In some cases, the text is quite long, and it becomes necessary to retain the original numbering of slips. Some numbering systems also include the archaeological source of slips. For example, in the case of Lǐyē Qín slips, the number 8-269 indicates that the slip 269 came from the eighth layer in the excavated ancient well, whereas a number like K1/25/50 indicates that slips 1, 25 and 50 were all excavated from a moat site. Some bamboo slips are written on both sides, and we will mark the front and back behind the numbering. If the original slips contain segments, we will refer to these segments with I, II, III or 1, 2, 3, etc. If the slips contain rows, we will number

the rows with “壹”, “貳”, “叁” or A, B, C, etc.

6. In the Bamboo Script, variant or loan characters used in the transcription will be indicated with the commonly used word put in parentheses ( ); the incorrect word will be noted with the correct one put in square brackets 〈 〉; missing words that can be added based on the context or format are put in heavy brackets 【 】; a smeared or unclear character is represented by a square □; if the number of unclear characters is uncertain, the sign …… is used; omitted characters or extra characters on the slips will be transcribed accordingly, but will be indicated in the Annotation. The fused mark and the iteration mark are also transcribed accordingly and indicated in the parentheses.

7. In order to accommodate the book layout, sometimes we need to re-size the photo of a bamboo or wood slip or adjust the coloration of the figure.

目　録
Contents

導 讀

一、秦簡概述

秦簡，泛指戰國時期及秦代用秦文字書寫的簡牘材料。20 世纪 70 年代以來，已有多個批次的秦簡材料被發現、公佈。到 2023 年末爲止，已完整公佈的秦簡牘材料包括：睡虎地 11 號秦墓竹簡，睡虎地 4 號秦墓木牘，青川郝家坪秦墓木牘，江陵岳山秦木牘，天水放馬灘秦簡，雲夢龍崗秦簡，周家臺秦簡，湖南大學嶽麓書院藏秦簡，北京大學藏秦簡等。部分公佈的秦簡牘材料包括：里耶秦簡，江陵王家臺秦簡，江陵楊家山秦簡，益陽兔子山秦簡等。這些簡牘的出土地、出土時間及具體内容等信息詳見表 1“已公佈秦簡一覽表”。要注意的是，有一些漢墓出土的文獻，也有可能是秦代書寫的，如馬王堆漢墓《五十二病方》等。但因秦漢之際文字變化不明顯，要準確地判定類似的文獻到底是秦簡還是漢簡並非易事，這裏爲避免將問題複雜化，暫且只羅列明確可判定爲秦簡的文獻。

表 1　已公佈秦簡一覽表

命　名	出土墓葬或收藏地	出土時間或入藏時間	具　體　内　容
睡虎地 11 號秦墓竹簡	湖北省雲夢縣睡虎地 11 號秦墓	1975 年	葉書；秦律十八種；效律；秦律雜抄；法律答問；封診式；語書；爲吏之道；日書甲種；日書乙種
睡虎地 4 號秦墓木牘	湖北省雲夢縣 4 號秦墓	1975—1976 年	書信木牘 2 枚
青川郝家坪秦墓木牘	四川省青川縣郝家坪 50 號秦墓	1979—1980 年	命書（16 號木牘正面）；不除道者及天數（16 號木牘背面）；不除道天數及折合款項（17 號木牘）
天水放馬灘秦簡	甘肅省天水市放馬灘 1 號秦墓	1986 年	日書甲種；日書乙種；木板地圖
江陵岳山秦木牘	湖北省江陵縣岳山 36 號秦墓	1986 年	日書木牘 2 枚
雲夢龍崗秦簡	湖北省雲夢縣龍崗 6 號秦墓	1989 年	律令
江陵楊家山秦簡	湖北省江陵縣荆州鎮黄山村楊家山 135 號秦墓	1991—1992 年	遣册
周家臺秦簡	湖北省荆州市沙市周家臺 30 號秦墓	1993 年	曆譜；日書；病方及其他
江陵王家臺秦簡	湖北省江陵縣荆州鎮郢北村王家臺 15 號秦墓	1993 年	歸藏；效律；日書；政事之常；災異占
里耶秦簡	湖南省龍山縣里耶鎮 J1 井、里耶古城護城壕	2002 年	主體爲文書

（續表）

命　名	出土墓葬或收藏地	出土時間或入藏時間	具　體　內　容
湖南大學嶽麓書院藏秦簡	湖南大學嶽麓書院	2007 年	質日；占夢書；爲吏治官及黔首；數書；律令
北京大學藏秦簡	北京大學	2010 年	質日；從政之經；道里書；公子從軍；隱書；酒令；算書；田書；九九術；製衣；禹九策；祓除；祠祝之道；日書；病方；白囊；善女子之方；泰原有死者；傭作文書等
益陽兔子山秦簡	湖南省益陽市赫山區三里橋社區	2013 年	秦二世詔書等

這些材料的基本情况，讀者可以參閲李均明先生等所著的《當代中國簡帛學研究（1949—2019）》。①

二、秦簡的學術價值

秦簡是解讀早期中國文明的重要材料。上述秦簡材料極大地推動了相關領域研究的進展，具有重要的學術價值，以下我們從幾個方面舉例談談相關問題。

文字學方面，秦簡對於漢字發展史、漢字職用史都具有重要研究價值。如隸變是漢字發展過程中極爲重要的階段，但早期的隸變研究限於材料，對一些問題的認識並不清晰，甚至存在一些錯誤的提法，如將隸變開始的時間定在秦統一後。戰國中期到秦末的秦簡材料，爲隸變研究提供了大量有價值的第一手資料，使相關問題的研究取得了極大的進展。代表性的論述如裘錫圭先生的《文字學概要》和趙平安先生的《隸變研究》等。② 趙平安先生提出了隸書形成的時間在戰國中期等新看法，認識更加科學。再如相比傳世文獻，秦簡材料爲我們認識戰國晚期及秦代的字詞關係面貌提供了真實資料。一方面，從中可以窺見戰國至秦代字詞關係的一些變化，進一步瞭解“書同文”的内涵，其中部分變化可參考本書第 44 篇對秦更名方的討論。另一方面，與戰國時期的楚簡及其他區系的文字材料比較，可以使我們進一步認識不同區系的文字材料在用字、記詞方面的不同，從而瞭解戰國時期漢語字詞關係的複雜面貌。③

語言學方面，秦簡材料對於我們認識戰國至秦代的漢語面貌具有重要意義。其中有大量的新詞新義，如嶽麓書院藏秦簡《爲獄等狀四種》中有“單”，是一種鄉民組織，類似的組織也見於東漢建初二年《侍廷里父老僤買田約束石券》，寫作“僤”，這個詞義在同時期傳世文獻中不見，可以補充《漢語大詞典》等辭書。有些詞語雖然見於傳世文獻，但出現較晚，秦簡可以提供更早用例，如義爲直視的“瞗”，傳世文獻最早見於《説文解

① 李均明等：《當代中國簡帛學研究（1949—2019）》，中國社會科學出版社 2019 年版，第 26—33 頁，第 202—210 頁。

② 裘錫圭：《文字學概要（修訂本）》，商務印書館 2013 年版，第 74—79 頁；趙平安：《隸變研究（修訂版）》，上海古籍出版社 2020 年版，第 7—12 頁。

③ 周波：《戰國時代各系文字間的用字差異現象研究》，綫裝書局 2012 年版，第 32—243 頁。

字》，而在放馬灘秦簡《日書》乙種 144 號簡即可見到。① 此類詞語可以提前辭書書證的時間，如《漢語大詞典》收録作爲神名的“北君”一詞，首引書證引自《論衡》，這個神名在放馬灘秦簡中即可見到。秦簡中一些詞語的用法可以糾正傳統上對這些詞語的認識。如“列”與“肆”，以往我們只知道這兩個詞與市場有關，卻不瞭解二者的具體區别。根據《爲獄等狀四種》，“列”是官府在市中劃出的空的商業用地，“肆”是在“列”上修治並蓋蓋兒而形成的商鋪，二者後來才逐漸混同泛指商鋪。秦簡中一些虛詞的用法也具有重要價值。如“與”和“及”、“如”和“若”等，在秦簡與楚簡中的用法存在明顯差異，使我們可以瞭解戰國時期語言的地域差異性。②

文獻學方面，秦簡爲我們呈現了一些以往同時期不見的文獻類别。如《法律答問》《封診式》等豐富了我們對法律文書多樣性的認識；再如《爲吏之道》《爲吏治官及黔首》《從政之經》等宦學文獻，使我們瞭解當時的官吏教育及官吏優劣的判定標準等③；再如《公子從軍》《酒令》等文學文獻，改變了我們以往對於秦代文學文獻的認識；再如《教女》，對於瞭解女箴類文獻的形成、發展具有重要意義；再如里耶秦簡所見的一些文書類别如録、課、志、簿、券、封檢與楬等，也豐富了我們對早期行政文書類别的認識。秦簡還爲我們呈現了一些文獻的形態特征。如通過里耶秦簡，研究者們整理出了秦代不同形態的券齒對應的數字，還弄清了“三辨券”等券的製作方式。④ 秦簡還爲我們呈現了文獻校勘的第一手資料。如秦簡抄寫存在脱漏現象，抄手可以採用多種手段進行補救。其中一種是可以將缺少的部分寫在一枚獨立的簡上，如睡虎地 11 號秦墓竹簡《日書》甲種 129—130 號簡載：“凡是有爲也，必先計月中閒日，句（苟）毋（無）直赤啻（帝）臨日，它日雖有不吉之名，毋（無）所大害。”《日書》乙種載：“凡且有爲也，必先計月中【閒日】，【苟毋】135 直赤啻（帝）臨 136 日，它日唯（雖）有不吉之名，大害 137。”136 號簡僅記有“直赤啻臨”四個字，“臨”字後留白，應該是抄寫者在抄寫時遺漏了這四個字，等到 137 號簡已書寫完成或書寫了一部分後才發現了這一脱漏，於是將脱漏的文字另外抄在 136 號簡上，編聯時將其編在 135 號簡與 137 號簡之間。抄手在抄寫這一篇時不僅有一處脱漏，另外如“毋（無）所大害”中的“毋所”也漏抄了，不過抄手並未採取補救措施。

歷史學方面，秦簡爲法律史、制度史、社會經濟史、思想文化史等領域的研究都提供了非常豐富的信息。首先，秦簡中有大量的法律文獻，而且通過一些行政文書也可窺見法律的實施情況，戰國及秦代法律史研究因此取得了空前的進展。比如在早期中國律與令是什麼關係，這是法律史中的一個難題。嶽麓書院藏秦簡有大量的經過嚴格編輯與整理的秦令。通過這些秦令，我們可以知道：令由皇帝頒布，涉及内容是非常廣泛的，有準則性

① 陳劍：《讀簡帛醫書零札四則》，《中醫藥文化》2022 年第 5 期。

② 周守晉：《出土戰國文獻語法研究》，北京大學出版社 2005 年版，第 119—129 頁，第 148—163 頁；張玉金：《出土戰國文獻虛詞研究》，人民出版社 2011 年版，第 251—280 頁，第 383—394 頁。

③ 雷戈：《爲吏之道——後戰國時代官僚意識的思想史分析》，《首都師範大學學報（社會科學版）》2005 年第 1 期；連劭名：《睡虎地秦簡〈爲吏之道〉與古代思想》，《江漢考古》2008 年第 4 期；張夢晗：《“新地吏”與“爲吏之道”——以出土秦簡爲中心的考察》，《中國史研究》2017 年第 3 期。

④ 張春龍、［日］大川俊隆、［日］籾山明：《里耶秦簡刻齒簡研究——兼論嶽麓秦簡〈數〉中的未解讀簡》，《文物》2015 年第 3 期。

規範，也有指向具體人或事的，還有少部分處罰性規範；除少部分秦令對於律篇的刑事規範予以補充外，大部分應歸屬在行政法範疇；條件成熟時，很多令會向律轉化，成爲正律的一部分。① 其次，秦簡中大量的秦代行政文書及法律文書，爲我們展示了秦帝國的行政運作形態。如通過里耶秦簡，我們知道了秦代由於種種原因，存在部分新佔領區官吏短缺的現象。據里耶 9-633 號簡所載“遷陵吏志”記載，遷陵縣官吏定員 103 人，除去有徭役者及缺員者，實際在崗位的只有 51 人。爲此，秦代官吏居守代理現象大量存在。當某一官署的主官空缺或臨時去職，令史及其他官署的主官等可以臨時代理該官署的主官行使職責。這一制度，保證了部分秦地方政府在不滿員的情況下得以維持高效運作。再次，秦簡也爲我們呈現了秦社會經濟的諸多方面。如里耶秦簡中所見的秦户籍簡，出現了一種以往不見的名爲“隸”的身份名稱。“隸”是一種依附於人的身份 ②，在户版上與家人並列，所在家庭對他的犯罪承擔連坐責任，並可能分得財產，成家分居，但他不爲所在家庭正式成員的犯罪連坐，又與奴婢有相似之處。③ 最後，秦簡爲我們考察秦思想文化史提供了大量材料。如通過秦簡《日書》，我們可以初步瞭解秦人的鬼神信仰。秦簡《日書》中記載了天神、地祇、人鬼、物魅等多種信仰對象，如土神（主管土建）、雨師（主管降雨）、父母與祖父母等祖先神、地蟲等。④ 此外，里耶秦簡、周家臺秦簡中都可見秦人進行“祠先農”的祭祀活動。⑤

歷史地理方面，秦簡爲我們認識戰國至秦代的地理沿革提供了重要信息。如里耶秦簡爲我們呈現了大量秦代郡縣 ⑥，學者據以勾勒了“洞庭郡”及屬縣的圖景 ⑦，而以往人們甚至不知道秦“洞庭郡”的存在。再如里耶秦簡爲我們完整呈現了遷陵縣及屬鄉、轄里的情況，使我們可以以遷陵縣爲個案解析秦代的“縣—鄉—里”三個層級的行政框架的設置。此外，如“道里書”等文獻，可以使我們更清晰地認識秦代的道路交通及水域等情況。⑧

三、如何讀懂秦簡

讀懂秦簡，至少要完成以下四項工作，即釋字、解詞、析句辨章、闡釋文意。下面我們就來結合本書的内容，談談讀者如何能夠完成這四項工作。

① 徐世虹等：《秦律研究》，武漢大學出版社 2017 年版，第 104 頁。

② 賈麗英：《小議“隸”的身份》，《中國社會科學報》，2009 年 9 月 10 日，第 5 版。

③ 陳偉：《秦簡牘校讀及所見制度考察》，武漢大學出版社 2017 年版，第 177 頁。

④ 沈剛：《睡虎地秦簡〈日書〉所見的秦時民間信仰活動探微》，《西安財經學院學報》2009 年第 1 期；晏昌貴：《日書與古代社會生活》，武漢大學出版社 2020 年版，第 299—338 頁。

⑤ 曹旅寧：《里耶秦簡〈祠律〉考述》，《史學月刊》2008 年第 8 期；吕亞虎：《試論秦漢時期的祠先農信仰》，《江西師範大學學報（哲學社會科學版）》2013 年第 5 期；沈剛：《秦簡所見地方行政制度研究》，中國社會科學出版社 2021 年版，第 399—411 頁。

⑥ 晏昌貴：《里耶秦簡牘所見郡縣名録》，《歷史地理》第 30 輯，上海人民出版社 2014 年版；晏昌貴：《里耶秦簡牘所見郡縣訂補》，《歷史地理研究》2019 年第 1 期。

⑦ 游逸飛：《里耶秦簡所見的洞庭郡：戰國秦漢郡縣制個案研究之一》，《中國文化研究所學報》2015 年第 61 期；鄭威：《出土文獻所見秦洞庭郡新識》，《考古》2016 年第 11 期；鄭威：《秦洞庭郡屬縣小議》，《江漢考古》2019 年第 5 期。

⑧ 晏昌貴：《秦簡牘地理研究》，武漢大學出版社 2017 年版，第 189—285 頁。

（一）釋字

秦簡主要用秦隸和小篆書寫，其中，用秦隸書寫的又是絶大多數。這就要求閲讀者掌握一定數量的秦隸、小篆字形。本書收録了一些秦簡圖版，並有對應的釋文，讀者可對照釋文閲讀、摹寫這些圖版。此外，學者們編寫了一些整理秦文字的文字編，如方勇先生的《秦簡牘文字編》、王輝先生的《秦文字編》、單曉偉先生的《秦文字字形表》等，讀者也可藉助這些文字編系統學習秦文字。有一些文字編是整理某一批秦簡材料中的文字的，如陳松長先生主編的《嶽麓書院藏秦簡（壹—叁）文字編》、蔣偉男先生的《里耶秦簡文字編》等，也可以參考。學習小篆離不開漢代人許慎的《説文解字》，因此學習《説文解字》中的篆文字形也是掌握秦文字的途徑。

秦簡中有些文字是用符號代替的，常見的有重文符、合文符、省代符三種。這三種符號往往都用上下兩個短横或兩個墨點標示，指示重文（文字的重複）、合文（將記録一個複音詞的兩個字合寫在一起，或形式上是一個字，但卻要讀爲該字和它的某個成字構件構成的複音詞）、省代時在形態上並無明顯差異，需要辨别具體所指。如本書第4篇《不日可增》載："黄=（黄黄）鳥邪"，"黄"字下方靠右的位置有兩個墨點，這是重文符，指"黄"字重複出現。再如《不日可增》載："吾欲爲怒烏=不=耐=（烏不耐，烏不耐），良=久=（良久良久），請人一桮（杯）。""烏不耐"與"良久"這五個字每個字下方靠右位置都有兩個墨點，指兩個詞語所用文字的重複。有時重文符可以多次連用。如睡虎地4號秦墓6號木牘中"急"字下有四個向右下方傾斜的斜筆，應該是兩個重文符連用，整理者釋爲"急急急"①，可從。類似的還有北京大學藏秦簡《病方》226號簡載："空==以=="，田天先生讀爲"空矣，空矣，空矣"②，可從。再如本書第25篇中的"顯大夫"，"大夫"即合寫爲"夫"，"夫"字下方右側用向右下方傾斜的兩個斜筆表示合文。類似的合文現象還有"粟米"合寫爲"粟"、"數婁（窶）"合寫爲"數"等。還有一些複音詞，只書寫第一個詞素或音節，第二個詞素或音節用省代符代替。如"是="可指"是謂"，"營="可指"營室"。這種省代需要依靠上下文或詞彙系統本身來辨識。③

本書收録的圖版與釋文畢竟有限，如果讀者想要參考其他釋文閲讀更多的秦簡圖版材料，要注意兩個問題：一是圖版的清晰度，二是釋文的準確性。

圖版選擇的核心原則是清晰。一批材料，可能有多種圖版，這時就要注意比較同一簡牘的不同圖版，選取最清晰的。以放馬灘秦簡爲例，早在天水放馬灘秦簡《日書》乙種出土後不久，何雙全先生就在《文物》1989年第2期上公佈了包括223—240號簡共18枚簡的圖版。其後，《書法》雜志1990年第4期上也公佈了少量簡的圖版，照片放大處理後較爲清晰，不過均爲片段。其後，《河西簡牘》《中國簡牘書法系列叢書・甘肅天水秦簡》也收録了少量該批簡的圖版。直到2009年，甘肅省文物考古研究所編寫的《天水放馬灘秦

① 《雲夢睡虎地秦墓》編寫組編著：《雲夢睡虎地秦墓》，文物出版社1981年版，第25頁。

② 田天：《北大藏秦簡〈醫方雜抄〉初識》，《北京大學學報（哲學社會科學版）》2017年第5期。

③ 陳劍：《關於"營="與早期出土文獻中的"替代符"》，復旦大學出土文獻與古文字研究中心網站"學術討論"板塊，http://www.fdgwz.org.cn/forum/forum.php?mod=viewthread&tid=4809&highlight=%E7%9C%81%E4%BB%A3%E7%AC%A6，2011年7月9日。

簡》一書才公佈了《日書》乙種的全部圖版，但由於簡牘保存情況較差，很多圖版上的字迹不清楚。2013 年，孫占宇先生編著的《天水放馬灘秦簡集釋》出版，公佈了絕大部分紅外圖版，但夾雜有部分原圖版。2014 年，孫占宇先生、晏昌貴先生撰著的《秦簡牘合集（肆）》出版，沿用了《天水放馬灘秦簡》一書所用的常規照片，並對應附上紅外照片，而且還附有 2：1 的放大圖版，後者於常規照片和紅外照片中選取相對清晰的作爲放大底版。有一點要提醒讀者，相對於常規照片多數紅外圖版的字形更爲清晰，但也有例外。一些秦簡很早就出土了，多種因素導致重新拍攝的紅外照片相比於早期拍攝的常規照片，整體或部分文字更模糊。

所參照的釋文的準確性，是正確釋讀圖版的關鍵。同一批材料，往往會存在不同的釋文，爲了保證釋文的準確性，讀者應盡量關注以下三種釋文。一是新的綜合整理本。如陳偉先生主編的《秦簡牘合集》，爲早期公佈的幾批秦簡重新拍攝了紅外綫照片，對釋文作了一些修訂，還收録了學者們對字詞的不同釋讀意見，在圖版、釋文、注釋上都有進步。二是校釋本。有時是整理者自己的校釋，如嶽麓書院藏秦簡是分批次公佈的，前三輯分批公佈後，整理者吸收學術界的意見做了釋文修訂本即《嶽麓書院藏秦簡（壹—叁）釋文修訂本》。有時是其他學者的修訂，如《里耶秦簡（壹）》《里耶秦簡（貳）》發行後，陳偉先生等著有《里耶秦簡牘校釋（第一卷）》《里耶秦簡牘校釋（第二卷）》，對《里耶秦簡（壹）》《里耶秦簡（貳）》的釋文做了修訂。三是集釋本。很多學者對某一批次的秦簡做了集釋工作，匯總了不同意見，如孫占宇先生所著的《天水放馬灘秦簡集釋》等。

（二）解詞

認識了文字，不代表就能夠正確地解讀詞語。一方面，秦簡所見字詞關係是較爲複雜的，一個字記録哪個詞，需要辨析；另一方面，一個詞語在語境中是何意義，也需要進行一定的考察。

首先要注意通假字。這裏所説的通假字指廣義通假，包括假借字與本字，假借字與假借字，也包括母字與分化字。以本書收録的第 3 篇《東採涇桑》爲例：

> 東菜（採）涇桑，可以食（飤）蠶。愛般適然，般獨安（宴）湛，食（飤）般已叔（就）歓（飲）子湛。寧見子般，不見子湛？黄$_=$（黄黄）鳥虖，醉（萃）吾蘭林。

“菜”從艸采聲，本義指蔬菜類植物，在本篇中假借用來記録採摘義；“安”從宀從女，本義指安居，在本篇假借用來記録宴請義；“叔”的古文字字形如何理解還存在争議，我們認爲其本義與拾取的動作有關，在本篇假借用來記録完成義的“就”。如果不能正確地辨識這些通假字，而將其讀爲上述字形通常記録的詞，就走入了秦簡釋讀的誤區。在秦簡中，類似的使用通假字的情況是較爲多見的。白於藍先生編有《簡帛古書通假字大系》，收録了古書類簡帛文獻中的大部分通假字，在釋讀秦簡時可以參考。

其次要注意異體字。如《東採涇桑》中的“歓”與“醉”兩個字，與古書習見的“飲”及“萃”，分别是兩組異體字。其中“醉”字很特殊，一方面該字不同於“萃”，改换了聲旁，另一方面用“醉”作爲該字的聲旁，可能又與本篇所述飲宴之事有關，主觀上取聲旁的醉義。

最後還要注意訛混字。秦簡中有一些字形容易訛混，如“列”與“死”。二者最重要的區别是左上方構件形態不同①，“死”的左上方是兩個小斜筆或拉直作一横筆，“列”的左上方則是三個豎筆或斜筆。秦簡中的“列”字常被訛寫爲“死”。類似的還有秦簡中的“冠”常被寫成“寇”②，“走”與“老”會出現互誤。③

通假字、異體字、訛混字都是從字詞關係的視角看釋讀秦簡需要注意的問題。本書在原文部分用符號標示了上述用字現象，在注釋部分也對部分特殊的用字現象進行了説明。

從詞義的視角看，正確閱讀秦簡需要將簡文中的詞一個個解釋清楚，這顯然不是一件容易的事情。因此，本書在每一篇選文後都有注釋來解釋疑難字詞供讀者參考。秦簡詞語的難懂之處主要有兩個方面，一是古今漢語的差異，二是文獻性質的特殊性。

秦簡語言屬於上古漢語的範疇，與現代漢語有著很大的差異，對於不熟悉古代漢語的人來説自然難懂。如第43篇《泰原有死者》載：“祠，毋以酒與羹沃祭，而沃祭前。”這裏的“沃”義爲澆灌，不熟悉古代漢語的讀者不借助注釋或其他工具書就很難講清“沃”的詞義。

即使熟悉古代漢語，秦簡仍然較難讀通，因爲秦簡文獻的性質大多較爲特殊。秦簡中有大量的法律文獻、行政文書、日書文獻、數學文獻、醫方文獻，這些文獻與讀者通常熟悉的史書、諸子文獻等存在較大的差異，也爲秦簡閱讀帶來了障礙。要想讀懂這些特殊性質的文獻，需要讀者先熟悉一些術語。如睡虎地11號秦墓《封診式》6—7號簡載：

> 有鞫
>
> 敢告某縣主：男子某有鞫，辭曰：“士五（伍），居某里。”可定名吏里，所坐論云可（何），可（何）辠（罪）赦，或（又）覆問毋（無）有，遣識者以律封守，當騰騰，皆爲報，敢告主。

這裏的“鞫”“辭”“坐”“論”“赦”“覆問”“封守”等都與司法行政有關，“敢告”“當騰騰”“報”等都是文書術語。從這一篇讀者們可以看到熟悉術語對於閱讀秦簡的重要性。本書在附録部分集中羅列了一些術語，供讀者參考。

（三）析句辨章

秦簡中雖然偶見標點符號，但秦簡所見標點符號並非如現代漢語標點符號那樣完整，

① 翁明鵬：《從秦簡牘“死”的用法説到“死”“列”在秦漢文字中的兩種區别特徵》，《簡帛》第21輯，上海古籍出版社2020年版。

② 王偉：《嶽麓書院藏秦簡（肆）242號簡文勘誤——兼論秦文字中用爲“冠”的“寇”字》，《簡帛》第20輯，上海古籍出版社2020年版。

③ 陳劍：《〈嶽麓簡（肆）〉校字拾遺》，中國文化遺産研究院編：《出土文獻研究》第19輯，中西書局2020年版。

還不足以據此分析句讀。因此，正確地添加標點仍是閱讀秦簡必須要解決的問題。有時，一個句子在何處添加標點會有不同認識，需要辨析。如本書第 12 篇《已腸辟方》載："取肥牛膽盛黑叔（菽），中盛之而係（繫）縣（懸）陰所，乾。"有學者將"中"屬上讀，有學者則將"中"屬下讀。我們同意後一意見，"中"可釋爲"内"，"中盛之"指用置於肥牛膽内的方式盛黑豆。

除了添加標點，析句還要正確地解釋句意。古今語法、修辭的不同，都是正確解釋句意的障礙。如第 4 篇《不日可增》中的"不日可增日可思"，"不日可增"即"日不可增"，翻譯時要注意此類特殊語序。再如第 27 篇《遷陵守丞敬告司空主書》載："謁告遷陵令官計者定以錢三百一十四。"秦簡中的"謁"義爲請求，其後往往直接加動詞，而隱藏請求的對象即"謁"後的動詞的施動者，在翻譯該句時一定要補出"請求的對象"才能解釋得通。有一些特殊的省略現象也要注意。如《遷陵守丞敬告司空主書》載："即走申行司空。"8-135 號簡相似的位置載有"即令走壬行司空"。因此，《遷陵守丞敬告司空主書》中的"即"字後省略了"令"。這一省略不只見有一次，另如里耶秦簡 9-1114 號簡載："即走筭行。"可見這一省略是習慣用法而非偶然的漏寫。再如第 18 篇《取禾程術》載："取禾程述（術）：以所已乾爲法，以生者乘田步爲貣（實），貣（實）如法一步。""實如法一步"的意義是"被除數中與除數相等的部分就是一步"，這在今天看來似乎是多餘的、無必要的解釋，但在當時的表述中卻是必要的。

除了析句，還要辨章。秦簡的辨章，除了一般意義上的分段問題，還包括篇章層次的劃分。如睡虎地 11 號秦墓竹簡《語書》，1—8 號簡是一個部分，9—14 號簡則是另一個部分，兩個部分的字體、寫法都不同，由不同的人書寫，但兩段文字在内容上又有密切聯繫。[①] 再如本書第 28 篇《遷陵守丞敦狐卻書》，該文書包含多個結構層次，詳見表 2 "《遷陵守丞敦狐卻書》結構層次"。

表 2 《遷陵守丞敦狐卻書》結構層次

序號	位　置	内　容
1	"九月庚辰"前	復述"八月丙子"文書的内容
2	"九月庚辰"至"其聽書從事"	"九月庚辰"日文書的主體内容
3	慶手。即令走壬行司空。	"九月庚辰"日文書的書手、傳遞者、傳遞目的地
4	【八】月戊寅走己巳以來。慶半。□手。	"八月丙子"日文書到達遷陵縣廷的時間及傳遞者；打開"八月丙子"日文書的官吏；"八月丙子"日文書的書寫者

此外，"八月丙子"日文書内還記述了"八月丙子"日之前司空與縣廷之間往來文書的内容。如果不能理清這一篇内部的複雜層次關係，就很容易出現誤讀。

部分秦簡的析句辨章要注意綴合編聯。有一些秦簡殘斷爲兩片甚至更多，這就需要我們首先綴合殘簡。同屬一篇的内容往往分別書寫在多枚秦簡上，出土時同屬一篇的秦簡常

① 黄盛璋：《雲夢秦簡辨證》，《考古學報》1979 年第 1 期。

散亂各處，這又需要我們將分散各處的同篇秦簡按照一定的次序重新編聯到一起。如本書第 15 篇《治暴心痛方》注釋⑨中所引的里耶秦簡“治暴心痛方”，由兩枚殘簡綴合後再與另一枚簡編聯。其中 8-1376 號簡與 8-1959 號簡由陳偉先生等綴合①，劉建民先生進一步指出綴合後的簡牘應與 8-876 號簡接排。②

秦簡的析句辨章還需要讀者熟悉秦簡文例。首先，讀者需要瞭解秦簡中的符號。雖然如上文所述秦簡中的符號並不能解決全部的句讀問題，但在有些時候，符號起著重要的標示作用。秦簡所見符號主要有如下類别：“▪”“■”（墨塊大小、高度、寬度不一）“└”“/”“｜”“—”“”“”“”“▲”“✔”等。③這些符號功能不一，可搭配使用。

其次，讀者需要瞭解簡牘書寫格式，包括篇題的書寫格式、分欄、留白（簡文中留出的一定空白）等。我們這裏談談秦簡篇題的書寫體例。一方面，秦簡篇題的書寫位置較爲多樣，詳見表 3“秦簡篇題書寫格式概覽”。

表 3　秦簡篇題書寫格式概覽④

序號	篇題書寫位置	例　證
1	首簡簡背	睡虎地 11 號秦墓《效律》篇題“效”、嶽麓書院藏秦簡“卅四年質日”等
2	末簡簡背	睡虎地 11 號秦墓《語書》《封診式》與《日書》乙種
3	首簡正面簡頭	睡虎地 11 號秦墓《封診式》第一篇篇題“治獄”
4	分别寫在首簡及其他簡簡頭	睡虎地 11 號秦墓《日書》甲種“土忌”
5	該篇第二枚簡簡頭（因爲首簡簡頭有墨塊）	《日書》乙種“盜”“失火”“生”
6	與正文接續在一起，無編繩分隔	放馬灘秦簡《日書》甲種“犬忌”

另一方面，篇題書寫的列數也可變化。多數篇題單列書寫，但有時篇題因爲空間的限制可分兩列書寫，如睡虎地 11 號秦墓《日書》乙種“穿户忌”，“穿户”與“忌”分兩列寫在一枚簡的簡首，正文卻單列書寫。

再次，讀者還要瞭解秦簡的誤寫例及校勘格式。如前文所述，秦簡書寫者會因形近而誤寫一些字形，從而造成文字訛混現象。還存在因上下文形近而訛的誤寫，如《嶽麓書院藏秦簡（肆）》124 號簡載：“金布律曰：市衝術者，没入其賣殹於縣官，吏循行弗得，貲一循〈盾〉。”第二個“循”字本來應該寫作“盾”，是受第一個“循”字的影響而出現的誤寫。⑤秦簡中也存在大量的衍文、脱文現象，還存在文字次序顛倒的錯誤。⑥此外，秦

① 陳偉：《里耶秦簡牘校釋（第一卷）》，武漢大學出版社 2012 年版，第 318 頁。

② 劉建民：《讀〈里耶秦簡（壹）〉醫方簡札記》，《簡帛》第 11 輯，上海古籍出版社 2015 年版。

③ 徐富昌：《睡虎地秦簡研究》，文史哲出版社 1993 年版，第 194—209 頁；王明欽：《王家臺秦墓竹簡概述》，艾蘭、邢文：《新出簡帛研究》，文物出版社 2004 年版，第 28—29 頁；孫占宇、魏芳：《放馬灘秦簡中的標識符號及其功用初探》，《簡帛研究二〇一六》（秋冬卷），廣西師範大學出版社 2017 年版；周海鋒：《秦律令文本形態淺析》，《簡帛》第 23 輯，上海古籍出版社 2021 年版。

④ 程鵬萬：《簡牘帛書格式研究》，上海古籍出版社 2017 年版，第 140—158 頁。

⑤⑥ 周海鋒：《秦律令文本形態淺析》，《簡帛》第 23 輯，上海古籍出版社 2021 年版。

簡中還存在“一字誤寫爲二字例”“二字誤寫爲一字例”等多種誤寫例。① 秦簡書寫者、閱讀者發現上述錯誤後，會採取一些手段進行更正校勘。可以刮削誤字後補上正確的文字，可以刮去衍文，可以如上所述在另一枚簡上補充脱文，也可以在脱文處右側小字補寫，還可以用雙行小字插入補寫。

最後，讀者還要瞭解秦簡的行文結構。有一些類型的秦簡文獻是有較爲格式化的行文體例的，掌握了行文結構，才能夠正確解讀這些文獻。如律令簡常在具體内容之後寫明所屬律名、令名或在一批律令中的次序，第 30 篇《除吏律》在簡文最後記録“除吏律”的律名，第 31 篇《寄長令》在簡文最後記録該令文的次序爲第 13 條。再如第 40 篇《出糧券》，同類型秦簡文獻往往先記録糧食的發放數量，然後記録發放時間、發放人及發放對象，最後記録發放行爲的監督者及文書的記録者。雖然在基本格式之外也會存在一些變體，但出糧券的基本要素大體如上所述。

（四）闡釋文意

能夠正確地釋詞解句，不代表就讀懂了秦簡。秦簡記録的是秦代文明的方方面面，也是秦人生活的方方面面。如何通過簡文探索秦文明，是更加複雜的課題。

本書第 43 篇《泰原有死者》載：

> 泰原有死者，三歲而復産，獻之咸陽，言曰：死人之所惡，解予死人衣。必令産見之，弗産見，鬼輒奪而入之少内。

以往學者們對於“死人之所惡，解予死人衣。必令産見之”的斷句及釋義有一定的争議。我們認爲，“解予死人衣”中的“解”可釋爲“解開”，在語境中指解開並脱掉衣服。在戰國至漢代的傳世文獻中此類用法多見，如：

> 解衣與弟子，夜半而死，弟子遂活。（《吕氏春秋・恃君覽・長利》）
> 今行者見大樹，必解衣縣冠倚劍而寢其下。（《吕氏春秋・慎行覽・壹行》）

上述辭例中的“解衣”都指脱衣。“予”與“死人衣”搭配，一般理解爲給予死者衣。但是結合“解”“予”連文看，“予”在語境中更有可能是與“解”産生了臨時性關聯的動作，特指脱掉死者的衣服後給死者穿上新衣。《儀禮・既夕禮》載：“疾病，外内皆埽，徹褻衣，加新衣。”鄭玄注：“故衣垢汙，爲來人穢惡之。”賈公彦疏：“則‘徹褻衣’據死者而言，則生者亦去故衣服新衣矣。‘徹褻衣’謂故玄端已有垢汙，故來人穢惡，是以徹去之。‘加新衣’者，謂更加新朝服。《喪大記》亦云：‘徹褻衣，加新衣。’鄭注云：‘徹褻衣，則所加者新朝服矣，互言之也。’”這是講當病人病情加重，面臨死亡之際，要爲他脱下不清潔的衣服，换上新衣服。“徹”與“加”，正對應於本篇的“解”與“予”。

---

① 暨慧琳：《先秦兩漢典籍類出土文獻特殊文例整理與研究》，復旦大學博士學位論文，2021 年，第 126—130 頁。

解釋“解予死人衣”，要聯繫下一句中的“必令産見之”。“死人之所惡，解予死人衣”，在一個句子中兩次出現“死人”，這是很不尋常的表述。人們通常會選擇用代詞代替第二處“死人”，但本篇卻並未如此處理。究其原因，第二處“死人”的使用恐怕是爲了與後文的“産”在時間上形成對應關係。“解予死人衣”是説死人所厭惡的是在人死後給他脱衣和穿衣，所厭惡者重心不在“解予衣”，而在於“解予衣”的時間爲人死後。對此後文補充説明“必令産見之”，即一定要在死者活著時見到爲他“解予衣”的行爲，“之”代指的是“解予衣”這個事。“必令産見之”並非如以往一般認爲的是在强調斂衣或陪葬之衣必須生前見到，而是在强調活著時就爲他更换葬衣。這樣解釋，解決了以往“必令産見之”所指事項缺失的問題，找到了前後兩個句子的邏輯聯繫。後文接下來再陳述“弗産見，鬼輒奪而入之少内”，是在交待爲什麽死人厭惡在他死後給他脱衣和穿衣，即爲什麽一定要讓他活著時見到這一過程，因爲死者如果不在活著時見到“解予衣”的過程，鬼差就會將衣服收入少内。

馬軼男指出放馬灘秦簡《丹》的性質是“指導喪葬、祭祀活動的文書”①，我們同意這一意見。《泰原有死者》與《丹》的性質相同，兩種文獻提及的喪葬、祭祀禁忌應該源於文獻創作者的某些意圖。《泰原有死者》强調死者厭惡在死後爲其脱衣、加衣，所作解釋是“弗産見，鬼輒奪而入之少内”，這顯然是恐嚇之語。那麽這一禁忌反映的深層意圖是什麽呢？

《漢書》卷六十七《朱雲傳》載：“雲年七十餘終於家。病不呼醫飲藥。遺言以身服斂，棺周於身，土周於槨，爲丈五墳，葬平陵東郭外。”朱雲要求家人在他死後以他身上所穿衣服斂葬，有節葬的意義。《漢書》特意記載此事，説明對於貴族、豪富階層來説這種情况很特殊，反映了朱雲的品質。我們换個視角看，這一事例也説明“以身服斂”的喪葬方式應該是存在於民間的。不在死者死後爲其脱衣、加衣，不正是“以身服斂”嗎？如果遵從《泰原有死者》的説法，就减少了喪葬儀式中爲死者進行的脱衣、加衣環節，只需保留彌留之際身上所穿衣服即可，自然會節省大量的喪葬用衣，避免了活人的財富向死人流轉。放馬灘秦簡《丹》載，“丹言曰：死者不欲多衣”，也有同樣的目的。②姜守誠認爲：“北大秦牘《泰原有死者》强調殮衣必須是死者生前所見過、用過的，其目的不外乎是爲了减少殯葬衣物的數量，藉此限制操辦喪事時的過度奢靡。”③雖然對簡文理解有偏差，但對於《泰原有死者》創作的目的卻説對了。不僅在隨葬衣服上加以限制，後文還提到，“死人所貴黄圈。黄圈以當金，黍粟以當錢，白菅以當繇”，也是出於節葬的考慮。④

李零曾指出，《泰原有死者》黄圈當金、黍粟當錢等説明死者地位不高，屬於較低的社會階層。⑤陳侃理進一步指出：“這類較低的社會階層也包括地方小吏和普通士人。他們一方面有以錢帛隨葬資格和欲求，一方面又會因此給生者造成沉重的負擔。以象徵物隨

① 馬軼男：《放馬灘秦簡〈丹〉篇文本性質的再思考》，《國學學刊》2019年第2期。

② 姜守誠：《放馬灘秦簡〈志怪故事〉中的宗教信仰》，《世界宗教研究》2013年第5期。

③ 姜守誠：《北大秦牘〈泰原有死者〉考釋》，《中華文史論叢》2014年第3期。

④ 陳侃理：《秦簡牘復生故事與移風易俗》，《簡帛》第8輯，上海古籍出版社2013年版。

⑤ 李零：《北大秦牘〈泰原有死者〉簡介》，《文物》2012年第6期。

葬，對他們而言最爲實際。”[1] 對於大量的社會底層群體而言，其全部的衣服大概也不會有幾件，如果按照相對富裕群體的喪葬方式穿著或陪葬大量衣服，即使部分或者都是舊衣，也是吃不消的。《墨子・節葬下》記載了當時社會底層爲厚葬習俗所累而“殆竭家室”的現象。因此，衣物上的節葬反映了當時社會底層的需求。

總之，“死人之所惡，解予死人衣。必令産見之”的斷句及釋義，是與當時的喪葬習俗緊密聯繫的，必須結合當時社會底層的節葬需求來理解。由此，讀者應該注意結合本書選文進一步剖析秦簡簡文的深層文義，進入秦文明的精彩世界。

上文我們初步討論了秦簡的基本情況、學術價值及如何閱讀秦簡，這些討論並未完全展開，只是提示讀者一些基本的信息及應該注意的事項。讀者如果能夠將導讀部分與後面的各組各篇結合閱讀，相信會有更深的體會。

① 陳侃理：《秦簡牘復生故事與移風易俗》，《簡帛》第 8 輯，上海古籍出版社 2013 年版。

Introduction

1. Overview of Qín Bamboo Slips

Qín bamboo slips refer to the excavated bamboo slips containing texts written in Qín style characters. Since the 1970s, multiple batches of Qín bamboo slips, covering a period from the Warring States Period to the Qín Empire, have been unearthed.

By the end of 2023, the following corpuses of Qín bamboo slips have been completely organized and published:

- Shuìhǔdì Qín tomb 11 bamboo slips 睡虎地 11 號秦墓竹簡
- Shuìhǔdì Qín tomb 4 wood slips 睡虎地 4 號秦墓木牘
- Qīngchuān Hǎojiāpíng Qín tomb wood slips 青川郝家坪秦墓木牘
- Jiānglíng Yuèshān Qín wood slips 江陵岳山秦木牘
- Tiānshuǐ Fàngmǎtān Qín bamboo slips 天水放馬灘秦簡
- Yúnmèng LóngGǎng Qín bamboo slips 雲夢龍崗秦簡
- Zhōujiātái Qín bamboo slips 周家臺秦簡
- Húnán University Yuèlù Academy corpus of Qín bamboo slips 湖南大學嶽麓書院藏秦簡

The editing work of Qín bamboo slips is still ongoing, the following corpuses are partially done:

- Lǐyē Qín bamboo slips 里耶秦簡
- Peking University corpus of Qín bamboo slips 北京大學藏秦簡
- Jiānglíng Wángjiātái Qín bamboo slips 江陵王家臺秦簡
- Jiānglíng Yángjiāshān Qín bamboo slips 江陵楊家山秦簡
- Yìyáng Tùzishān Qín bamboo slips 益陽兔子山秦簡

It should be noted that some of the unearthed documents from early Hàn tombs could also be Qín bamboo slips, as during the transition from the Qín to the Hàn Dynasty, there were insignificant changes in script style. Thus, it is difficult to decide whether the bamboo slips entitled *Fifty-two Disease Prescriptions* (*Wǔshièr bìngfāng* 五十二病方) from Mǎwángduī Hàn tomb belongs to Qín or Hàn. In order to avoid complicating the issue, only the documents that can be clearly determined to be Qín bamboo slips are used in this book. Readers can also refer to a recent review written by Lǐ Jūnmíng 李均明 et al. (2019).

2. The Academic Value of Qín Bamboo Slips

Qín bamboo and wood slips represent authentic and original documentary sources of Qín society and state, before and after the great unification. They are undoubtedly valuable materials for studying China during that period and they have contributed greatly to the research of many related academic disciplines, as briefly discussed below.

2.1 Paleography: *lìbiàn* 隸變, a change of script style from small seal to clerical script, is an extremely important stage in the evolution and development of Chinese characters. Early research in *lìbiàn* was hampered by a lack of source materials. Now the unearthed Qín bamboo slips have filled this gap, and it has been conclusively shown that *lìbiàn* occurred long before the Qín unification. Representative scholarly works are, for example, Qiú Xīguī's 裘錫圭 *Chinese Writing*（*Wénzìxué gàiyào* 文字學概要）and Zhào Píng'an's 趙平安 *Research on Lìbiàn*（*Lìbiàn yánjiū* 隸變研究）. Qín bamboo slips are also valuable for scholars to learn how words（*cí* 詞）were formed with individual characters（*zì* 字）during pre-imperial and imperial Qín times, and to learn the regional differences in the use of words by comparing bamboo slips excavated from different states.

2.2 Philology: Qín bamboo slips are also of great value for evaluating how the written Chinese changed over one hundred years, from the Warring States Period to the Qín Dynasty. With those materials, we can witness the appearance of new words or new assigned meanings for existing characters. For example, now we know the character "*dān* 單," which appeared in *Four Kinds of Prisons and Other Forms*（*Wéiyù děng zhuàng sìzhǒng* 爲獄等狀四種）in the Yuèlù Academy corpus of Qín slips, refers to a local village organization. This helps us to understand an Eastern Hàn Dynasty text *Buying Field Binding Stone Coupons*（*Shìtíng lǐ fùlǎo dàn mǎitián yuēshù shíquàn* 侍廷里父老僤買田約束石券）, where the character "*dàn* 僤" was used as a variant of "*dān* 單," referring to a village organization.

In some cases, although a character was listed in a dictionary（e.g., *Great Dictionary of Chinese* 漢語大詞典 *Hànyǔ dà cídiǎn*）, the appearance of that character in Qín bamboo slips provides a much earlier source evidence. For example, *běijūn* 北君, the name of a god, was listed in the *Great Dictionary of Chinese* as a name that came from *Lùnhéng* 論衡, a well-known book of the Hàn Dynasty. Now we see this name in the Fàngmǎtān Qín bamboo slips, clearly, a source much earlier than Hàn. Many examples from Qín bamboo slips also help us to clarify the meaning of certain words in traditional texts. For example, *liè* 列 and *sì* 肆, in the past we only knew that these two words were related to the market place, but did not understand the specific difference between the two words. According to *Four Kinds of Prisons and Other Forms*, *liè* 列 is an empty lot designated by the local government for commercial use, and *sì* 肆 is a stall or a shop established on such a lot. Gradually the two characters were used to refer to market place. The usage of some function words in Qín bamboo slips is also of great value. For example, *yǔ* 與 and *jí* 及, *rú* 如 and *ruò* 若, etc., have obvious differences in usage in Qín bamboo slips and Chǔ bamboo slips, so that we can understand the regional differences of language in the Warring States Period.

2.3 Textual Research: the Qín bamboo slips present us with some types of ancient texts and documents that we have not seen before. For example, *Answers to Questions Concerning Qín Statutes* (*Fǎlǜ dáwèn* 法律答問) and *Models for Sealing and Physical Examinations* (*Fēngzhěn shì* 封診式) have enriched our understanding of the diversity of legal documents. Other documents such as *The Way of Being an Official* (*Wéilì zhīdào* 爲吏之道), *Being Officials Governing Government Office and Commoners* (*Wéilì zhìguān jí qiánshǒu* 爲吏治官及黔首), and *Practice in Politics* (*Cóngzhèng zhījīng* 從政之經) have shown us how an official was trained at that time and the criteria for judging the quality of officials. Literary texts such as *The Young Master Joins the Army* (*Gōngzǐ cóngjūn* 公子從軍) and *Wine Order* (*Jiǔlìng* 酒令) have given us a flavor of Qín literature that one rarely sees in the received traditional texts. The text such as *Teaching Females* (*Jiàonǚ* 教女) has greatly contributed to our understanding of the genesis of a literary genre known as models for females (*nǚzhēn* 女箴). Some texts such as *lù* 録 , *kè* 課 , *zhì* 志 , *bù* 簿 , *quàn* 券 , *fēngjiǎn* 封檢 and *jié* 楬 that we see in Lǐyē Qín bamboo slips offer us a glimpse of the many different forms of administrative documents of that time.

The Qín Bamboo slips have also revealed many features of Qín administrative documents regarding format and style. For example, through the Lǐyē Qín bamboo slips, the researchers have figured out how the numbers correspond to the different forms of coupon teeth (*quàn chǐ* 券齒), and they also clarified the production methods of coupons such as Sānbiàn coupons (*sānbiàn quàn* 三辨券). Qín bamboo slips also present us with first-hand information on document collation and proofreading. If there are omissions of characters in bamboo slips, scribes can use various remedial means to correct them. One of them is to write the missing part on an independent slip and then to insert the independent slip between the original two slips.

2.4 History: the Qín bamboo slips provide a wealth of information in areas like legal history, institutional history, social and economic history, and ideological and cultural history. A large number of legal documents and administrative documents in the Qín bamboo slips show how the law was implemented at that time. They also clarify many issues in legal history. For example, the relationship between statutes (*lǜ* 律) and decrees (*lìng* 令) in the Qín Dynasty was previously ill-understood. Now, with many collated Qín decrees and orders in the collection of the Yuèlù Academy corpus of Qín slips, we know that the decrees are promulgated by the emperor that cover a very wide range of issues, from criminal justice to administrative and personnel matters; when the situations are ripe many orders and decrees would be transformed into statutes and become a part of orthodox laws (*zhènglǜ* 正律). The presence of legal documents also shows us how the government at the local level operated in the Qín Empire. For example, for various reasons, there was a shortage of officials in some newly occupied areas. The text *Records of Qiānlíng Officials* (*Qiānlíng lìzhì* 遷陵吏志) in Lǐyē Qín slip No.9-633 shows that there should have been 103 officials in Qiānlíng County 遷陵縣 , but only 51 were on duty. We then find out that the vacant government positions at the local level were filled with temporary or acting personnel. Thus, if the chief officer of branch A is absent, the chief official of branch B can serve as an acting one to manage branch A. Obviously such an arrangement ensured a smooth and efficient operation during the time of great expansion of the empire.

Texts from Qín bamboo slips also present us with many aspects of Qín society and economy. For example, in the Qín household registration bamboo slips as seen in the Lǐyē Qín bamboo slips, one sees a new kind of identity title called *Lì* 隸, which was listed as a family member on the household board. The nature of this status *Lì* 隸 in a family has drawn a lot of academic attention.

Qín bamboo slips also provide materials for investigating the cultural history. For example, we can get a good understanding of the ghosts and gods that were popular in the society through several types of *Day Book* (*Rìshū* 日書), such as heaven, emperor, sun, moon and stars, gods of land, water gods, rain masters and other gods, there are gods such as doors and households, a large number of ancestor gods, human ghosts, and other ghosts. In addition, in Lǐyē Qín bamboo slips and Zhōujiātái Qín bamboo slips, it can be seen that Qín people have already had the sacrificial rituals performed to God of Agriculture (*xiānnóng* 先農).

2.5 Geography: Useful information related to the Qín geography can be obtained from the Qín bamboo slips. For example, the Lǐyē Qín slips describe many prefectures and counties, particularly in and around Dòngtíng Commandery 洞庭郡. This commandery was not even mentioned in the received historical texts. Moreover, the detailed information in Lǐyē Qín bamboo slips on Qiānlíng County, its subordinate townships, and jurisdictions, have allowed us to reconstruct the three-level administrative framework of "county-township-lǐ" (*xiàn—xiāng—lǐ* 縣—鄉—里) in the Qín Dynasty. In addition, documents such as *Dàolǐ shū* 道里書 can give us a clearer understanding of the traffic on roads and rivers in the Qín Dynasty.

3. How to Read Qín Bamboo Slips

Reading of Qín bamboo slips includes four steps: (1) interpreting the individual character; (2) understanding the words; (3) analyzing and parsing sentences and chapters; (4) interpreting the meaning of the text. The following provides some instructions.

3.1 Interpreting Characters

Qín bamboo slips are mostly written in Qín clerk script (*lì* 隸), some in the little seal script (*xiǎozhuàn* 小篆). We have included photos of the original bamboo slips. We have also included the transcription, so that the readers can become acquainted with the Qín script. For more advanced readers, the following books can be consulted: *Collection of Characters in Qín Bamboo Slips Text* (*Qín jiǎndú wénzì biān* 秦簡牘文字編) by Fāng Yǒng 方勇, *Collection of Qín Character* (*Qín wénzì biān* 秦文字編) by Wáng Huī 王輝, and *Qín Character Glyph Table* (*Qín wénzì zìxíng biǎo* 秦文字字形表) by Shàn Xiǎowěi 單曉偉. Learning the seal script in *Shuōwén Jiězì* 說文解字,

written by Xǔ Shèn 許慎 of the Hàn Dynasty, is also a good way to master Qín characters.

Sometime a character in the bamboo slips can be replaced by a certain sign as an abbreviation. The most common ones are: the repetitive sign or iteration mark (*chóngwén fú* 重文符), the fused mark (*héwén fú* 合文符), and the abbreviation mark (*shěngdài fú* 省代符). These three marks are often indicated just with two short horizontal lines or two ink dots. It is upon the reader to distinguish from the context which function the marks serve. For example, in Piece 4 *The Day Cannot Be Added* (*Bù rì kě zēng* 不日可增) contains "黄₌鳥邪" (*huáng₌ niǎo xié*). The sign "₌" is an iteration mark. So, the word "*huáng₌*" actually is to be read as "*huáng huáng* 黄黄". Similarly, in the same piece, words such as "*wū₌ bù₌ nài₌* 烏₌不₌耐₌" and "*liáng₌ jiǔ₌* 良₌久₌" should be read as "*wū bù nài, wū bù nài* 烏不耐，烏不耐" and "*liángjiǔ liángjiǔ* 良久良久" respectively. When two characters are fused together, they are indicated with fused marks. For example, for the term *xiǎn dàfū* 顯大夫 in Piece 25, the two characters *dàfū* 大夫 is written as a single word *fū* 夫 ; however, two slanted lines to the right of the word *fū* 夫 indicate that this is a fused word *dàfū* 大夫 . Similarly, *sùmǐ* 粟米 (millet rice) would be fused as *sù* 粟 , and *shùlóu* 數婁 (窶) fused as *shù* 數 . Also, for some two-character words, only the first character is written, and the second one is replaced by an abbreviation mark. For example, "*shì₌* 是₌" in No.114 of the Qín bamboo slips in Fàngmǎtān, refers to *shìwèi* 是謂 (is called), and "*yíng₌* 営₌" in No.143 of Zhōujiātái Qín bamboo slips refers to *yíngshì* 営室 . This kind of omission needs to be recognized from the context or the lexical system itself.

Two issues are essential for reading Qín bamboo slips, one is the clarity of the photographs of the slips, the other is the accuracy of the transcription of each slip script. Both rely on the quality and scholarship of the published work. We have tried our best to select the clearest photographs from all available sources. With regard to the transcription of slip characters, we have paid attention to the following three kinds of scholarly work. The first is the comprehensive compilation of Qín bamboo slips, like *The Collection of Qín Bamboo Slips and Documents* (*Qín jiǎndú héjí* 秦簡牘合集) edited by Chén Wěi 陳偉 . The second is the revised edition of a corpus of Qín bamboo or wood slips based on extensive feedback from scholars in the field, like *Qín Bamboo Slips Collected by Yuèlù Academy* (*1-3*) *Revised Interpretation* [*Yuèlù shūyuàn cáng qínjiǎn Ⅰ—Ⅲ shìwén xiūdìng běn* 嶽麓書院藏秦簡（壹—叁）釋文修訂本]. The third is the collection of interpretations and opinions of scholars on each of a specific batches of bamboo slips, like *Tiānshuǐ Fàngmǎtān Qín Bamboo Collection and Interpretation* (*Tiānshuǐ fàngmǎtān qínjiǎn jíshì* 天水放馬灘秦簡集釋) edited by Sūn Zhànyǔ 孫占宇 .

3.2 Interpreting Words

To know each character does not mean one understands the word formed with each character. On the one hand, there is an issue of the relationship between the character and the word formed with that character (or script); on the other hand, the effect of the context on the interpretation of a word should be examined and considered. First, we need to pay attention to borrowed graphs (*tōngjiǎzì* 通假字), which broadly refers to loan characters. Here, we use Piece 3 as an example:

> 東菜（採）涇桑，*Dōng cài (cǎi) jīng sāng*
> 般獨安（宴）湛，*bān dú ān (yàn) zhàn*
> 食（飤）般已叔（就）歓（飲）子湛。*shí (sì) bān yǐ shū (jiù) yǐn (yǐn) zǐ zhàn*

The characters underlined are so-called borrowed graphs, meaning that the character was borrowed to represent another character, either due to phonetic similarity or due to convenience. In this way, correct interpretation of these words will have to rely on the context. The use of borrowed graphs in Qín was quite common. Readers can refer to the *Book Series of Borrowed Graphs in Ancient Texts on Bamboo and Silk* (*Jiǎnbó gǔshū tōngjiǎzì dàxì* 簡帛古書通假字大系) compiled by Bái Yúlán 白于藍 .

Next, we need to pay attention to the so-called variant scripts (*yìtǐzì* 異體字). For example, the two characters "歓" and "醉" in Piece 3 are variant script of *yǐn* 飲 and *cuì* 萃 , respectively. The use of "醉" here is interesting in that a character *zuì* 醉 (drunkenness) was used as a phonetic sign in the variant, which nicely meshes with the context of drinking and banquet as described in this piece.

Finally, there are the so-called confused and mistaken characters (*éhùnzì* 訛混字), referring to characters that look very similar and thus are quite easily confused and therefore misused. For example, in the Qín bamboo slips, the script for characters *liè* 列 (column) is easy confused with the script *sǐ* 死 (death). Similarly, *guān* 冠 (crown, cap) and *kòu* 寇 (enemy), *zǒu* 走 (walk) and *lǎo* 老 (old) are all easily confused when written as Qín scripts.

Since identification of borrowed graphs, variant characters, and confused and mistaken characters is crucial for correct reading of the bamboo slips, we have indicated these characters in the Bamboo Script section in each chapter and explained these characters in the Annotation section.

There are two main reasons why Qín bamboo slips are difficult to understand: one is the difference between ancient and modern Chinese, and the other is the particularity of the literature. The language of the Qín bamboo slips belongs to the category of ancient Chinese, so it is naturally difficult for people who are not familiar with ancient Chinese to understand. For example, the text in Piece 43 *A Dead Person at Tàiyuán* (*Tàiyuán yǒu sǐzhě* 泰原有死者) contains: "When making offerings to the family, do not pour wine or broth on the sacrificial offerings to moisten them, pour them in front of the offerings." (祠，毋以酒與羹沃祭，而沃祭前。) The term *wò* 沃 here means pouring or watering. Without annotation or good dictionaries, it can be difficult to clarify the meaning of *wò* 沃 here.

Even if you are familiar with ancient Chinese, it still can be difficult to read the Qín bamboo slips, because the nature of most of the Qín bamboo slips are quite specialized, including legal documents, administrative documents, documents of divination and fortune-telling, mathematics, and medical texts, which even students of Chinese history or ancient literature are not familiar with. Many specialized terms used in these documents bring significant obstacles to the reading of the Qín bamboo slips. We have addressed those difficulties whenever they arise in the book.

3.3 Analyzing and Parsing Sentences and Chapters

In most cases, punctuation marks were not used in Qín bamboo slips. Thus, it becomes crucial to know how to parse and punctuate a sentence and how to distinguish one chapter from the other.

In some cases, different punctuation leads to completely different interpretation of the text. For example, in Piece 12 *A Recipe for Treating Dysentery* (*Yǐ chángpì fāng* 已腸辟方) , the text reads: "Take fat ox gallbladder to hold black beans, hang it in the dark to dry." (*Qǔ féi niú dǎn chéng hēi shū, zhōng chéng zhī ér jì xuán yīn suǒ, gān* 取肥牛膽盛黑叔，中盛之而係縣陰所，乾。) A punctuation mark can be put either before or after the character *zhōng* 中 , which will lead to different understandings of the sentence.

In addition to sentence punctuation, careful sentence analysis is necessary. The differences in grammar and rhetoric between ancient Qín and our time can also hinder correct interpretation of sentence. For example, in Piece 4 *The Day Cannot Be Added* (*Bù rì kě zēng* 不日可增), the phrase *bù rì kě zēng* 不日可增 should be understood as *rì bù kě zēng* 日不可增 , meaning the day cannot be added. Another example is Piece 27 *Official Dispatch from Acting Assistant Magistrate of Qiānlíng Named Jìng to the Minister of Convict Labor* (*Qiānlíng shǒuchéng jìng gào sīkōng zhǔshū* 遷陵守丞敬告司空主書), the term *yè* 謁 actually means to request someone to inform. As such "someone" is a hidden object of the verb *yè* 謁 and should be identified during translation to make sense of the text.

There are some special omissions to be aware of. For example, in Piece 27, there is a line: "*Jí zǒu shēn xíng sīkōng* 即走申行司空" on slip No.8-36. However, on slip No.8-135, the text reads "*Jílìng zǒu rén xíng sīkōng* 即令走壬行司空", which means to order Rén 壬 to send documents to Sīkōng 司空 . Clearly, the character *lìng* 令 was omitted on slip No.8-36. Similar omission of *lìng* 令 can also be seen in other slips like Lǐyē Qín bamboo slip No.9-1114. Therefore, we know that such omission is a customary usage in Qín language rather than accidental. In Piece 18 *Method of Crop Measurement* (*Qǔhé chéng shù* 取禾程術), it stated at the end that "The part of dividend that equals to the divisor is one step" (*Shí rúfǎ yībù* 實如法一步). This seems to be redundant to readers, but it was again a customary usage at that time. In addition to analyzing sentences, you also need to be able to distinguish between section sequences, which includes not only the general sense of segmentation, but also the division of events.

In some cases, a bamboo slip was broken into two or multiple pieces, and they must be correctly rejoined. For example, a recipe of treatment of heartburn discussed in Annotation 9 of

Piece 15 came from three separate damaged slips rejoined by two scholars.

In some cases, a document or text was written on many bamboo slips and sewn together with a hemp or silk string. As they were buried underground for over two thousand years, most of the time, the unearthed bamboo slips were loosely scattered, and painstaking work is required to align them in correct sequence for recovering the original text.

The analysis of sentences and sections on bamboo slips also requires readers to be familiar with the styles and format of Qín bamboo slips. Firstly, one needs to understand the symbols in Qín bamboo slips that the scribe used for various purposes including punctuation. The symbols that readers can find on bamboo slips shown in tableau of this book include: "▪" "■" (various sizes) " ┗" "/" " | " "—" "⌇" "⌒" "⋈" " ▲" "✔". Secondly, one needs to know the format of the bamboo slips, including the title, column division, function of the blank space (certain blank spaces left in the bamboo slips), etc. In addition, the number of columns written for the title can also be changed. Most of the titles are written in a single column, but sometimes the titles can be written in two columns on one slip due to space constraints. Thirdly, readers also need to know that scribal errors abound, and how the scribes correct those errors during proofreading. In that case, the scribe would, for example, scrape off the wrong character and replace it with the correct one. If they found words were missing, they would add the missing words in small characters. Finally, one needs to know the type and style of certain Qín documents. For legal documents, whether statutes or decrees, the title of the statute or order would be written at the end. In the case of dealing with a batch of laws and decrees, the number of a particular statute in that batch would be indicated too. For example, at the end of Piece 30, *Statutes on Staff Appointment* (*Chúlì lǜ* 除吏律), the title *Chúlì lǜ* 除吏律 was added at the end. In Piece 31 *Orders on Adoption* (*Jìzhǎng lìng* 寄長令), the number 13 put at the end indicates that this particular order is the Article 13 in this batch of orders. Another example is Piece 40, *Voucher of Food Delivery* (*Chūliáng quàn* 出糧券) which starts with the amount of grain distributed, the time of distribution, the issuer and the recipient, and finally records the supervisor of the distribution and the person who recorded the document. This format is quite standard for the same type of Qín vouchers.

3.4 Interpreting the Meaning of the Text

The Qín bamboo slips record all aspects of the civilization of the Qín, as well as all aspects of the life of the Qín people. Understanding the texts on the bamboo slips would enable us to peer into Qín society that existed two-thousand years ago. The following gives one example on how to achieve that goal through one piece in this book.

A line in Piece 43, *A Dead Person at Tàiyuán* states: "*Sǐrén zhī suǒ wù, jiěyǔ sǐrén yī. bì lìng chǎn jiàn zhī.* 死人之所惡，解予死人衣。必令產見之。" (What the dead dislike: having their clothes changed after their demise. [The living] must let the to-be-dead see the clothes before they die.) In the past, scholars had some disputes about the interpretation of "*jiěyǔ sǐrén yī*."

Here, the character "*jiě* 解" can be interpreted as "untie," which means to untie and take off the clothes. This kind of usage is common in documents transmitted from the Warring States Period to the Hàn Dynasty. However, regarding the character *yǔ* 予 in "*jiěyǔ sǐrén yī*," it is unclear what it means. In traditional literature like *Yílǐ* 儀禮 one sees the phrase "*chè xiè yī, jiā xīn yī* 徹褻衣，加新衣" (remove dirty clothes, add new clothes). Careful examination of the context, we can be certain that *yǔ* 予 is used here as a verb, meaning to give. The use of *jiě* 解 and *yǔ* 予 together here is equivalent to the use of *chè* 徹 and *jiā* 加 in ancient literature such as the *Yílǐ* 儀禮 .

Mǎ Yìnán 馬軼男 has pointed out that the nature of the *Dān* 丹 in Fàngmǎtān Qín tomb is a document to guide funeral and sacrificial activities. The nature of *A Dead Person at Tàiyuán* and *Dān* are quite similar in that the funeral and sacrificial rituals and taboos mentioned in the two documents not only provide guidelines, but also reflect certain intentions of the document creators. *A Dead Person at Tàiyuán* emphasizes that the dead hate to undress and add clothes after death, and the explanation is "otherwise, the ghosts (underworld officials) will snatch it from you", which is obviously a threatening language. So, what is the underlying intention reflected in this taboo?

Hànshū 漢書 volume 67 *Zhū Yún Zhuàn* 朱雲傳 describes that before he died, Zhū Yún 朱雲 asked his family to bury him with the clothes he was wearing. Clearly, burying someone with the clothes the person was wearing probably was a practice among commoners at that time, but for a rich person of high status, Zhū Yún's request for not changing dress before burial is unusual, and obviously gained attention at that time for this kind of moderation. Do not change the dress of the dead before burying serves the purpose of moderation of funerals, and probably is the underlying intention of *A Dead Person at Tàiyuán*, as the practice would then minimize the transfer of wealth from the living to the dead. In the article *Dān* in Fàngmǎtān Qín bamboo slips, it also mentioned that the dead do not want more clothes. It also has the same purpose to reduce the number of funeral clothes and limit the excessive extravagance in arranging funerals.

It can also be noted that in *A Dead Person at Tàiyuán* it is advocated that as burial goods, yellow circles (i.e., soy beans), millet and cogon grass should be used for they represent, respectively, gold, money, and silk in the underworld. A number of scholars have suggested that for the lower middle class of the Qín society during the Warring States Period, on the one hand, they have the qualifications and desires to be buried with money and silk, but on the other hand, this would have caused a heavy burden onto the living. Hence burial with symbolic items with a good justification as provided in *A Dead Person at Tàiyuán* would solve the problem. After all, for a large number of low-level commoners, there may be only a few pieces of clothes in their possession. Burial practice with a large number of clothes, even old clothing, can be a significant burden to poor families. The Chapter: *Moderation in Funerals* in the *Mòzǐ* 墨子・節葬下 describes the death of a common man whose funeral exhausted the wealth of his family. Hence, moderation in funerals reflected the need of the bottom of society.

In short, to read correctly the sentence "*Sǐrén zhī suǒ è, jiěyǔ sǐrén yī. bì lìng chǎnjiàn zhī.* 死人之所惡，解予死人衣。必令産見之。" (What the dead dislike: having their clothes changed after their demise. [The living] must let the to-be-dead see the clothes before they die.), one needs to understand the funerary practice of commoners at that time. Therefore, readers who study the selected bamboo texts in this book should pay further attention to connect the text with the society and culture of Qín time to gain a better understanding of the complex world of Qín civilization.

In summary, we briefly reviewed the basics of the scholarship of Qín bamboo slip research and how to read Qín bamboo slips. We hope the information provided will be helpful to the readers before and after they embark their journey into the ancient Qín world as revealed in the following 44 pieces of texts.

第一組　葉書
Group 1　The Chronicle

簡介
Introduction

《葉書》類文獻最早見於睡虎地 11 號秦墓竹簡，最初整理者稱之爲《大事記》，後改爲《編年記》。李零改稱爲《葉書》，以爲即牒書，但從秦文字的用字習慣看讀“葉”爲“牒”較爲可疑。陳偉懷疑“葉”讀爲“世”，“世書”是記録世系之書。睡虎地秦墓竹簡《葉書》主要内容包括兩部分，第一部分是秦昭王元年（公元前 306 年）至秦始皇三十年（公元前 217 年）期間君王更替以及各自在位年份，第二部分是在對應的年份下分别記録的一些國家大事及墓主的私事，國家大事包括國君的即位、死亡以及國家戰争等，墓主私事包括直系親屬的生死年份及喜擔任政府職務、處理的政務等。分兩欄書寫。

湖北省荆州市出土的印臺 M60 漢墓簡牘與松柏 M1 漢墓簡牘中也出現了類似的材料。印臺 M60 漢墓簡牘也分兩欄書寫，内容爲從秦昭王開始到漢文帝初年之間的君王更替及各自在位年份，還有對應的國家大事，可見自名《葉書》。松柏 M1 漢墓簡牘則記載了秦昭王至漢武帝七年之間的君王更替及各自在位年份。何有祖認爲漢簡中的《葉書》只是空白表格，其重點是提供時間坐標，因爲將被用來記録各個家族不同世代成員所構成的家族世系

圖 1　散落在人骨架上的睡虎地秦墓竹簡
Figure 1　Bamboo slips unearthed from Qín tomb 11 at Shuìhǔdì
（引自《湖北雲夢睡虎地十一號秦墓發掘簡報》3 頁）

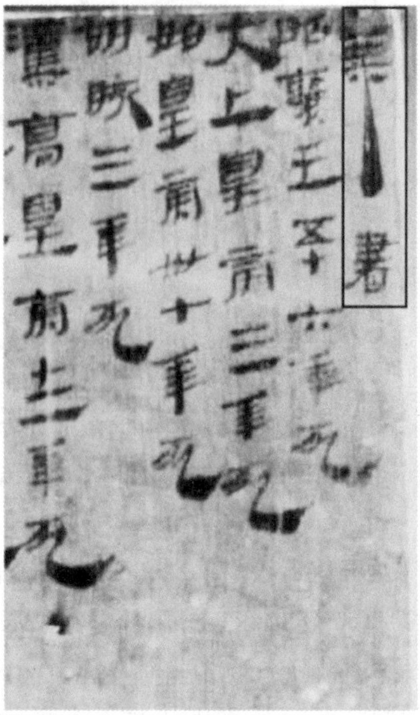

圖 2　松柏漢墓中的"葉書"自名（兩字外圍的框線爲筆者所加）
Figure 2　The Sōngbǎi Hàn slip with title of *Yèshū*（two characters encircled）
（引自 https://www.sohu.com/picture/423008243）

而得名。胡家草場漢簡中有一種自題爲《歲紀》的文獻，由多枚簡牘編聯而成，記載内容也從秦昭王開始，按君主更替次序每枚簡牘記載一年，而且記録該年發生的重要事務，與《葉書》内容有相似之處。

Documents in Group 1 were first discovered in the bamboo slips unearthed from Qín tomb 11 at Shuìhǔdì in Yúnmèng, Húběi Province. Scholars initially called them *The Chronicles of Events*（*Dàshìjì* 大事記）, a title that was later changed to *The Chronicles*（*Biānniánjì* 編年記）. Lǐ Líng 李零, a prominent historian of early China at Peking University, changed the title to *Yèshū* 葉書, thinking that it was itemized documents（*Diéshū* 牒書）. Chén Wěi 陳偉, a leading specialist in Chinese paleography and history at Wuhan University, suspects that *Yèshū* should be read as *Shìshū* 世書, meaning annals or chronicles. The Chronicle discovered at Shuìhǔdì consists of two parts: the first one is the list of kings from the first year of Qín Zhāowáng, King Zhāo of the state of Qín（306 BCE）to the thirteenth year of the First Emperor of Qín（217 BCE）; the second part lists events that occurred during each corresponding year, including major national events and the private affairs of the tomb owner. National events include enthronements and deaths of kings, and wars. The private affairs include births and deaths of immediate family members, as well as career advancements in local government. Each slip is divided into two segments, upper and lower part.

Similar materials are found in Yìntái M60 Hàn slips and Sōngbǎi M1 Hàn slips unearthed in Jīngzhōu, Húběi Province. Yìntái M60 Hàn slips are also written in two segments, the content of which is the change of kings and the years of their respective reigns from the beginning of King Zhāo of Qín to the early years of Emperor Wén of the Hàn Dynasty, as well as the corresponding national events; and the slips were entitled as *Yèshū* by the scriber. The Sōngbǎi M1 Hàn slips record the change of kings and their respective reign years between King Zhāo of Qín and Emperor Wǔ of the Hàn Dynasty. Hé Yǒuzǔ 何有祖 believes that the *Yèshū* in the Hàn bamboo slips is just a blank table, and its focus is to provide time frames, so it is named because it will be used to record the family lineage composed of members of different generations of each family. There is a self-titled *Suìjì* 歲紀 in the Hàn bamboo slips of the Hújiā cǎochǎng 胡家草場 , which is composed of many slips, recording contents that started from King Zhāo of Qín, and each slip recorded important events that took place in that year and arranged according to the order of monarchs, with some overlaps with the contents of *Yèshū*.

篇目來源
Text Source

第 1 篇　喜（節選：睡虎地秦墓竹簡《葉書》1—19 號）

1. *Chronicle of Xǐ*（selected from Shuìhǔdì Qín tomb 11 bamboo slips, *Yèshū*, No.1-19）

參考文獻
References

陳偉：《秦漢簡牘〈葉書〉芻議》，《簡帛》第 10 輯，上海古籍出版社 2015 年。

陳偉主編：《秦簡牘合集釋文注釋修訂本（壹）》，武漢大學出版社 2016 年。

何有祖：《里耶 16-9 號簡“枼”與秦漢簡中的〈葉〉、〈葉書〉》，簡帛網，http://bsm.org.cn/show_article.php?id=3206，2018 年 8 月 16 日。

李零：《視日、日書和葉書——三種簡帛文獻的區别和定名》，《文物》2008 年第 12 期。

李忠林：《秦至漢初（前 246 至前 104）曆法研究——以出土曆簡爲中心》，《中國史研究》2012 年第 2 期。

凌文超：《秦代傅籍標準新考》，《文史》2019 年第 3 輯。

單印飛：《秦代縣級屬吏的遷轉路徑——以里耶秦簡爲中心》，《魯東大學學報》2018 年第 1 期。

睡虎地秦墓竹簡整理小組：《睡虎地秦墓竹簡》，文物出版社 1990 年。

蘇建洲：《説睡虎地秦簡〈葉書〉“喜揄史”的“揄”》，復旦大學出土文獻與古文字研究中心，http://www.gwz.fudan.edu.cn/Web/Show/4396，2019 年 3 月 6 日。

王婧凝：《論睡虎地秦簡編年記的内容和性質——兼論相關以年系事類出土文獻》，《秦漢研究》第 16 輯，西北大學出版社 2021 年。

孝感地區第二期亦工亦農文物考古訓練班：《湖北雲夢睡虎地十一號秦墓發掘簡報》，《文物》1976 年第 9 期。
袁延勝:《荊州胡家草場漢簡〈歲紀〉研究》,《中原文化研究》2022 年第 3 期。
雲夢睡虎地秦墓編寫組:《雲夢睡虎地秦墓》，文物出版社 1981 年。
張培瑜:《根據新出曆日簡牘試論秦和漢初的曆法》,《中原文物》2007 年第 5 期。

照片、隸定本
Photo, Transcription

圖表 1　第一組　睡虎地 11 號秦墓竹簡《葉書》1—8 號簡第 1 欄；
第二組　睡虎地 11 號秦墓竹簡《葉書》1—8 號簡第 2 欄（我們將節選的簡牘分欄編聯，方便讀者閱讀）

Tableau 1: The first group, Shuìhǔdì Qín tomb 11 bamboo slips *Yèshū*, No.1-8, segment 1;
The second group, Shuìhǔdì Qín tomb 11 bamboo slips *Yèshū*, No.1-8, segment 2. Here we put all selected portions in columns for the convenience of reading

圖表 2　睡虎地 11 號秦墓竹簡《葉書》9—19 號簡第 2 欄

Tableau 2: Shuìhǔdì Qín tomb 11 bamboo slips *Yèshū*, No.9-19, segment 2

圖表 1　Tableau 1

第一組　睡虎地 11 號秦墓竹簡《葉書》1—8 號簡第 1 欄	
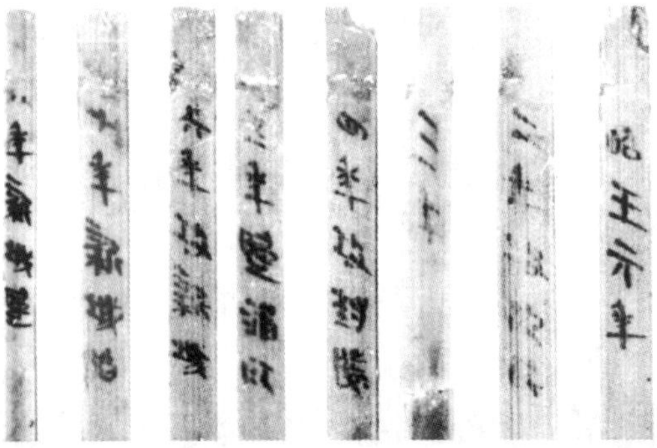	昭王元年 二年攻皮氏 三年 四年攻封陵 五年歸蒲反 六年攻新城 七年新城陷 八年新城歸
第二組　睡虎地 11 號秦墓竹簡《葉書》1—8 號簡第 2 欄	
	五十四年 五十五年 五十六年後九月昭死正月遬産 孝文王元年立即死 莊王元年 莊王二年 莊王三年莊王死 今元年喜傅

圖表 2　Tableau 2

睡虎地 11 號秦墓竹簡《葉書》9—19 號簡第 2 欄

二年
三年卷軍八月喜揄史
四年□軍十一月喜除安陸□史
五年
六年四月爲安陸令史
七年正月甲寅鄢令史
八年
九年
十年
十一年十一月獲産
十二年四月癸丑喜治獄鄢

一、喜
1. Chronicle of Xǐ

原文
Bamboo Script

1 壹　昭王 ① 元年。
2 壹　二年，攻皮氏 ②。
3 壹　三年。
4 壹　四年，攻封陵。
5 壹　五年，歸蒲反（坂 / 阪）。
6 壹　六年，攻新城。
7 壹　七年，新城陷。
8 壹　八年，新城歸。
……
1 貳　五十四年。
2 貳　五十五年。
3 貳　五十六年，後九月 ③，昭 ④ 死。正月，遬（速）⑤ 産 ⑥。
4 貳　孝文王元年，立即死。
5 貳　莊王元年。
6 貳　莊王二年。
7 貳　莊王三年，莊王死。
8 貳　今 ⑦ 元年，喜傅 ⑧。
9 貳　二年。
10 貳　三年，卷軍 ⑨。八月，喜揄史 ⑩。
11 貳　四年，□軍。十一月，喜除 ⑪ 安陸□史。
12 貳　五年。
13 貳　六年，四月，爲安陸令史 ⑫。
14 貳　七年，正月甲寅，鄢令史。
15 貳　八年。
16 貳　九年。
17 貳　十年。
18 貳　十一年，十一月，獲産。
19 貳　十二年，四月癸丑，喜治獄鄢。
……

注釋
Annotation

① 昭王：秦昭王。這段簡文中出現了秦王政（即秦始皇）在内的秦國四代國君，按順序依次爲秦昭王（在位 56 年）、秦孝文王（在位 1 年）、秦莊王（在位 3 年）、秦王政（即秦始皇）。據《史記・秦本紀》，秦族源自顓頊氏，舜時賜姓嬴氏，周孝王時秦嬴（即非子）因蓄養馬匹有功被封於秦邑。公元前 770 年，秦襄公因護送周平王東遷有功，被封爲諸侯，秦成爲諸侯國之一。到秦始皇時統一天下，秦二世時秦亡。本書所載秦簡的書寫年代早至秦武王時，晚至秦二世時。下面列出秦武王至秦二世的世系情況，方便讀者以此爲時間坐標了解本書所記秦簡。具體如下：

1. 秦二世，公元前 209 年—公元前 207 年。
2. 秦始皇，公元前 221 年—公元前 210 年；秦王政，公元前 246 年—公元前 221 年。
3. 秦莊襄王（即本文中的莊王），公元前 249 年—公元前 247 年。
4. 秦孝文王，公元前 250 年。
5. 秦昭襄王（即本文中的昭王），公元前 306 年—公元前 251 年。
6. 秦武王，公元前 310 年—公元前 307 年。

② 皮氏：地名。後文的封陵、蒲反（古書作蒲坂、蒲阪）、新城等都是地名。

③ 後九月：中國早期曆法包含多種，秦國採用的是顓頊曆，一年之中以十月爲歲首，依次爲十月、十一月、十二月、正月（端月）、二月、三月、四月、五月、六月、七月、八月、九月。在部分年份置閏月，將閏月置於九月之後稱爲“後九月”。據學者研究，秦王政與秦二世統治期間，在秦王政元年、四年、七年、十年、十二年、十五年、十八年、二十年、二十三年、二十六年、二十九年、三十一年、三十四年、三十七年以及秦二世二年有“後九月”。由於秦出土文獻的不斷發現，現在已經基本理清了秦王政至漢初這段時間的曆朔情況，具體可參見參考文獻中所列張培瑜、李忠林等的研究。

④ 昭：昭王的省稱，或是漏寫“王”字。

⑤ 遬：即“速”，喜的弟弟。

⑥ 産：出生。

⑦ 今：指秦王政。

⑧ 傅：秦漢男子成年後，需要到官府登記，有了爲國家從事勞役的資格，這被稱爲“傅”。採取的方式是民衆申報，官方詢問並登記其生年，再根據生年計算年齡，登記時間一般在八月。秦早期採用身高爲傅籍標準，男性以六尺七寸爲界限，後來以年齡爲標準，一般認爲在 18 歲時傅籍。

⑨ 卷軍：卷爲地名，卷軍指在卷地發生了戰爭。

⑩ 揄史：選拔爲史。“史”與“佐”是秦基層吏員的主要構成部分。張家山漢簡《二年律令・史律》記録了“史”的培養。“史”的孩子 17 歲時學史，3 年後考試，能背誦、書寫 5000 字以上，能夠成爲史。《葉書》記載墓主喜 19 歲成爲史，如 17 歲學史，19 歲時正好經歷 3 年的學習，與《二年律令》的記載相合。秦時“史”的主要職責是書寫

文書，其有一定的升遷途徑，如據里耶秦簡 8-269 號簡記載，一個名爲釦的“史”在鄉擔任史 9 年多，又在田部擔任史 4 年多，然後成爲“令史”。《葉書》中的墓主喜也由史提拔爲令史，之後又處理案件（大概擔任了獄史）。

⑪ 除：被任命爲。

⑫ 令史：職務名。史的一種，在史中地位更高，往往承擔更多書寫之外的行政任務，如負責某曹的事務、監察諸官署的行政行爲、參與帶隊緝捕盜賊，甚至常常代理縣屬官署的負責人。

1. 昭王 *zhāo wáng*: King Zhāo of Qín. This piece of bamboo text features four monarchs of the state of Qín in the following order: King Zhāo of Qín (reigned for 56 years), King Xiàowén of Qín (reigned for 1 year), King Zhuāng of Qín (reigned for 3 years), and the king of Qín named Zhèng (the First Emperor of Qín). According to Sīmǎ Qiān's Historical Records, the Qín royal lineage originated from the famous Zhuānxū clan, and was given the surname Yíng during the reign of the Great Shùn. At the time of the King Xiào of the Zhōu Dynasty, Qín Yíng (that is, Fēizǐ) was enfeoffed in a place called Qín because of his merit in raising horses. In 770 BCE, because of his meritorious deeds in escorting King Píng of Zhōu to move the capital to Luòyáng, he was named a vassal and became one of the vassal states of the Zhōu Dynasty. King Zhèng of Qín united China in 221 BCE by defeating all other vassal states and proclaimed himself Qín Shǐhuáng, First Emperor of the Qín. The Qín Empire perished in the hand of the Second Emperor of Qín.
   The bamboo slips collected in this volume range in date from the time of King Wǔ of Qín to the time of the Second Emperor of Qín. And cover the reign periods of the following kings of the Qín state: King Wǔ of Qín (Qín Wǔwáng), 310-307 BCE; King Zhāoxiāng of Qín (Qín Zhāoxiāng Wáng or Zhāo Wáng), 306-251 BCE; King Xiàowén of Qín (Qín Xiàowén Wáng), 250 BCE; King Zhuāngxiāng of Qín (Qín Zhuāngxiāng Wáng or Zhuāng Wáng), 249-247 BCE; King Zhèng of Qín (Qín Wáng Zhèng), 246-221 BCE; the First Emperor of Qín, 221-210 BCE; The Second Emperor of Qín (Qín Ershì), 209-207 BCE.
2. 皮氏 *pí shì*: place name Píshì. Fēnglíng 封陵 , Púfǎn 蒲反 (or Púbǎn 蒲阪), and Xīnchéng 新城 mentioned below are all place names.
3. 後九月 *hòu jiǔ yuè*: literally, after the month 9 or post-month 9. In early China, different calendric systems might be adopted by different vassal states. The Qín calendric system chose the month 10 as the beginning of a year, such as October, November, December, the first month (*duānyuè*), February, March, April, May, June, July, August, and September. In years when an intercalary month needed to be added, it is always placed after month 9, and thus called *hòujiǔyuè*, i.e., post-month 9.
4. 昭 *zhāo*: abbreviation of Zhāowáng 昭王 . Alternatively, the word wáng 王 may be missing.
5. 遬 *sù*: equivalent to Sù 速 , the younger brother of Xǐ.

6. 産 *chǎn*: to be born, to give birth.
7. 今 *jīn*: lit. "now or current," refers to the current king, i.e., King Zhèng of Qín.
8. 傅 *fù*: when man became an adult, he needed to register with the government to be qualified to serve the county as a laborer. This qualification was *fù* 傅 or *fùjí* 傅籍. The registration was usually held in the month 8. In the Warring States Period, the height of 6 chǐ and 7 cùn was adopted as the standard for qualifying *fùjí* in the state of Qín. Later, the age of 18 years old was used as the criteria for gaining *fùjí*.
9. 卷軍 *juǎn jūn*: *juǎn* 卷 is the name of a place Juǎn. Juǎn *jūn* means a war broke out in the area of Juǎn.
10. 揄史 *yú shǐ*: to be selected for public office as scribe (*shǐ* 史). Scribes and Assistants (*zuǒ* 佐) are both grass-roots officials of Qín bureaucratic system. The way scribe was cultivated and trained was described in *Statutes on Scribes*, which is a part of *Statutes and Ordinances of the Second Year* in Zhāngjiāshān Hàn bamboo slips. The son of scribe started to learn how to become scribe at the age of seventeen, took an exam three years later; if he could recite and write more than 5000 words, he would be qualified to become scribe. The tomb owner Xǐ became scribe at the age of 19, exactly 3 years after learning the trade of scribe. The major duty of scribe in the Qín Dynasty was to write or copy documents, and there were certain promotion paths. For example, according to the records of Lǐyē Qín Slips No.8-269, an official named Kòu 釦 served as a scribe in the township for more than 9 years, and served as a scribe in the department of agriculture for more than 4 years, and then became a Prefectural Clerk (*lìngshǐ* 令史). The tomb owner Xǐ in *Yèshū* was also promoted from scribe to Prefectural Clerk, and then handled the criminal justice case, probably acted as the Judiciary Scribe (*yùshǐ* 獄史, lit. "scribe of the jail").
11. 除 *chú*: to be appointed as.
12. 令史 *lìng shǐ*: Prefectural Clerk, a position at the level above scribe, responsible for administrative tasks in addition to scribing. For example, they could be in charge of certain Bureau in the government, supervise various offices, and command police to pursue criminal offenders. They can also act as a deputy of a county government.

寬式隸定
Loose Transcription

昭王元年。
二年，攻皮氏。
三年。
四年，攻封陵。
五年，歸蒲坂。

六年，攻新城。
七年，新城陷。
八年，新城歸。
……
五十四年。
五十五年。
五十六年，後九月，昭死。正月，速産。
孝文王元年，立即死。
莊王元年。
莊王二年。
莊王三年，莊王死。
今元年，喜傅。
二年。
三年，卷軍。八月，喜揄史。
四年，□軍。十一月，喜除安陸□史。
五年。
六年，四月，爲安陸令史。
七年，正月甲寅，鄢令史。
八年。
九年。
十年。
十一年，十一月，獲産。
十二年，四月癸丑，喜治獄鄢。
……

白話文

Vernacular Chinese

昭王元年。
二年，攻打皮氏。
三年。
四年，攻打封陵。
五年，歸還蒲坂。
六年，攻打新城。
七年，新城陷落。
八年，新城回歸楚國。
……

五十四年。
五十五年。
五十六年，後九月，昭王死。一月，速出生。
孝文王元年，立爲王就死了。
莊王元年。
莊王二年。
莊王三年，莊王死。
秦王政元年，喜傅籍。
二年。
三年，卷地發生戰爭。八月，喜選拔爲史。
四年，某地發生戰爭。十一月，喜被任命爲安陸縣某史。
五年。
六年，四月，成爲安陸縣令史。
七年，正月甲寅，成爲鄢縣令史。
八年。
九年。
十年。
十一年，十一月，獲出生。
十二年，四月癸丑，喜處理鄢縣的案件。
……

英文翻譯
English Translation

First year of King Zhāo.
Second year: [King Zhāo] attacked the Píshì area.
Third year.
Fourth year: [King Zhāo] attacked the Fēnglíng area.
Fifth year: [King Zhāo] returned to the Púbǎn area.
Sixth year: [King Zhāo] attacked Xīnchéng City.
Seventh year: Xīnchéng City was occupied.
Eighth year: Xīnchéng City was recaptuned by Chǔ.
[...]
Year fifty-four.
Year fifty-five.
Year fifty-six: in the post-month 9 (i.e., leap month), King Zhāo died. In the first month, Sù was born.

First year of King Xiàowén: the King died immediately following installation.
First year of King Zhuāng.
Second year of King Zhuāng.
Third year of King Zhuāng: King Zhuāng died.
First year of the current king [i.e., King named Zhèng, later known as the First Emperor of Qín] : Xǐ registered as an adult.
Second year.
Third year: war broke out in the area of Juǎn. In the eighth month, Xǐ was appointed as scribe.
Fourth year: war [broke out somewhere] . (Place name is unclear) In the eleventh month, Xǐ was appointed as a certain class of scribe in Ānlù County.
Fifth year.
Sixth year: in the fourth month, [Xǐ] became Prefectural Clerk (*lìngshǐ*) of Ānlù County.
Seventh year: on the *jiǎyín* day of the first month, [Xǐ] became Prefectural Clerk of Yān County.
Eighth year.
Ninth year.
Tenth year.
Eleventh year: in the eleventh month, Huò was born.
Twelfth year: on the *guǐchǒu* day of the fourth month, Xǐ handled criminal cases of Yān County.
[…]

練習
Practice

釋讀圖表 3 中的幾枚《葉書》簡。(睡虎地秦墓竹簡《葉書》23、32、33、45 號)
Read slips in Tableau 3. (Shuìhǔdì Qín tomb 11 bamboo slips, *Yèshū*, No.23, 32, 33, 45)

圖表 3　Tableau 3

睡虎地《葉書》45	睡虎地《葉書》33		睡虎地《葉書》32		睡虎地《葉書》23	
上	下	上	下	上	下	上
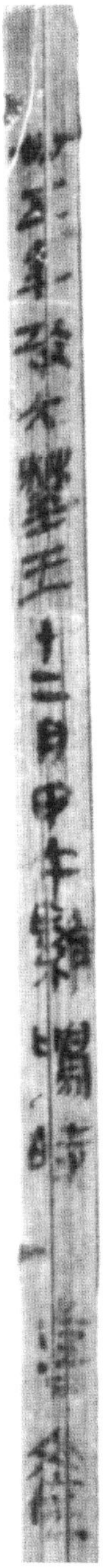	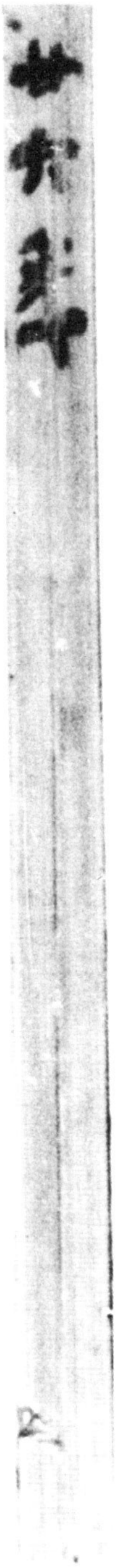		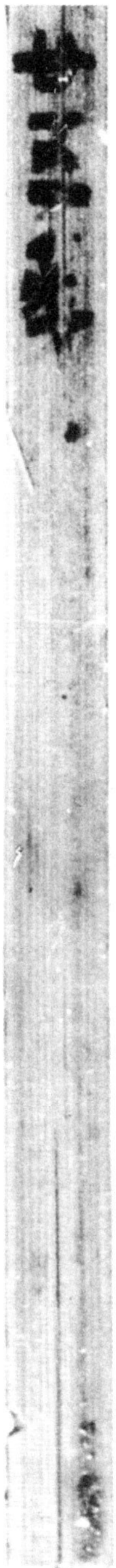	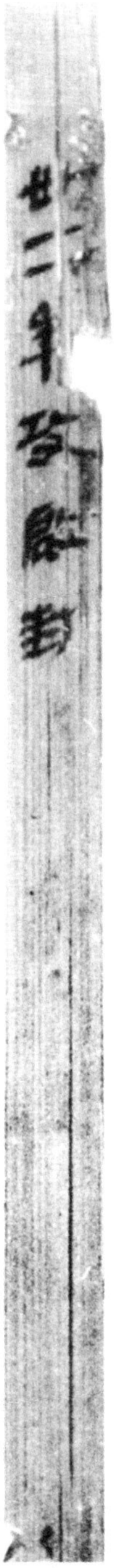	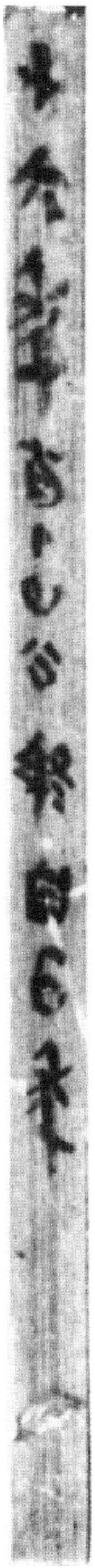	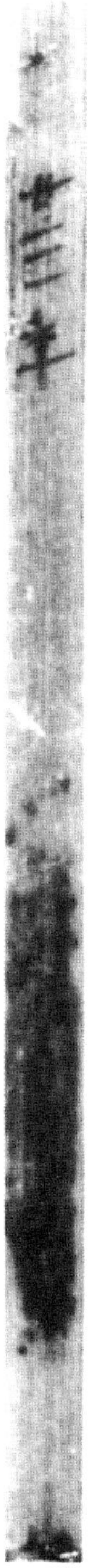

第二組　質日
Group 2　Zhìrì

簡介
Introduction

質日，是一種可以用於查檢歲時節日、記録事務及配合日書類文獻占卜吉凶的文獻。其内容主要包含月名大小、朔日干支、節氣等曆日信息及部分日期下對應的公私事務。以往或被稱爲“曆譜”。一般一枚簡分爲六欄，每一欄記載一日的干支，部分干支下記載該日所從事的事務。從次序上看，往往是偶數月居前，奇數月居後，如果該年存在後九月，則居於最後。

目前能看到的秦簡牘“質日”主要有周家臺 30 號秦墓《三十四年質日》，嶽麓書院藏秦簡《二十七年質日》《三十四年質日》《三十五年私質日》，都是秦始皇時期的“質日”。北大藏秦簡中也有兩篇“質日”，據整理者介紹，這兩篇分别是秦始皇三十一年、三十三年的“質日”，大體内容類似。值得注意的是這兩種“質日”在部分干支下還可見到記載當日的建除。建除是古代數術家按一定的規律將干支日規定爲建日、除日等 12 種日名，分别對應一定的人事宜忌，用以擇日。這也進一步説明“質日”配合《日書》使用的功能。此外，由於存在《三十五年私質日》的題名，“質日”可能還存在公私之别，即還存在官府用“質日”。

漢墓中也多見“質日”類文獻，如睡虎地 M77 號墓《元年質日》《七年質日》等。

The term *zhìrì* 質日 (lit. “inquire the day”) refers to a group of documents in Qín and pre-Qín bamboo slips that were used as calendars to check dates, festivals, and to record special events or daily affairs, in conjunction with *rìshū* 日書 that were used to deal with divination and fortune-telling. The content of *zhìrì* mainly includes calendar information such as the names of the solar and lunar months, the stem-branch signs of the first day in a month, and the twenty-four solar terms. They also included dates of important private affairs and public events. In the past, *zhìrì* may simply be called Calendar. Generally, a piece of bamboo is divided into six segments, each segment records the day’s stem branch, and in some cases the affairs that occurred on that day. It appears that the records were arranged to have the even-numbered months first, to be followed by the odd-numbered months. For the leap year the leap month (*hòujiǔyuè* 後九月) would be put at the end.

In the vast corpus of Qín bamboo slips the following slips are of the type of *zhìrì*: *Calendar of Thirty-fourth Year* unearthed from Qín tomb 30 at Zhōujiātái, Jīngzhōu, Húběi Province; *Calendar of Twenty-Seventh Year* in the Yuèlù Academy corpus of Qín slips; *Calendar of Thirty-fourth Year* in the Yuèlù Academy corpus of Qín slips; *Private Calendar of Thirty-fifth Year* in the Yuèlù Academy corpus of Qín slips. All of them belong to the time period of the First Emperor of Qín. There are also two examples of *zhìrì* in the Peking University corpus of Qín bamboo slips; unfortunately, they have not yet been fully published. They are *zhìrì* of the years 31 and 33 of the First Emperor of Qín, and they are roughly similar in content. It is worth noting that these two examples of *zhìrì* contain information about the so-called *jiànchú* 建除（see below）under certain dates.

The word *jiànchú* is an astrological term. According to astrologists in pre-Qín time, the *gānzhī* 干支 days were assigned with 12 names called *jiànrì* 建日, *chúrì* 除日, etc. Each name corresponds to certain taboos for certain affairs. The assignment helped laymen and astrologers to choose the proper day for performing certain personal or public affairs. This also further illustrates the function of *zhìrì* in conjunction with *rìshū*. In addition, given the existence of the *Private Calendar of Thirty-fifth Year*, there may be a distinction between private and government *zhìrì*.

There are also many documents of *zhìrì* in Hàn tombs, such as *Calendar of the First Year* and *Calendar of the Seventh Year* in Shuìhǔdì Hàn tomb 77.

篇目來源
Text Source

第 2 篇　三十四年質日（節選：周家臺 30 號秦墓竹簡 29—58 號）

2. *Calendar of Thirty-fourth Year*（selected from Zhōujiātái Qín tomb 30 bamboo slips, No.29-58）

參考文獻
References

陳侃理：《出土秦漢曆書綜論》，楊振紅、鄔文玲主編：《簡帛研究二〇一六》（秋冬卷），廣西師範大學出版社 2016 年。

陳偉主編：《秦簡牘合集釋文注釋修訂本（叁）》，武漢大學出版社 2016 年。

程少軒：《周家臺秦簡〈日書〉與〈卅六年日〉編聯補説》，《簡帛》第 8 輯，上海古籍出版社 2013 年。

郭濤：《秦代南郡“陰”地考》，《中國歷史地理論叢》2015 年第 4 期。

郭濤：《周家臺 30 號秦墓竹簡“秦始皇三十四年質日”釋地》，《歷史地理》第 26 輯，上海人民出版社 2012 年。

温俊萍：《嶽麓書院藏秦簡〈質日〉研究綜述》，《簡牘學研究》第 7 輯，甘肅人民出版社 2018 年。

照片、隸定本
Photo, Transcription

圖表 1　周家臺 30 號秦墓竹簡 29、30、35、36 號簡

Tableau 1: Zhōujiātái Qín tomb 30 bamboo slips, No.29, 30, 35, 36

圖表 2　周家臺 30 號秦墓竹簡 53、54、57、58 號簡

Tableau 2: Zhōujiātái Qín tomb 30 bamboo slips, No.53, 54, 57, 58

圖表 1　Tableau 1

周家臺《質日》36			周家臺《質日》35			周家臺《質日》30			周家臺《質日》29		
隸定	照片（下）	照片（上）	隸定	照片（下）	照片（上）	隸定	照片（下）	照片（上）	隸定	照片（下）	照片（上）
甲戌 甲戌 壬申治 辛未 庚午 庚午			癸酉 癸酉 辛未治後府 庚午 己巳 己巳			戊辰 戊辰 丙寅治競陵 乙丑 甲子 甲子			十一月丁卯 正月丁卯嘉平視事 三月乙丑治競陵 五月甲子 七月癸亥 九月癸亥		

圖表 2　Tableau 2

周家臺《質日》58			周家臺《質日》57			周家臺《質日》54			周家臺《質日》53		
隸定	照片（下）	照片（上）	隸定	照片（下）	照片（上）	隸定	照片（下）	照片（上）	隸定	照片（下）	照片（上）
丙申 甲午并左曹 癸巳 壬辰 壬辰	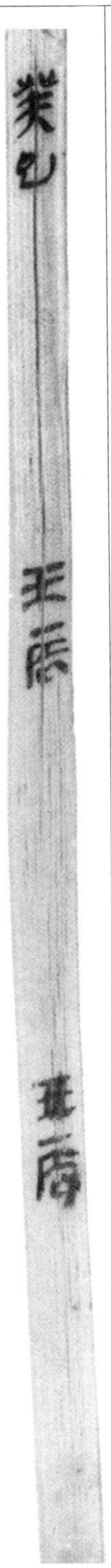		乙未 乙未宿尋平 癸巳 壬辰 辛卯 辛卯			壬辰 壬辰宿迣離涌東 庚寅 己丑 戊子 戊子	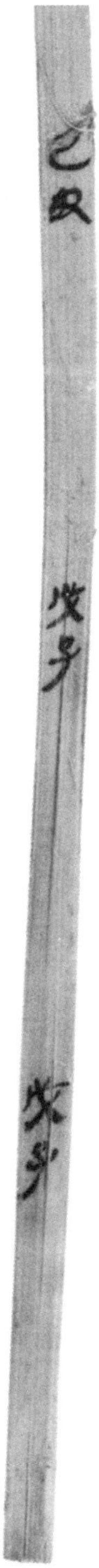		辛卯 辛卯宿迣羅涌西 己丑論脩賜 戊子 丁亥 丁亥		

二、三十四年質日
2. Calendar of Thirty-fourth Year

原文

Bamboo Script

十一月 丁卯 ①	正月丁卯 嘉平 ② 視事 ③。	三月乙丑 治競（竟）陵。	五月 甲子	七月 癸亥	九月 癸亥	29
戊辰	戊辰	丙寅 治競（竟）陵。	乙丑	甲子	甲子	30
己巳	己巳	丁卯 宿□上。	丙寅	乙丑	乙丑	31
庚午	庚午	戊辰 宿路陰。	丁卯	丙寅	丙寅	32
辛未	辛未	己巳 宿江陵。	戊辰	丁卯	丁卯	33
壬申	壬申	庚午 到江陵。	己巳	戊辰	戊辰	34
癸酉	癸酉	辛未 治後府 ⑩。	庚午	己巳	己巳	35
甲戌	甲戌	壬申 治。	辛未	庚午	庚午	36
乙亥	乙亥	癸酉 治。	壬申	辛未	辛未	37
丙子	丙子	甲戌	癸酉	壬申	壬申	38
丁丑	丁丑	乙亥	甲戌	癸酉	癸酉	39
戊寅	戊寅	丙子	乙亥	甲戌	甲戌	40
己卯	己卯	丁丑	丙子	乙亥	乙亥	41
庚辰	庚辰	戊寅	丁丑	丙子	丙子	42
辛巳	辛巳	己卯	戊寅	丁丑	丁丑	43
壬午	壬午	庚辰	己卯	戊寅	戊寅	44

（續表）

癸未	癸未	辛巳 賜⑪。	庚辰	己卯	己卯	45
甲申	甲申	壬午	辛巳	庚辰	庚辰	46
乙酉	乙酉	癸未 奏⑫上。	壬午	辛巳	辛巳	47
丙戌	丙戌	甲申 史𢕟⑬（徹）行。	癸未	壬午	壬午	48
丁亥	丁亥 史除④不坐⑤掾曹⑥。 從公⑦，宿長道⑧。	乙酉	甲申	癸未	癸未	49
戊子	戊子 宿迣羸邑北上蒲。	丙戌 後事已。	乙酉	甲申	甲申	50
己丑	己丑 宿迣離涌西。	丁亥 治競（竟）陵。	丙戌	乙酉	乙酉	51
庚寅	庚寅 宿迣□□郵⑨北。	戊子	丁亥	丙戌	丙戌	52
辛卯	辛卯 宿迣羅涌西。	己丑 論⑭脩、賜⑮。	戊子	丁亥	丁亥	53
壬辰	壬辰 宿迣離涌東。	庚寅	己丑	戊子	戊子	54
癸巳	癸巳 宿區邑。	辛卯	庚寅	己丑	己丑	55
甲午	甲午 宿競（竟）陵。	壬辰	辛卯	庚寅	庚寅	56
乙未	乙未 宿尋平。	癸巳	壬辰	辛卯	辛卯	57
丙申		甲午 并⑯左曹⑰。	癸巳	壬辰	壬辰	58

注釋

Annotation

① 這組簡的閱讀要從29號簡第1欄的十一月丁卯開始，然後是30號簡第1欄的戊辰，

依次到 58 號簡第 1 欄的丙申，這是該年十一月的完整紀日。然後再從 29 號簡第 2 欄的正月丁卯開始，以此類推。丁卯、戊辰等採用天干（包括甲、乙、丙、丁、戊、己、庚、辛、壬、癸）、地支（包括子、丑、寅、卯、辰、巳、午、未、申、酉、戌、亥）的搭配來紀日，60 日爲一個周期，這些搭配也可用來紀年。具體搭配名見附録一。因内容多有重複，照片、隸定本部分只選取 8 枚簡牘圖片。

② 嘉平：即臘日，在秦漢時代是一個非常重要的節日。秦代以十二月二十五日爲臘日，西漢時則以冬至後的某個戌日（日名中含有戌的日子叫作戌日，如甲戌、丙戌等）爲臘日。本簡中正月丁卯日下言“嘉平”，我們懷疑指此日開始嘉平假期結束。

③ 視事：治事，處理政務。

④ 除：人名。

⑤ 坐：坐曹治事。

⑥ 掾曹：掾指官府中的佐助官吏，曹是某官署内分科辦事的機構，掾曹即處理與佐助官吏相關事務的曹。秦代在縣廷設有多種曹，如司空曹、倉曹、户曹、獄東曹等，這些曹分别負責對應的官署或事務的文書統計、行政監督等，要注意的是，倉曹不等於倉，後者是獨立的官署。曹的負責人往往由令史擔任。

⑦ 公：官府主官的敬稱。

⑧ 長道：地名。本篇多見官吏所居地名，如迣、贏邑、上蒲、離涌、羅涌、區邑、尋平、竟陵、江陵、路陰等。這裏的竟陵、江陵爲縣名，其他地名性質不一，但應該都是小於縣的居民聚居區。

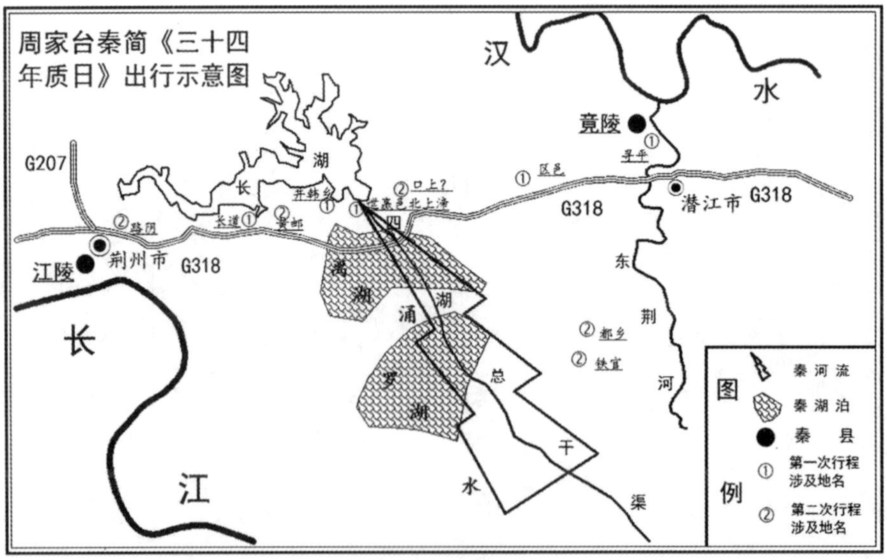

圖 1　部分地名位置示意

Figure 1　Map of places mentioned in the text

（引自郭濤：《周家臺 30 號秦墓竹簡“秦始皇三十四年質日”釋地》248 頁）

⑨ 郵：秦漢時期每隔一定的里程設置在重要交通線路上的機構，主要職能是傳遞文書和爲往來官吏提供飲食、車馬及炊具等器具。

⑩ 後府：官署名，具體執掌不明。

⑪ 賜：疑爲人名。

⑫ 奏：奏記，一種文書的名字，在嶽麓書院藏秦簡律令中“奏”與“對”“請”對稱，是不同性質的呈遞給上級的文書。

⑬ 嬃：人名。

⑭ 論：論罪。

⑮ 脩、賜：均是人名。

⑯ 并：歸併。

⑰ 左曹：曹名。

1. The reading of this group of bamboo slips starts from the day *dīngmǎo* 丁卯 of month 11 in the first segment (slip No.29), then *wùchén* 戊辰 in the first segment (slip No.30), and *bǐngshēn* 丙申 in the first segment (slip No.58). This would complete the full chronology of month 11 of that year. Then start from *dīngmǎo* of the first month in the second segment (slip No.29), and so on. There are ten *gān* 干 (stems, heavenly stems) : *jiǎ, yǐ, bǐng, dīng, wù, jǐ, gēng, xīn, rén, guǐ* and twelve *zhī* 支 (branches, earthly branches) : *zǐ, chǒu, yín, mǎo, chén, sì, wǔ, wèi, shēn, yǒu, xū, hài*. The combination of one *gān* and one *zhī* in an orderly manner form 60 *gānzhī* pairs, which were used in ancient China for naming each day in a 60-day cycle. The *gānzhī* system was also used to record years 1 to 60 in a 60-year cycle. The table in Appendix 1 lists these 60 pairs of *gānzhī* combinations.
2. 嘉平 *jiā píng*: a festival called *Làrì* 臘日 . According to the same slip, the twenty-fifth day of the twelfth month of that year is *Làrì* in the Qín Dynasty.
3. 視事 *shì shì*: handling matters, handling administrative or official matters.
4. 除 *chú*: personal name Chú.
5. 坐 *zuò*: that is *zuòcáo* 坐曹 (lit. “to sit in the bureau”) ; the term was used to mean “handling administrative duties.”
6. 掾曹 *yuàn cáo*: *Yuàn* 掾 refers to the supporting staff in a government office like secretaries or assistants. *Cáo* 曹 (Bureaus) refers to branch offices under certain office departments called *shǔ* 署 . *Yuàncáo* are thus staff members in a branch office. The Qín established many bureaus at the County Court level.
7. 公 *gōng*: honorific title of a superior or head of an office.
8. 長道 *cháng dào*: place name. The place names mentioned in this chapter are either county or places smaller than county. Jìnglíng and Jiānglíng are counties, but other places are smaller than county.
9. 郵 *yóu*: In the Qín and Hàn Dynasties, posts were set up on important transportation routes at certain distance, serving as a transit point for transmitting official documents and supply station for providing food, horse and carriage and cooking utensils for officials.

10. 後府 *hòu fǔ*: name of a certain bureaucratic office, but the function is unclear.
11. 賜 *cì*: personal name here.
12. 奏 *zòu*: a certain kind of official documents.
13. 䢁 *chè*: personal name.
14. 論 *lùn*: lit. "to discuss." Here *lùn* refers to *lùnzuì* 論罪 , to discuss penalties for the crime committed by someone, to prosecute.
15. 脩 *xiū*, 賜 *cì*: both are personal names.
16. 并 *bìng*: here it means *guībìng* 歸併 , to merge, to combine.
17. 左曹 *zuǒ cáo*: Left Bureau.

寬式隸定
Loose Transcription

十一月 丁卯	正月丁卯 嘉平視事。	三月乙丑 治竟陵。	五月 甲子	七月 癸亥	九月 癸亥	29
戊辰	戊辰	丙寅 治竟陵。	乙丑	甲子	甲子	30
己巳	己巳	丁卯 宿□上。	丙寅	乙丑	乙丑	31
庚午	庚午	戊辰 宿路陰。	丁卯	丙寅	丙寅	32
辛未	辛未	己巳 宿江陵。	戊辰	丁卯	丁卯	33
壬申	壬申	庚午 到江陵。	己巳	戊辰	戊辰	34
癸酉	癸酉	辛未 治後府。	庚午	己巳	己巳	35
甲戌	甲戌	壬申 治。	辛未	庚午	庚午	36
乙亥	乙亥	癸酉 治。	壬申	辛未	辛未	37
丙子	丙子	甲戌	癸酉	壬申	壬申	38
丁丑	丁丑	乙亥	甲戌	癸酉	癸酉	39
戊寅	戊寅	丙子	乙亥	甲戌	甲戌	40

（續表）

己卯	己卯	丁丑	丙子	乙亥	乙亥	41
庚辰	庚辰	戊寅	丁丑	丙子	丙子	42
辛巳	辛巳	己卯	戊寅	丁丑	丁丑	43
壬午	壬午	庚辰	己卯	戊寅	戊寅	44
癸未	癸未	辛巳 賜。	庚辰	己卯	己卯	45
甲申	甲申	壬午	辛巳	庚辰	庚辰	46
乙酉	乙酉	癸未 奏上。	壬午	辛巳	辛巳	47
丙戌	丙戌	甲申 史徹行。	癸未	壬午	壬午	48
丁亥	丁亥 史除不坐掾曹。從公， 宿長道。	乙酉	甲申	癸未	癸未	49
戊子	戊子 宿𨒅贏邑北上蒲。	丙戌 後事已。	乙酉	甲申	甲申	50
己丑	己丑 宿𨒅離涌西。	丁亥 治竟陵。	丙戌	乙酉	乙酉	51
庚寅	庚寅 宿𨒅□□郵北。	戊子	丁亥	丙戌	丙戌	52
辛卯	辛卯 宿𨒅羅涌西。	己丑 論脩、賜。	戊子	丁亥	丁亥	53
壬辰	壬辰 宿𨒅離涌東。	庚寅	己丑	戊子	戊子	54
癸巳	癸巳 宿區邑。	辛卯	庚寅	己丑	己丑	55
甲午	甲午 宿竟陵。	壬辰	辛卯	庚寅	庚寅	56
乙未	乙未 宿尋平。	癸巳	壬辰	辛卯	辛卯	57
丙申		甲午 并左曹。	癸巳	壬辰	壬辰	58

白話文
Vernacular Chinese

十一月 丁卯	正月丁卯 嘉平假期結束，開始治事。	三月乙丑 在竟陵縣處理政務。	五月 甲子	七月 癸亥	九月 癸亥	29
戊辰	戊辰	丙寅 在竟陵縣處理政務。	乙丑	甲子	甲子	30
己巳	己巳	丁卯 住在某上。	丙寅	乙丑	乙丑	31
庚午	庚午	戊辰 住在路陰。	丁卯	丙寅	丙寅	32
辛未	辛未	己巳 住在江陵縣。	戊辰	丁卯	丁卯	33
壬申	壬申	庚午 到達江陵縣。	己巳	戊辰	戊辰	34
癸酉	癸酉	辛未 在後府處理政務。	庚午	己巳	己巳	35
甲戌	甲戌	壬申 處理政務。	辛未	庚午	庚午	36
乙亥	乙亥	癸酉 處理政務。	壬申	辛未	辛未	37
丙子	丙子	甲戌	癸酉	壬申	壬申	38
丁丑	丁丑	乙亥	甲戌	癸酉	癸酉	39
戊寅	戊寅	丙子	乙亥	甲戌	甲戌	40
己卯	己卯	丁丑	丙子	乙亥	乙亥	41
庚辰	庚辰	戊寅	丁丑	丙子	丙子	42
辛巳	辛巳	己卯	戊寅	丁丑	丁丑	43
壬午	壬午	庚辰	己卯	戊寅	戊寅	44
癸未	癸未	辛巳 賜。	庚辰	己卯	己卯	45
甲申	甲申	壬午	辛巳	庚辰	庚辰	46
乙酉	乙酉	癸未 呈上奏記。	壬午	辛巳	辛巳	47

（續表）

丙戌	丙戌	甲申 名爲徹的史出行。	癸未	壬午	壬午	48
丁亥	丁亥 名爲除的史不在掾曹處理事務。跟隨主官某住在長道。	乙酉	甲申	癸未	癸未	49
戊子	戊子 住在迣地贏邑北部的上蒲。	丙戌 後府之事完畢。	乙酉	甲申	甲申	50
己丑	己丑 住在迣地離涌的西部。	丁亥 在竟陵縣處理政務。	丙戌	乙酉	乙酉	51
庚寅	庚寅 住在迣地某鄢的北部。	戊子	丁亥	丙戌	丙戌	52
辛卯	辛卯 住在迣地羅涌的西部。	己丑 論脩、賜之罪。	戊子	丁亥	丁亥	53
壬辰	壬辰 住在迣地離涌的東部。	庚寅	己丑	戊子	戊子	54
癸巳	癸巳 住在區邑。	辛卯	庚寅	己丑	己丑	55
甲午	甲午 住在竟陵縣。	壬辰	辛卯	庚寅	庚寅	56
乙未	乙未 住在尋平。	癸巳	壬辰	辛卯	辛卯	57
丙申		甲午 合併左曹。	癸巳	壬辰	壬辰	58

英文翻譯
English Translation

dīngmǎo of month 11	*dīngmǎo* of month 1, on the jiāpíng day, started office work	*yǐchǒu* of month 3, in Jìnglíng County, performed official duties	*jiǎzǐ* of month 5	*guǐhài* of month 7	*guǐhài* of month 9	29
wùchén	*wùchén*	*bǐngyín* in Jìnglíng County, performed official duties	*yǐchǒu*	*jiǎzǐ*	*jiǎzǐ*	30

(continued)

jǐsì	*jǐsì*	*dīngmǎo* stayed at …Shàng	*bǐngyín*	*yǐchǒu*	*yǐchǒu*	31
gēngwǔ	*gēngwǔ*	*wùchén* stayed at Lùyīn	*dīngmǎo*	*bǐngyín*	*bǐngyín*	32
xīnwèi	*xīnwèi*	*jǐsì* stayed at Jiānglíng County	*wùchén*	*dīngmǎo*	*dīngmǎo*	33
rénshēn	*rénshēn*	*gēngwǔ* arrived at Jiānglíng County	*jǐsì*	*wùchén*	*wùchén*	34
guǐyǒu	*guǐyǒu*	*xīnwèi* worked at Hòufǔ handling administrative matters	*gēngwǔ*	*jǐsì*	*jǐsì*	35
jiǎxū	*jiǎxū*	*rénshēn* handling administrative matters	*xīnwèi*	*gēngwǔ*	*gēngwǔ*	36
yǐhài	*yǐhài*	*guǐyǒu* handling administrative matters	*rénshēn*	*xīnwèi*	*xīnwèi*	37
bǐngzǐ	*bǐngzǐ*	*jiǎxū*	*guǐyǒu*	*rénshēn*	*rénshēn*	38
dīngchǒu	*dīngchǒu*	*yǐhài*	*jiǎxū*	*guǐyǒu*	*guǐyǒu*	39
wùyín	*wùyín*	*bǐngzǐ*	*yǐhài*	*jiǎxū*	*jiǎxū*	40
jǐmǎo	*jǐmǎo*	*dīngchǒu*	*bǐngzǐ*	*yǐhài*	*yǐhài*	41
gēngchén	*gēngchén*	*wùyín*	*dīngchǒu*	*bǐngzǐ*	*bǐngzǐ*	42
xīnsì	*xīnsì*	*jǐmǎo*	*wùyín*	*dīngchǒu*	*dīngchǒu*	43
rénwǔ	*rénwǔ*	*gēngchén*	*jǐmǎo*	*wùyín*	*wùyín*	44
guǐwèi	*guǐwèi*	*xīnsì* Cì	*gēngchén*	*jǐmǎo*	*jǐmǎo*	45
jiǎshēn	*jiǎshēn*	*rénwǔ*	*xīnsì*	*gēngchén*	*gēngchén*	46
yǐyǒu	*yǐyǒu*	*guǐwèi* submitted memos and reports	*rénwǔ*	*xīnsì*	*xīnsì*	47
bǐngxū	*bǐngxū*	*jiǎshēn* official Chè made a trip	*guǐwèi*	*rénwǔ*	*rénwǔ*	48

(continued)

dīnghài	*dīnghài* official Chú not in the bureau, went with superior, stayed at Chángdào	*yǐyǒu*	*jiǎshēn*	*guǐwèi*	*guǐwèi*	49
wùzǐ	*wùzǐ* stayed at Shàngpú, north of Yíngyì, Zhìdì	*bǐngxū* finished matters of Hòufū	*yǐyǒu*	*jiǎshēn*	*jiǎshēn*	50
jǐchǒu	*jǐchǒu* stayed at the west of Líyǒng of Zhìdì	*dīnghài* handling administrative matters at Jìnglíng County	*bǐngxū*	*yǐyǒu*	*yǐyǒu*	51
gēngyín	*gēngyín* stayed at the northern post of Zhìdì	*wùzǐ*	*dīnghài*	*bǐngxū*	*bǐngxū*	52
xīnmǎo	*xīnmǎo* stayed at the west of Luóyǒng, Zhìdì	*jǐchǒu* prosecuted the crime of Xiū and Cì	*wùzǐ*	*dīnghài*	*dīnghài*	53
rénchén	*rénchén* stayed at the east of Líyǒng, Zhìdì	*gēngyín*	*jǐchǒu*	*wùzǐ*	*wùzǐ*	54
guǐsì	*guǐsì* stayed at Qūyì	*xīnmǎo*	*gēngyín*	*jǐchǒu*	*jǐchǒu*	55
jiǎwǔ	*jiǎwǔ* stayed at Jìnglíng County	*rénchén*	*xīnmǎo*	*gēngyín*	*gēngyín*	56
yǐwèi	*yǐwèi* stayed at Xúnpíng	*guǐsì*	*rénchén*	*xīnmǎo*	*xīnmǎo*	57
bǐngshēn		*jiǎwǔ* combined the Left Bureau	*guǐsì*	*rénchén*	*rénchén*	58

練習
Practice

釋讀圖表 3 中的幾枚質日簡。(周家臺 30 號秦墓竹簡 51、52、55、56 號簡)

Read the slips in Tableau 3. (Zhōujiātái Qín tomb 30 bamboo slips, No.51, 52, 55, 56)

圖表 3　Tableau 3

周家臺《質日》56		周家臺《質日》55		周家臺《質日》52		周家臺《質日》51	
下	上	下	上	下	上	下	上

第三組　酒令
Group 3　Wine Order

簡介
Introduction

見於北京大學藏秦簡。寫在一枚竹牘和兩枚木牘上，與一枚行酒令的木骰同出，最初被稱爲“飲酒歌詩”，後李零據文義改稱爲《酒令》。李零指出：酒令是酒席宴上的詩歌，行令求答，答不上來受罰。這種詩歌，可以吟誦，可以清唱，可以配樂，可以伴舞。《酒令》具有重要的文學史意義。一方面，《酒令》與北京大學藏秦簡《公子從軍》都屬詩賦類文獻。以往對秦焚書坑儒是否封禁詩賦類的作品看法不一。現在看來，至少秦代並不完全禁絶詩賦類文獻。另一方面，劉釗推測《酒令》是秦代民謠“相”的變體。何家興進一步推斷:《酒令》作爲民間歌謠，屬於“秦時雜賦”，是“成相雜辭”(用一種叫“相”的樂器給歌曲打拍子，進行説唱的賦體。由三言、四言和七言搭配而成，基本句式是3+3+7+4+7，每一句都押韻）的早期形態。《酒令》的格式與“相”類的賦的基本格式還是有差異的，與“相”的關係或許還可進一步討論，但其作爲文學的一個類别承上啟下是毋庸置疑的。

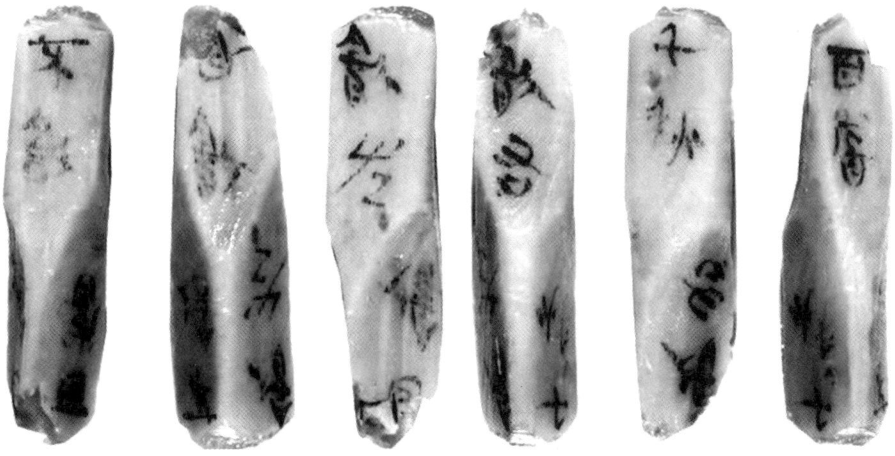

圖 1　木骰各截面示意（内容依次爲：不歙，自歙，歙左，歙右，千秋，百嘗）
Figure 1　Wooden dice for the drinking game
（引自李零:《北大藏秦簡〈酒令〉》19 頁）

Jiǔlìng 酒令 , literally “*Wine Order*,” refers to a drinker’s wager game. The texts of *jiǔlìng* are found in the Peking University corpus of Qín bamboo slips. They were written on one bamboo slip and two wood slips. All three slips were unearthed together with a wooden dice for the drinking game. They were first named *Wine Drinking Songs*. Lǐ Líng 李零 , upon a more careful study of the texts, later changed the name to *Wine Order*. According to Lǐ Líng, wine orders refer to the poems used at banquets to proffer orders and solicit correct answers from banquet participants. In case answers were incorrect, some penalty, like drinking more wine, would follow. This kind of poetry can be chanted and either sung a cappella or with musical and dance accompaniment.

Wine Orders were an important part of elite life with literary and historical significance. Wine orders like *The Young Master Joins the Army* (*Gōngzǐ cóngjūn* 公子從軍) are all written in the form of poetry. The existence of such poems clearly shows that despite the disdain for and the harsh treatment of Confucian scholars, poetry and odes were not completely forbidden in Qín times. Scholars like Liú Zhāo 劉釗 have speculated that wine orders are a variant of folk ballads called *xiàng* 相 (a musical instrument used to mark the beat in songs) in the Qín Dynasty. Hé Jiāxīng 何家興 has further speculated that *Wine Orders*, as a form of folk ballads, belong to the miscellaneous *fù* 賦 of the Qín Dynasty, which is a precursor or early form of *Chéngxiàng zácí* 成相雜辭 (a musical instrument called *xiàng* 相 was used to tap the beat of song of a style called *fù*. Lines in the *fù* are either three, four or seven characters long; these lines are often combined into a 3+3+7+4+7 pattern, with each line rhyming). Although the *Wine Orders* are different in form from the *fù* and the relationship with *xiàng* may need further study, there is no doubt that the different poetic forms of the *Wine Orders, fù*, and *Chéngxiàng zácí* are all linked with each other.

篇目來源
Text Source

第 3 篇　東採涇桑（北京大學藏秦《酒令》竹牘）

3. *Plucking Mulberry at Jīng* (Peking University corpus of Qín manuscripts, bamboo slip of *Wine Order*)

第 4 篇　不日可增（北京大學藏秦《酒令》木牘 1）

4. *The Day Cannot Be Added* (Peking University corpus of Qín manuscripts, wood slip 1 of *Wine Order*)

第 5 篇　歓不醉（北京大學藏秦《酒令》木牘 2）

5. *Not Drunken* (Peking University corpus of Qín manuscripts, wood slip 2 of *Wine Order*)

參考文獻
References

何家興:《秦簡〈酒令〉的文學史意義》,《湖南師範大學學報》2019 年第 5 期。

李零:《北大藏秦簡〈酒令〉》,《北京大學學報》2015 年第 2 期。

商之彝:《北大藏秦簡〈酒令〉零識》, 簡帛網, http://www.bsm.org.cn/show_article.php?id=2111, 2014 年 12 月 16 日。

照片、隸定本
Photo, Transcription

圖表 1　北京大學藏秦《酒令》竹牘；北京大學藏秦《酒令》木牘 1；北京大學藏秦《酒令》木牘 2

Tableau 1: Peking University corpus of Qín manuscripts, bamboo slip of *Wine Order*, wood slip 1 of *Wine Order*, wood slip 2 of *Wine Order*

圖表 1　Tableau 1

㱃不醉（北大藏《酒令》木牘 2）		不日可增（北大藏《酒令》木牘 1）		東採涇桑（北大藏《酒令》竹牘）	
隸定	照片	隸定	照片	隸定	照片
㱃不醉非江漢殹醉不歸夜未半殹趣〃駕雞未鳴 殹天未旦一家翁濡年尚少不大爲非勿庸譙心 不翕〃從野草斿		不日可增日可思檢〃枝髮中夜自來吾欲爲怒 烏〃不〃耐〃良〃久〃請人一桮黃〃烏邪醉吾冬栂		東菜涇桑可以食蠶愛般適然般獨安 湛食般巴叔㱃子湛寧見子死 □見子□黃〃烏虖醉吾蘭林	

三、東採涇桑
3. Plucking Mulberry at Jīng

原文
Bamboo Script

東菜①（採）涇桑②，可以食（飤）③蠶。愛般適然④，般獨安⑤（宴）湛，食（飤）般巴叔⑥（菽）歙⑦（飲）子湛。寧見子死，□見子□？黄₌⑧（黄黄）鳥虖，醉⑨（萃）吾蘭林⑩。

注釋
Annotation

① 菜：通“採”，採摘。
② 涇桑：涇水邊上桑樹的葉。
③ 食：讀爲“飤”，飼養。
④ 適然：應當的，恰當的。
⑤ 安：通“宴”，宴請。
⑥ 巴叔：巴豆。
⑦ 歙：通“飲”。
⑧ 黄₌：“黄”的重文，讀爲“黄黄”。秦簡牘中，“₌”可以作爲重文符、合文符（如“粟米”寫作“粟₌”）、省代符（如“是謂”寫作“是₌”）等使用。
⑨ 醉：通“萃”，聚集。用了雙關的手法，也可指醉。
⑩ 蘭林：即林蘭，也叫木蘭、杜蘭，一種落葉喬木。此處因爲押韻寫作蘭林。

1. 菜 *cài*: equivalent to *cǎi* 採 , meaning to pick, to pluck.
2. 涇桑 *jīng sāng*: mulberry trees and leaves at the bank of Jīng River.
3. 食 *shí*: equivalent to *sì* 飤 , meaning to feed.
4. 適然 *shì rán*: equivalent to *dāngrán* 當然 , meaning surely, of course.
5. 安 *ān*: equivalent to *yàn* 宴 , meaning to entertain, to treat.
6. 巴叔 *bā shū*: croton.
7. 歙 *yǐn*: equivalent to *yǐn* 飲 , meaning to drink.
8. 黄₌ *huáng huáng*: the sign “₌” is the iteration mark, indicating here that the character “*huáng* 黄” should be read twice, to emphasize that the color is very yellow.
9. 醉 *cuì*: the word is equivalent to *cuì* 萃 , meaning to gather, to collect. Here, it refers to *zuì* 醉 , meaning “drunkenness” as a pun.

10. 蘭林 *lánlín*: same as *línlán* 林蘭 , also known as *mùlán* 木蘭 or *dùlán* 杜蘭 . All these names refer to magnolia trees. Here the tree was called lánlín for rhyming purposes.

寬式隸定
Loose Transcription

東採涇桑，可以飤蠶。愛般適然，般獨宴湛，食般巴菽飲子湛。寧見子死，□見子□？黄黄鳥虖，萃吾蘭林。

白話文
Vernacular Chinese

採摘東面涇水邊上桑樹的葉，可以用來餵蠶。湛喜歡般是應當的，般只宴請湛……鳥兒黄黄，聚集在我的木蘭樹上。

英文翻譯
English Translation

On the east bank of the Jīng River, I pluck leaves of the mulberry trees; they can be used to feed silkworms. Zhàn likes Bān, that's how things ought to be. Bān only feasts with Zhàn …… Birds ever so yellow, gathering/drunken on my magnolia tree.

四、不日可增
4. The Day Cannot Be Added

原文
Bamboo Script

不日可增①日可思②，檢=（鬑鬑）③柀（披）④髮，中夜⑤自來。吾欲爲怒烏=不=耐=⑥（烏不耐，烏不耐），良=久=（良久良久），請人一桮⑦（杯）。黄=（黄黄）烏邪⑧，醉（萃）吾冬栂⑨（梅）。

注釋
Annotation

① 不日可增：即“日不可增”。
② 思：愛惜。
③ 檢=：即“鬑鬑”，形容頭髮長。
④ 柀：通“披”。
⑤ 中夜：時稱名，即午夜。
⑥ 烏不耐：何無奈。
⑦ 桮：同“杯”。
⑧ 邪：同“耶”。
⑨ 栂：同“梅”。

1. 不日可增 *bù rì kě zēng*: equivalent to *rì bù kě zēng* 日不可增, lit. “day cannot be increased,” meaning that the day past cannot come back.
2. 思 *sī*: to cherish.
3. 檢= *jiǎn jiǎn*: equivalent to *liánlián* 鬑鬑, describing long hair.
4. 柀 *bǐ*: equivalent to *pī* 披, meaning scattered, spread out.
5. 中夜 *zhōng yè*: midnight.
6. 烏不耐 *wū bù nài*: equivalent to *hé wú nài* 何無奈, meaning helpless, or “what can be done” “nothing can be done.” The sign “=” is an iteration mark. So the “*wū bù nài*” would be repeated once.
7. 桮 *bēi*: equivalent to *bēi* 杯, cup.
8. 邪 *xié*: equivalent to *yē* 耶, interrogative word in classical Chinese.
9. 栂 *méi*: equivalent to *méi* 梅, plum.

寬式隸定
Loose Transcription

不日可增日可思，鬑鬑披髪，中夜自來。吾欲爲怒烏不耐，烏不耐，良久良久，請人一杯。黄黄鳥邪，萃吾冬梅。

白話文
Vernacular Chinese

去日不可再來，明日應該愛惜。披着長髮，午夜時自己到來。我想發怒卻無可奈何，無可奈何，太久太久，請他喝一杯。鳥兒黄黄，聚集在我的冬梅樹上。

英文翻譯
English Translation

The days past will not come back, each day is to be cherished.
Long hair spreading, at midnight he shows up by himself.
I want to get angry [at him] , but what can be done?
What can be done? After a long, long time, offer him a drink.
Birds ever so yellow, gathering/drunken on my winter plum tree.

五、歓不醉
5. Not Drunken

原文
Bamboo Script

歓（飲）不醉，非江漢殹。醉不歸，夜未半殹。趣₌（趣趣）① 駕，雞未鳴殹天未旦。一家翁濡（孺）② 年尚少，不大爲非勿庯譙 ③。心不翕₌（翕翕）④，從野草斿 ⑤（游）。

注釋
Annotation

① 趣₌：快的狀態，這裏指催促。或認爲形容急忙。
② 濡：通“孺”，指小孩。翁孺泛指一家老小。或認爲通“嫗”，翁嫗指老頭老太太。
③ 譙：責備。或認爲通“憔”，義爲焦慮。
④ 翕₌：失意。
⑤ 斿：通“游”。

1. 趣₌ *cù cù*: to describe something moving fast, here it means to press, to hasten or to urge.
2. 濡 *rú*: equivalent to *rú* 孺 , meaning little kids. The term *wēngrú* 翁孺 refers broadly to a family of young and old. Alternatively, the word *rú* might be equivalent to *yù* 嫗 , meaning old lady. Then, *wēngyù* 翁嫗 refers to the old man and the old woman.
3. 譙 *qiào*: to scold, to blame. Alternatively, the word may be equivalent to *qiáo* 憔 , meaning to worry.
4. 翕₌ *xī xī*: frustrated, disappointed, to feel dejected.
5. 斿 *yóu*: equivalent to *yóu* 游 , to tour, to play, to wander.

寬式隸定
Loose Transcription

飲不醉，非江漢殹。醉不歸，夜未半殹。趣趣駕，雞未鳴殹天未旦。一家翁孺年尚少，不大爲非勿庯譙。心不翕翕，從野草游。

白話文
Vernacular Chinese

喝不醉啊，除非長江漢水啊。醉了不回家，還没到午夜呢。快些駕車啊，趁着雞没叫啊天未亮。一家老少年紀還小啊，不做什麼壞事所以不要責備。心不要失意啊，跟着野草隨風飄摇。

英文翻譯
English Translation

Will not get drunken, unless [I consumed as much as the amount of] *Yangtze* and *Hàn* rivers.
Will not go back home, as it is not even midnight yet.
Drive home quickly, rooster has not crowed and dawn has not yet broken.
The whole family are still young, they committed no wrong, [so] don't chastise them.
Don't torment yourself, just follow what the wild grass does, swaying in the wind.

圖 2　成都昭覺寺東漢歌舞宴樂畫像石
Figure 2　Stone portrait of a feast party scene of the Eastern Hàn Dynasty in Zhāojué Temple, Chéngdū
（引自 http://www.handanwenhua.net/zuojia/2021-07-21/4587.html）

練習
Practice

釋讀圖表 2 中的北京大學藏秦簡《公子從軍》選簡。（編號依據整理者編號，圖版選自《北京大學藏秦代簡牘書迹選粹》，爲紅外放大圖版，每枚簡分三段拍攝）
Read the slips in Tableau 2. (Selected from Peking University corpus of Qín bamboo slips, *The Young Master Joins the Army*)

圖表 2　Tableau 2

《公子從軍》8 紅外圖片			《公子從軍》6 紅外圖片			《公子從軍》3 紅外圖片		
（三）	（二）	（一）	（三）	（二）	（一）	（三）	（二）	（一）

第四組　日書
Group 4　Day Book

簡介
Introduction

日書，是一種屢見於秦漢簡牘的時日宜忌占測文獻。作爲篇題，最早見於睡虎地《日書》乙種 259 號簡簡背，之後作爲篇名的“日書”還見於睡虎地 77 號漢墓簡牘、孔家坡 8 號漢墓簡牘等。日書中包含用於查檢的實用表格、具體的時日宜忌、晝夜劃分、五行生克、相宅、禳夢、驅鬼術等多方面的内容。楚簡、秦簡、漢簡中都有日書，秦簡中的日書見於湖北雲夢睡虎地 11 號墓秦簡、甘肅天水放馬灘 1 號墓秦簡、湖北江陵岳山 36 號墓秦簡、湖北荆州周家臺 30 號墓秦簡、湖北江陵王家臺 15 號墓秦簡、北京大學藏秦簡等。

《史記》有《日者列傳》，可見當時占卜風俗的盛行。《日者列傳》記載：“臣爲郎時，與太卜待詔爲郎者同署，言曰：‘孝武帝時，聚會占家問之，某日可取婦乎？五行家曰可，堪輿家曰不可，建除家曰不吉，叢辰家曰大凶，曆家曰小凶，天人家曰小吉，太一家曰大吉。辯訟不決，以狀聞。制曰：避諸死忌，以五行爲主。’”皇帝娶親也需擇日，而占卜分爲若干流派，提供了不同的意見，可見占卜之術流變的複雜情況。

Rìshū 日書 , lit. “*day book*,” is a genre of texts dealing with dates, taboos, and divinatory matters, equivalent to almanacs or hemerological texts. *Rìshū* were circulated widely from the late Warring States Period to the Hàn Dynasty. The earliest bamboo slip in which this term was used appears in Shuìhǔdì *Rìshū* B, No.259. Later the title of *Rìshū* also appears in the slips of Hàn tomb 77 at Shuìhǔdì and the slips of Hàn tomb 8 at Kǒngjiāpō, among many other texts. *Rìshū* contain useful tables for checking the dates, taboos on any specific day, and other information related to *fēngshuǐ* 風水 , decoding bad dreams, exorcising demons, etc. The bamboo slips of the states of Chǔ, Qín, and Hàn all have *rìshū*. Qín bamboo slip *rìshū* can be found in Shuìhǔdì Qín tomb 11 bamboo slips, in Yúnmèng, Húběi Province; Fàngmǎtān Qín tomb 1 bamboo slips in Tiānshuǐ, Gānsù Province; Yuèshān Qín tomb 36 bamboo slips in Jiānglíng, Húběi Province; Zhōujiātái Qín tomb 30 bamboo slips in Jīngzhōu, Húběi Province; Wángjiātái Qín tomb 15 bamboo slips in Jiānglíng, Húběi Province; and Peking University corpus of Qín bamboo slips.

Shǐjì 史記 has a chapter called *Biography of Diviners* (*Rìzhě lièzhuàn* 日者列傳), indicating the custom of divination was very popular at that time. That chapter records a story that Sīmǎ Qiān 司馬遷 heard from his diviner colleagues at the office the following story: Once, the emperor was considering to get married. He gathered a few diviners and ask for their opinion about whether a particular date is appropriate. The *Wǔxíng* 五行 school diviner said: “Yes, good!” The *Kānyú* 堪輿 school diviner said: “No, no good!” The *Jiànchú* 建除 school diviner said: “ It is not auspicious.”

The *Cóngchén* 叢辰 school diviner said: "Worst omen!" The *Lì* 曆 school diviner said: "Bad omen!" The *Tiānrén* 天人 school diviner said: "Somewhat auspicious!" The *Tàiyī* 太一 school diviner said: "Hugely auspicious!" They argued with each other, and could not reach a consensus. The emperor then ordered: "To avoid death or taboo, the *Wǔxíng* school is a better choice." This story shows that even an emperor had to deal with diviners of so many different schools and that the situation at that time could indeed be very complicated.

篇目來源
Text Source

第 6 篇　除（節選：睡虎地秦墓竹簡《日書》乙種 26 壹，29 壹，44 壹，45 壹）
6. *Almanacs*（selected from Shuìhǔdì Qín tomb 11 bamboo slips, *Rìshū B*, slips 26, 29, 44, 45）
第 7 篇　人字（睡虎地秦墓竹簡《日書》甲種 150—154 號簡）
7. *Bearing a Child*（Shuìhǔdì Qín tomb 11 bamboo slips, *Rìshū A*, slips 150-154）
第 8 篇　出邦門（睡虎地秦墓竹簡《日書》甲種 111 號簡背面，112 號簡背面）
8. *Walking Out of City Gate*（Shuìhǔdì Qín tomb 11 bamboo slips, *Rìshū A*, slips 111 back and 112 back）
第 9 篇　夢（睡虎地秦墓竹簡《日書》乙種 189—195 號簡）
9. *Dream*（Shuìhǔdì Qín tomb 11 bamboo slips, *Rìshū B*, slips 189-195）
第 10 篇　戎曆日（周家臺秦墓竹簡《日書》131—144 號簡）
10. *Róng Calendar Day*（Zhōujiātái Qín tomb 30 bamboo slips, *Rìshū*, slips 131-144）

參考文獻
References

陳偉：《讀沙市周家臺秦簡札記》，《楚文化研究論集》第 5 輯，黃山書社 2003 年。
陳偉主編：《秦簡牘合集釋文注釋修訂本（二）（三）》，武漢大學出版社 2016 年。
方勇：《秦簡劄記四則》，簡帛網，http://bsm.org.cn/?qinjian/5207.html，2009 年 3 月 20 日。
［日］工藤元男著、曹峰譯：《睡虎地秦簡所見秦代國家與社會》，上海古籍出版社 2010 年。
湖北省荆州市周梁玉橋遺址博物館：《關沮秦漢墓簡牘》，中華書局 2001 年。
胡平生、李天虹：《長江流域出土簡牘與研究》，湖北教育出版社 2004 年。
胡文輝：《秦簡〈日書・出邦門篇〉新證》，《文博》1998 年第 1 期。
孔慶典：《10 世紀前中國紀曆文化源流：以簡帛爲中心》，上海人民出版社 2011 年。
劉樂賢：《睡虎地秦簡日書研究》，文津出版社 1994 年。
劉樂賢：《簡帛數術文獻探論》，湖北教育出版社 2003 年。
劉青：《放馬灘秦簡〈日書〉乙種集釋》，武漢大學碩士學位論文，2010 年。
劉昭瑞：《論"禹步"的起源及禹巫、道的關係》，《梁釗韜與人類學》，中山大學出版社

1991 年。
龍永芳:《周家臺秦簡〈日書〉之“戎曆”圖符説》,《出土文獻研究》第 7 輯，上海古籍出版社 2005 年。
吕亞虎:《戰國秦漢簡帛文獻所見巫術研究》，科學出版社 2010 年。
馬繼興:《馬王堆古醫書考釋》，湖南科學技術出版社 1992 年。
饒宗頤:《秦簡中的五行説與納音説》,《古文字研究》第 14 輯，中華書局 1986 年。
施謝捷:《簡帛文字考釋札記》,《簡帛研究》第 3 輯，廣西教育出版社 1998 年。
睡虎地秦墓竹簡整理小組:《睡虎地秦墓竹簡》，文物出版社 1990 年。
孫機:《漢代物質文化資料圖説（增訂本）》，上海古籍出版社 2011 年。
唐强:《周家臺秦簡〈日書〉三閉臆解》，簡帛網，http://bsm.org.cn/?qinjian/8230.html，2020 年 3 月 4 日。
王洪震:《漢畫像石》，新世界出版社 2011 年。
王偉:《嶽麓書院藏秦簡（肆）242 號簡文勘誤——兼論秦文字中用爲“冠”的“寇”字》,《簡帛》第 20 輯，上海古籍出版社 2020 年。
王學理:《秦物質文化通覽》，科學出版社 2015 年。
王子今:《睡虎地秦簡〈日書〉甲種疏證》，湖北教育出版社 2003 年。
晏昌貴:《〈日書〉札記十則》,《楚地出土簡帛文獻思想研究（一）》，湖北教育出版社 2002 年。
周波:《秦漢簡〈日書〉校讀札記》，復旦大學出土文獻與古文字研究中心網站，http://fdgwz.org.cn/Web/Show/111，2010 年 3 月 17 日。
周天游:《秦漢雄風》，浙江人民美術出版社 1999 年。

照片、隸定本
Photo, Transcription

圖表 1　睡虎地秦墓竹簡《日書》乙種 26，29，44，45
Tableau 1: Shuìhǔdì Qín tomb 11 bamboo slips, *Rìshū* B, slips 26, 29, 44, 45
圖表 2　睡虎地秦墓竹簡《日書》甲種 150—154 號簡
Tableau 2: Shuìhǔdì Qín tomb 11 bamboo slips, *Rìshū* A, slips 150-154
圖表 3　睡虎地秦墓竹簡《日書》甲種 111 號簡背面，112 號簡背面；
睡虎地秦墓竹簡《日書》乙種 189—191 號簡
Tableau 3: Shuìhǔdì Qín tomb 11 bamboo slips, *Rìshū A*, slips 111 back and 112 back;
Rìshū B, slips 189-191
圖表 4　睡虎地秦墓竹簡《日書》乙種 192—195 號簡
Tableau 4: Shuìhǔdì Qín tomb 11 bamboo slips, *Rìshū B*, slips 192-195
圖表 5　周家臺秦墓竹簡《日書》131—135 號簡第 3 欄
Tableau 5: Zhōujiātái Qín tomb 30 bamboo slips, *Rìshū*, slips 131-135, segment 3

圖表 6　周家臺秦墓竹簡《日書》136 第 3 欄，137—140 號簡第 2 欄

Tableau 6: Zhōujiātái Qín tomb 30 bamboo slips, *Rìshū*, slip 136, segment 3; slip 137-140, segment 2

圖表 7　周家臺秦墓竹簡《日書》141—144 號簡第 2 欄

Tableau 7: Zhōujiātái Qín tomb 30 bamboo slips, *Rìshū*, slips 141-144, segment 2

圖表 1　Tableau 1

睡虎地《日書》乙 45		睡虎地《日書》乙 44		睡虎地《日書》乙 29		睡虎地《日書》乙 26	
隸定	照片	隸定	照片	隸定	照片	隸定	照片
虛日不可以臧=蓋=它人必發之毋可有爲也用得必復出		剽日不可以使人及畜六畜它毋有爲也		四月建巳徐午吉未實申窞酉敫戌衝子虛丑吉寅卯閉辰		正月建寅余卯吉辰實巳窞午徼未衝申剽酉虛戌吉亥實子閉丑	

圖表 2　Tableau 2

睡虎地《日書》甲 150—154 號簡	
第 2 欄	第 1 欄
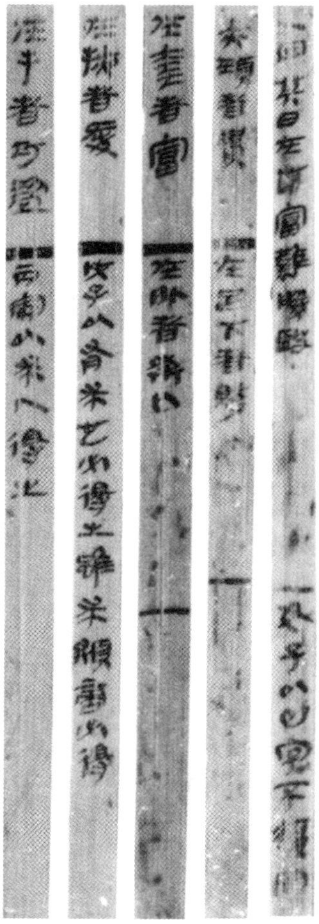	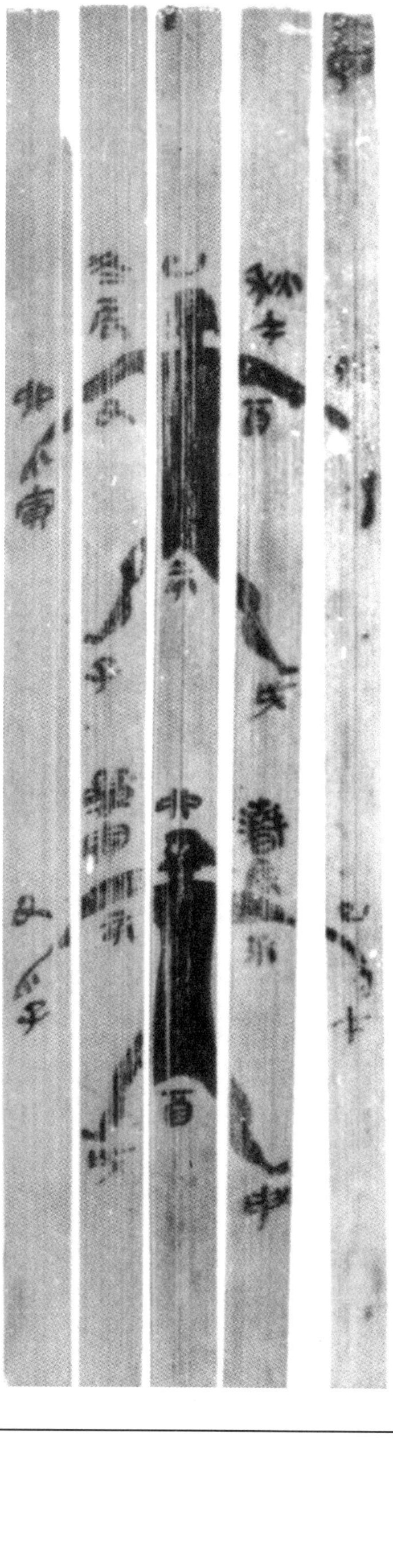
人字其日在首富難勝毆　女子以巳字不復字 150 夾頸者貴　在足下者賤 151 在奎者富　在外者奔亡 152 在掖者愛 153 在手者巧盜 154	

圖表 3　Tableau 3

睡虎地《日書》乙 191		睡虎地《日書》乙 190		睡虎地《日書》乙 189		睡虎地《日書》甲 111 背下，112 背上		睡虎地《日書》甲 111 背上	
隸定	照片	隸定	照片	隸定	照片	隸定	照片	隸定	照片
戊己夢黑吉得喜也		夢丙丁夢喜也木金得也		甲乙夢被黑裘衣寇喜人水中及谷得也		毋咎先爲禹除道即五畫地掓其畫中央土		行到邦門困禹步三勉壹步謼皋敢告曰某行	
						而懷之			

圖表 4　Tableau 4

睡虎地《日书》乙 195		睡虎地《日书》乙 194		睡虎地《日书》乙 193		睡虎地《日书》乙 192	
隸定	照片	隸定	照片	隸定	照片	隸定	照片
之宛奇强歙食賜某大畐不錢則布不壐則絮		凡人有惡夢覺而擇之西北鄉擇髮而駟祝曰綍敢告壐宛奇某有惡夢老來		壬癸夢日喜也金得也		庚辛夢青黑喜心木水得也	

圖表 5　Tableau 5

周家臺《日書》135 第 3 欄		周家臺《日書》134 第 3 欄		周家臺《日書》133 第 3 欄		周家臺《日書》132 第 3 欄		周家臺《日書》131 第 3 欄	
隸定	照片	隸定	照片	隸定	照片	隸定	照片	隸定	照片
衡・入月二日六日八日十二日十四日十八日廿日廿		晝者竆・入月一日七日十三日十九日廿五日大		一日直一者大衡直周者小衡直周中三		此所謂戎磨日毆從朔日始數之晝當			

圖表 6　Tableau 6

周家臺《日書》140 第 2 欄		周家臺《日書》139 第 2 欄		周家臺《日書》138 第 2 欄		周家臺《日書》137 第 2 欄		周家臺《日書》136 第 3 欄	
隸定	照片	隸定	照片	隸定	照片	隸定	照片	隸定	照片
人不得利以舉大事		•凡大奭之日利以遠行絕邊競攻毄亡		二日廿七日廿八日廿九日竈日		十日十一日十五日十六日十七日廿一日廿二日廿一		四日廿六日卅日小奭•入月三日四日五日九日	

圖表 7 Tableau 7

周家臺《日書》 144 第 2 欄		周家臺《日書》 143 第 2 欄		周家臺《日書》 142 第 2 欄		周家臺《日書》 141 第 2 欄	
隸定	照片	隸定	照片	隸定	照片	隸定	照片
閉		•凡竆日不利有爲殹亡人得是謂三		女吉氏謂小徹利以羉謀		•凡小徹之日利以行作爲好事取婦嫁	

六、除
6. Almanacs

原文
Bamboo Script

正月，建寅，余[①]（除）卯，吉辰，實巳，窞午，徹未，衝申，剽酉，虚戌，吉亥，實子，閉丑。（26壹）

四月，建巳，徐（除）午，吉未，實申，窞酉，敫戌，衝【亥，剽】[②]子，虚丑，吉寅，【實】[③]卯，閉[④]辰。（29壹）

剽日，不可以使人及畜六畜[⑤]，它毋有爲[⑥]也。（44壹）

虚日，不可以臧₌蓋₌（藏蓋，藏蓋）[⑦]，它人必發[⑧]之。毋可有爲也。用[⑨]得，必復出。（45壹）

注釋
Annotation

① 余：通“除”，神煞名。本篇自題爲“徐”，在27號簡上部，也通“除”。秦簡中多見此種建除家的擇日文獻，題爲“除”或“秦除”。一般包含兩部分，一部分記録12個神煞在12個月裏分别所處地支爲何，一部分記録各個神煞日的宜忌情況，兩部分配合使用。建、余（除）、吉、實、窞、徹、衝、剽、虚、吉、實、閉是一套神煞名。還可見其他神煞體系，完整的如放馬灘秦墓竹簡《日書》甲種所載：
建日：良日殹。可爲嗇夫，可以祝祠，可以畜大生（牲），不可入黔首。（13）
除日：逃亡，不得，癉疾死。可以治嗇夫，可以徹言君子、除罪。（14）
盈日：可築閒（閑）牢，可入生（牲）。利築宫室、爲小嗇夫，有疾難瘳。（15）
平日：可取（娶）妻、祝祠、賜客，可以入黔首，作事吉。（16壹）
定日：可以臧（藏）、爲府，可以祝祠。（17壹）
摯（執）日：不可行。行遠，必執而于公。（18壹）
彼（破）日：毋可以有爲殹，雖（唯）利彼（破）水。（19壹）
危日：可以責人及摯（執）人、毄（擊）人、外政（征）。（20壹）
成日：可以謀事，可起衆及作有爲殹，皆吉。（21壹）
收：可以氏馬牛畜生（牲）盡可，及入禾粟，可以居處。（21貳）
開日：逃亡，不得。可以言盜，盜必得。（18貳）
閉日：可以波（陂）渴（堨），入人奴妾。（20貳）

② 此處漏寫了“亥”與“剽”兩個字。

③ “實”字因簡牘殘斷不見。

④ 閉：書手將字中的構件“才”誤寫爲“牛”。
⑤ 六畜：一般指牛、馬、羊、豬、犬、雞。
⑥ 有爲：有所作爲，即做事。
⑦ 臧蓋：臧，通“藏”。藏蓋，收藏。
⑧ 發：開啟，這裏指找到收藏之物。
⑨ 用：介詞，在，其後省略了虛日。

1. 余 *yú*: equivalent to *chú* 除 , the name of one of the twelve spirits governing fortune or evil (*shénshà* 神煞). Quite a few of Qín bamboo slips are entitled with *chú* or *Qínchú* 秦除 , which usually contains two parts: one part lists the corresponding earth branch (*dìzhī* 地支) for each spirit, the other part lists compatible and incompatible activities, or taboos for each spirit day. Thus, *chú* or *Qínchú* are almanacs of the Qín Dynasty. Here, *jiàn* 建 , *chú* 余 , *jí* 吉 , *shí* 實 , *dàn* 窞 , *jiǎo* 徼 , *chōng* 衝 , *piāo* 剽 , *xū* 虚 , *jí* 吉 , *shí* 實 , *bì* 閉 are twelve names that constitute a set of spirits. In some slips another set of twelve spirits is listed. One of the most complete almanac listings appears in the Fàngmǎtān Qín tomb 1 bamboo slips in Tiānshuǐ, Gānsù Province.
2. Here, the two characters *hài* 亥 and *piāo* 剽 are missing.
3. Here, the character *shí* 實 is missing due to fragmentation of the slip.
4. 閉 *bì*: the scribe mistakenly wrote the internal component *cái* 才 as *niú* 牛 .
5. 六畜 *liù chù*: literally six animals, the term generally refers to cattle, horses, sheep, pigs, dogs, and chickens.
6. 有爲 *yǒu wéi*: to do something.
7. 臧蓋 *zāng gài*: the character *zāng* 臧 is equivalent to *cáng* 藏 . *Cánggài* means to hoard, to collect.
8. 發 *fā*: to open. Here it refers to finding the hoarded things.
9. 用 *yòng*: a preposition, meaning at or on a certain day. The name of the spirit day *xūrì* 虚日 is omitted here.

寬式隸定

Loose Transcription

正月，建寅，除卯，吉辰，實巳，窞午，徼未，衝申，剽酉，虛戌，吉亥，實子，閉丑。

四月，建巳，除午，吉未，實申，窞酉，敫戌，衝亥，剽子，虛丑，吉寅，實卯，閉辰。

剽日，不可以使人及畜六畜，它毋有爲也。

虛日，不可以藏蓋，藏蓋，它人必發之。毋可有爲也。用得，必復出。

白話文
Vernacular Chinese

正月，建日爲寅日，除日爲卯日，吉日爲辰日，實日爲巳日，窞日爲午日，徹日爲未日，衝日爲申日，剽日爲酉日，虛日爲戌日，吉日爲亥日，實日爲子日，閉日爲丑日。

四月，建日爲巳日，除日爲午日，吉日爲未日，實日爲申日，窞日爲酉日，徹日爲戌日，衝日爲亥日，剽日爲子日，虛日爲丑日，吉日爲寅日，實日爲卯日，閉日爲辰日。

剽日，不可以役使他人及畜養六畜，其他的事情不要做。

虛日，不可以收藏東西，收藏，其他人一定會找到它。不要做事。在這一日有所得，一定會再次失去。

英文翻譯
English Translation

In the first month [of the lunar calendar] , the first day *jiànrì* is the *yín* day; *chúrì* is the *mǎo* day; *jírì* is the *chén* day; *shírì* is the *sì* day; *dànrì* is the *wǔ* day; *jiǎorì* is the *wèi* day; *chōngrì* is the *shēn* day; *piāorì* is the *yǒu* day; *xūrì* is the *xū* day; *jírì* is the *hài* day; *shírì* is the *zǐ* day; and *bìrì* is the *chǒu* day.

In the fourth month [of the lunar calendar] , *jiànrì*, the first day, is the *sì* day; *chúrì* is the *wǔ* day; *jírì* is the *wèi* day; *shírì* is the *shēn* day; *dànrì* is the *yǒu* day; *jiǎorì* is the *xū* day; *chōngrì* is the *hài* day; *piāorì* is the *zǐ* day; *xūrì* is the *chǒu* day; *jírì* is the *yín* day; *shírì* is the *mǎo* day; and *bìrì* is the *chén* day.

On the day of *piāorì*, do not enslave others or raise animals, and do not do other things.

On the day of *xūrì*, do not hoard, if you hoard, others will definitely find it. Don't engage in anything. Whatever you gain on this day will surely be lost again.

七、人字
7. Bearing a Child

原文
Bamboo Script

圖 1 人字圖
Figure 1 *Rénzì* Figure
（引自《秦簡牘合集釋文注釋修訂本（貳）》397 頁）

人字①
人字，其日在首，富難勝②毆（也）。（150 貳）
夾頸者貴。（151 貳）
在奎③者富。（152 貳）
在掖④者愛⑤。（153 貳）
在手者巧盜⑥。（154 貳）
在足下者賤。（151 叄）
在外⑦者奔亡。（152 叄）
女子以巳字，不復字。（150 叄）

注釋
Annotation

① 人字：篇名。與人字圖配合使用，根據新生兒所生的季節的地支日在人字圖上的位置，占測新生兒未來的命運。字，生子。
② 富難勝：富得難以超越。勝，超越。
③ 奎：《说文解字・大部》："奎，兩髀之間。" 髀，大腿，故奎指大腿之間。

④ 掖：通“腋”，腋窩。
⑤ 愛：招人喜歡。
⑥ 巧盜：巧指工巧，盜指將來會成爲盜賊。
⑦ 外：肩。

1. 人字 *rén zì: rén* 人 means human, *zì* 字 means bearing a child. *Rénzì*, used as the title here, means giving birth or bearing a child. According to Qín custom, the fortune of a newborn is predicted from the birth dates (which season and which day of the twelve earth branches) that are marked around a human figure as shown in Rénzì Figure (Fig. 1) above.
2. 富難勝 *fù nán shèng*: lit. “wealth difficult to surpass”, meaning unsurpassed wealth.
3. 奎 *kuí*: according to *Shuōwén jiězì*, the word means area between the two thighs.
4. 掖 *yē*: equivalent to the word *yè* 腋 , meaning armpit.
5. 愛 *ài*: likable.
6. 巧盜 *qiǎo dào: qiǎo* 巧 means handy, dexterous; *dào* 盜 means theft, thief.
7. 外 *wài*: shoulder.

寬式隸定
Loose Transcription

人字：
人字，其日在首，富難勝也。
夾頸者貴。
在奎者富。
在腋者愛。
在手者巧盜。
在足下者賤。
在外者奔亡。
女子以巳字，不復字。

白話文
Vernacular Chinese

人生子：
人生子，其出生日期在頭部，有難以超越之財富。
夾着脖子的尊貴。
在兩腿中間的富裕。
在腋下的招人喜歡。

在手的工巧而爲盜賊。
在腳下的低賤。
在肩膀之上的逃亡。
女子在巳日生孩子，不再生子。

英文翻譯
English Translation

Bearing a Child
Bearing a child at dates indicated at the top head area: the child will have unsurpassed wealth.
At dates indicated around the neck area: [the child] will enjoy a noble stature.
At dates indicated between the areas of legs: [the child] will be rich.
At dates indicated underneath the armpit: [the child] will be likable.
At dates indicated at hands: [the child] will be dexterous, or may be adept at theft.
At dates indicated at the bottom of feet: [the child] will have a humble and lowly life.
At dates indicated at the shoulder: [the child] will lead a life on the road or be a fugitive.
A woman who gives birth to children on the day of *sì* will not bear children again.

八、出邦門①
8. Walking Out of City Gate

原文
Bamboo Script

行到邦門困②，禹步③三，勉④壹步，譁（呼）⑤："皋⑥，敢告曰：某⑦行毋咎，先爲禹除道⑧。"即五畫⑨地，掓⑩其畫中央土（111背）而懷⑪之。（112背）

注釋
Annotation

① 出邦門：篇題，又見於睡虎地秦墓竹簡《日書》乙種和放馬灘秦簡《日書》甲種等，文字略有差異。類似的內容還見於傳世古書《增補玉匣記》等。邦門，城邑之門。
② 困：門檻。
③ 禹步：一種巫術步法。
④ 勉：盡力。或認爲通"邁"。
⑤ 譁：通"呼"，喊叫。
⑥ 皋：擬聲詞。
⑦ 某：即禹步而呼的人的名字。
⑧ 先爲禹除道：放馬灘簡作"爲禹前除道"，義爲先爲禹清除道路上的危險邪祟。
⑨ 五畫：五筆畫的某種符號。或認爲畫出東西南北中五方，或認爲畫縱橫交錯的十字形符號，或認爲是五條橫畫。後世方術中的"四縱五橫"可能與此有關。

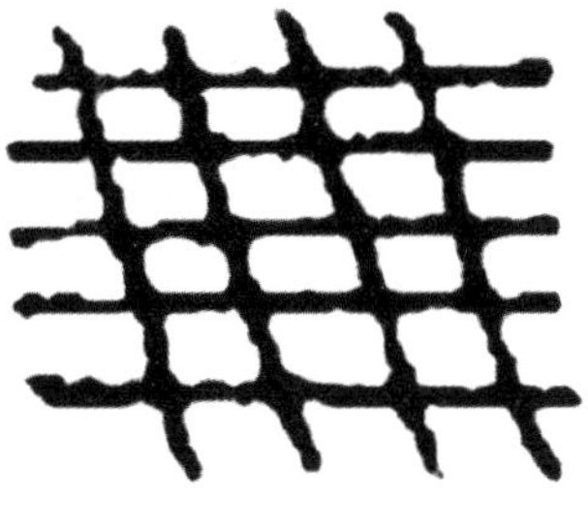

圖 2 "四縱五橫"圖
Figure 2　*Sìzòng wǔhéng*, a diagram of four vertical and five horizontal lines
（引自《靈寶玉鑒》卷八）

⑩ 掓：拾。
⑪ 懷：懷藏。

1. 出邦門 *chū bāng mén*: walking out of city gate. Similar pieces, with slight variations, are

also seen in bamboo slips *Rìshū* from the Qín tombs at Shuìhǔdì and Fàngmǎtān. And texts with similar content are also found in received ancient books like *Zēngbǔ yùxiájì* 增補玉匣記 (Expanded Record of the Jade Casket, a popular almanac attributed to the third-century immortal Xǔzhēnjūn 許真君) .The term *bāngmén* 邦門 means city gate.

2. 困 *kùn*: threshold, sill.
3. 禹步 *Yǔ bù*: lit. "the step or pace of Yǔ 禹 step," basic dance step of religious Daoism.
4. 勉 *miǎn*: to strive, to make great effort.
5. 謼 *hū*: equivalent to *hū* 呼 , to yell, to cry out.
6. 皋 *gāo*: an onomatopoeia.
7. 某 *mǒu*: referring to the person who makes Yǔ steps and who yells out.
8. 先爲禹除道 *xiān wèi yǔ chú dào*: meaning to remove dangerous things or evil on the road for Yǔ. The sentence was written as "*wèi yǔ qián chú dào* 爲禹前除道" in the Fàngmǎtān Qín bamboo slips.
9. 五畫 *wǔ huà*: to draw some kind of special symbol in five strokes. It may also relate to the so-called *Sìzòng wǔhéng* 四縱五横 , a Daoist diagram of four vertical and five horizontal lines.
10.
敊 *shū*: to pick up.
11. 懷 *huái*: to conceal.

寬式隸定
Loose Transcription

行到邦門閫，禹步三，勉壹步，呼："皋，敢告曰：某行毋咎，先爲禹除道。"即五畫地，敊其畫中央土而懷之。

白話文
Vernacular Chinese

行走到城邑之門的門檻處：走禹步三次，盡力走一步，大叫："發出皋的聲音，冒昧告説：某出行没有災禍，先爲禹清除道路。"就在地上畫上某種符號，拾起所畫符號中央的土而懷藏它。

英文翻譯
English Translation

[When traveling] , on reaching the threshold-bar of the city gate, perform the Pace of Yǔ thrice. Strive for another step, then, call out with a sound like *Gaaah*, [say] I dare make a declaration: Let so-and-so [to be filled in with the name of the traveler] travel and not suffer odium; he removes the dangerous things or evil on the road for Yǔ. Immediately draw a five-stroke (*wǔhuà*) symbol on the ground; pick up the soil from the center of the symbol and conceal it [in the bosom] .

九、夢
9. Dream

原文
Bamboo Script

夢①

甲乙夢被黑裘、衣、寇②（冠），喜。人③〈入〉水中及谷，【得】也。（189 壹）

丙丁夢□，喜也。木金，得也。（190 壹）

戊己夢黑，吉，得、喜也。（191 壹）

庚辛夢青黑，喜心④。木水，得也。（192 壹）

壬癸夢日〈白〉⑤，喜也。金，得也。（193 壹）

凡人有惡夢，覺而擇⑥（釋）之，西北鄉⑦（嚮）擇（釋）髮⑧而駟⑨（呬），祝曰："綼⑩（皋），敢告壐⑪（爾）宛奇⑫，某有惡夢，老來□（194）之，宛奇强⑬歓（飲）食，賜某大畐⑭（富），不錢則布⑮，不壐⑯（繭）則絮。"（195 壹）

注釋
Annotation

① 夢：篇題。全篇先講對不同的天干日夢到不同事物的占測，然後記載驅惡夢的方法，該方法又見於睡虎地秦墓竹簡《日書》甲種。

② 寇：秦隸書中"冠"與"寇"的寫法混同。

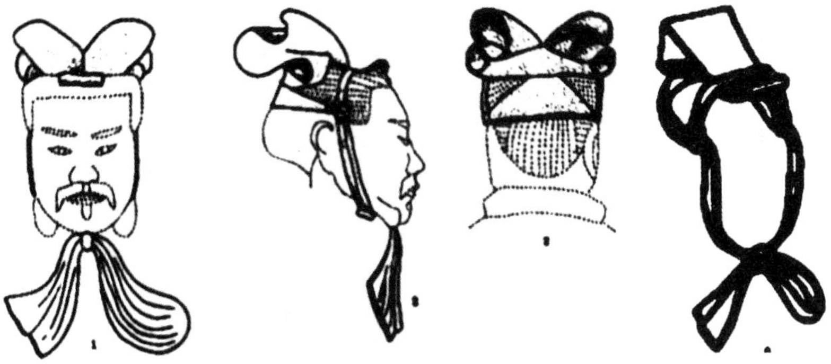

圖 3　秦兵馬俑所戴的冠

Figure 3　Crown worn by Qín Terracotta Soldiers

（引自王學理：《秦物質文化通覽》476 頁）

③ 人："入"的誤寫。

④ 心：疑爲"也"的誤寫。

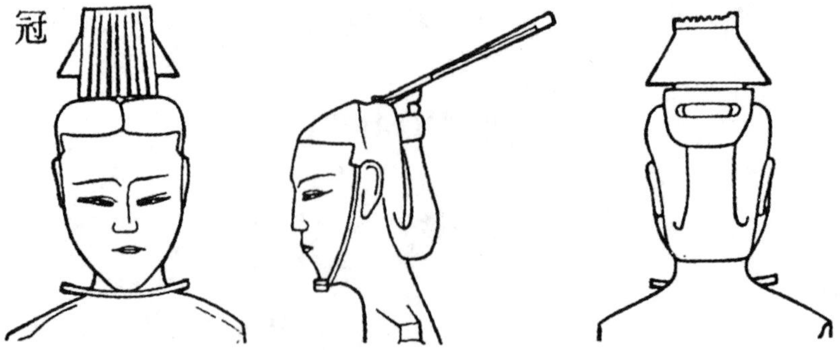

圖 4　馬王堆漢墓中所見的冠
Figure 4　Crown recovered from the Mǎwángduī Hàn tomb
（引自孫機：《漢代物質文化資料圖説》（增訂本）267 頁）

⑤ 日：“白”的誤寫。
⑥ 擇：通“釋”，解除。
⑦ 鄉：通“嚮”，方向。
⑧ 擇髮：即釋髮，解開頭髮。
⑨ 駟：通“呬”，呼吸。這裏應該指調整呼吸，是祝禱前的準備。
⑩ 皞：通“皋”，擬聲詞。
⑪ 壐：通“爾”，你。
⑫ 宛奇：傳世文獻或作“窮奇”，神獸名。《山海經》中記載的“窮奇”形象或類似有翼的老虎，或類似牛。

圖 5　漢畫像石中的“翼虎”
Figure 5　“Winged tiger” in the Hàn Dynasty stone relief
（引自王洪震：《漢畫像石》204 頁）

⑬ 强：努力。
⑭ 畐：通“富”，富有。
⑮ 布：秦時一定規制的“布”可以作爲通行貨贝，秦律中規定：“布袤八尺，福（幅）廣二尺五寸。布惡，其廣袤不如式者，不行。”（睡虎地“金布律”66 號）“錢十一當一

圖6　秦“半兩”錢
Figure 6　Qín currency “*bànliǎng*” coin
（引自周天游：《秦漢雄風》36 頁）

布。”（睡虎地“金布律”67 號）
⑯ 璽：通“繭”。

1. 夢 *mèng*: dream, the title of this piece. The whole piece deals first with the divination of dreams, based on the heavenly stem of each day. The second part describes the method on how to deal with nightmares. A similar method was also mentioned in the Shuìhǔdì Qín tomb 11 bamboo slips *Rìshū* A.
2. 寇 *kòu*: this word was confused with the word *guān* 冠 , meaning “crown.”
3. 人 *rén*: the word should have been written as *rù* 入 , meaning “to enter.”
4. 心 *xīn*: the word was mistakenly written, it is suspected to be *yě* 也 , a particle, just like in previous sentences.
5. 日 *rì*: the word is a typographic error. From the context, the word should have been *bái* 白 , meaning “white.”
6. 擇 *zé*: the word is equivalent to *shì* 釋 , meaning “to release.”
7. 鄉 *xiāng*: equivalent to *xiàng* 嚮 , meaning “direction.”
8. 擇髮 *zé fà*: equivalent to *shì fà* 釋髮 , indicating to release hair, i.e., unbind the hair.
9. 駟 *sì*: the word is equivalent to *xì* 呬 , meaning “to breathe.” Here it means to adjust the breath before the prayer.
10. 綼 *gāo*: the word is equivalent to *gāo* 皋 , an onomatopoeia.
11. 璽 *xǐ*: equivalent to *ěr* 爾 , meaning “you.”
12. 宛奇 *wǎn qí*: name of a legendary beast Wǎnqí. It was also written as *qióngqí* 窮奇 in the received ancient texts.
13. 强 *qiáng*: to work hard.
14. 畐 *fú*: equivalent to *fù* 富 , to be rich, to have wealth.
15. 布 *bù*: in the Qín Dynasty, the regulation was that cloth measuring eight feet by two and half feet and of good quality can be used as currency. According to the *Statutes on Finance* (Shuìhǔdì Qín tomb 11 bamboo slips, No.67), one piece of cloth is worth 11 Qín coins.
16. 璽 *xǐ*: equivalent to *jiǎn* 繭 , cocoon.

寬式隸定
Loose Transcription

夢

甲乙夢被黑裘衣冠，喜，入水中及谷，得也。

丙丁夢□，喜也。木金，得也。

戊己夢黑，吉，得、喜也。

庚辛夢青黑，喜心。木水，得也。

壬癸夢白，喜也。金，得也。

凡人有惡夢，覺而釋之，西北鄉釋髮而呬，祝曰："皋，敢告爾宛奇，某有惡夢，老來□之，宛奇強飲食，賜某大富，不錢則布，不繭則絮。"

白話文
Vernacular Chinese

夢

甲乙日夢到穿着黑裘、穿黑衣、戴黑冠，有喜事。進入水中和山中水流，有所得。

丙丁日夢到某，有喜事。所做之事涉及五行中的木與金，有所得。

戊己夢黑色，吉利，有所得，有喜事。

庚辛日夢到青黑色，有喜事。所做之事涉及五行中的木與水，有所得。

壬癸日夢到白色，有喜事。所做之事涉及五行中的金，有所得。

凡是人有惡夢，醒來解除它，面朝西北解散頭髮而調整呼吸，祝禱說："發出皋的聲音，冒昧告知宛奇，我有惡夢，……宛奇盡力吃掉它，賜給我大富，不是錢就是布，不是繭就是絮。"

英文翻譯
English Translation

Dream

On the days of *jiǎ* and *yǐ*, if dreaming of wearing black fur and wearing a black crown, auspicious. Go into the water or the mountain stream, and you will get something.

On the days of *bǐng* and *dīng*, if dreaming of ..., auspicious. If what you dream is related to wood or gold, you will have gains.

On the days of *wù* and *jǐ*, if dreaming of black color, auspicious, there will be gains, and there will be happiness.

On the days of *gēng* and *xīn*, if dreaming of livid color, there will be happy events. If what you dream is related to wood or water, there will be gains.

On the days of *rén* and *guǐ*, if dreaming of white color, there will be happy events. If what you dream is related to gold, there will be gains.

Anyone who has a nightmare, to get rid of it after waking up, face northwest, unbind the hair, adjust the breathing, pray and say: Gaaah! I take the liberty to tell Wǎnqí that I have a nightmare, ... Wǎnqí please try your best to devour it and give me a great deal of wealth, with either money or cloth, cocoon or silk floss.

十、戎曆日
10. Róng Calendar Day

原文
Bamboo Script

圖表 7
戎曆日示意

此所謂戎磨日②殹（也）。從朔日始數之，畫當（132 叁）一日③。直一④者，大徶（徹）⑤。直周⑥者，小徶（徹）。直周中三（133 叁）畫⑦者，窮（窮）⑧。入月一日、七日、十三日、十九日、廿五日，大（134 叁）徶（徹）。入月二日、六日、八日、十二日、十四日、十八日、廿日、廿（135 叁）四日、廿六日、卅日，小徶（徹）。入月三日、四日、五日、九日（136 叁）、十日、十一日、十五日、十六日、十七日、廿一日、廿二日、廿一（137 貳）二〈三，誤寫爲一二〉日、廿七日、廿八日、廿九日，窮（窮）日。（138 貳）

凡大徶（徹）之日，利以遠行，絶邊竸（境）⑨，攻毄（擊）。亡（139 貳）人不得。利以舉大事⑩。（140 貳）

凡小徶（徹）之日，利以行作⑪，爲好事⑫，取（娶）婦、嫁（141 貳）女，吉。氏（是）謂小徶（徹），利以竆（羈）謀⑬。（142 貳）

凡窮（窮）日，不利有爲殹。亡人得。是謂三（143 貳）閉⑭。（144 貳）

注釋
Annotation

① 該篇整理者命名“戎磨日”。該篇第一支簡是一組圖形，後文據此計算大徹日、小徹日、窮日的日期。

② 戎磨：數術術語。一般認爲磨通“曆”，戎，或認爲義爲大，或認爲指兵車，有待進一步研究。

③ 畫當一日：指 131 號簡中的圖形中的每種筆畫當一日，具體而言單獨的橫筆是一日，方框中的三橫分别是一日，方框數兩次，分别對應一日。5 組橫筆及方框共 30 日。

④ 直一：對應一。一，指單獨的橫筆，共 5 個，對應後文大徹日的 5 個日期。

⑤ 大徶：徶同“徹”，義爲通，大徹指“大通”，從後文的占文看，無論大徹還是小徹，諸事多通達順利，都是吉日。

⑥ 周：指圖形中的長方形框。

⑦ 周中三畫：指框中的 3 個橫筆。

⑧ 窮：同“窮”，這裏作爲日名，取義困窘。從後文的占文看，窮日諸事多不利。

⑨ 絶邊竟：絶，過。邊竟，即邊境。
⑩ 大事：或認爲泛指重要的事，或認爲特指兵役之類事務。
⑪ 行作：勞作。
⑫ 好事：和好之事，如通使、會盟。
⑬ 鳿謀：鳿，同“羈”，通“寄”，謀，通“媒”，羈謀即託人作媒。
⑭ 三閉：指框中的 3 個横筆被閉塞於框中。

1. This piece has been given the title as “Róng Calendar Day” (*Rónglìrì*) by modern editors of the bamboo slip text. The first slip in this piece is a set of figures for diviners to calculate and determine dates that belong to big auspicious days (*dàchèrì*), little auspicious days (*xiǎochèrì*), and days in trouble (*qióngrì*).
2. 戎磿 *róng lì*: the word *lì* 磿 is equivalent to *lì* 曆, a special term used in numerology, probably referring to a method used to devise almanacs. The original meaning of the term is not clear.
3. 畫當一日 *huà dāng yī rì*: lit. “one stroke is equivalent to one day.” Specifically, in the figure shown on slip No.131, one transverse stroke is one day, whether it is independent or within boxes. Together there are 30 strokes corresponding to 30 days.
4. 直一 *zhí yī*: the term refers to 5 single strokes in the figure. They correspond to the big auspicious days.
5. 大徹 *dà chè*: the word *chè* 徹 is equivalent to *chè* 徹, meaning “through, all right, smooth, success.” *Dàchè* means “big success,” indicating it is a big auspicious day.
6. 周 *zhōu*: periphery or circumference. Here it refers to the periphery of the rectangular box in the graph.
7. 周中三畫 *zhōu zhōng sān huà*: the 3 transverse lines or strokes within the rectangular box.
8. 竆 *qióng*: the archaic form of *qióng* 窮, meaning “stranded, hard.” Here it refers to days in which bad or difficult things happen.
9. 絶邊竟 *jué biān jìng*: *jué* 絶, meaning “to cross, to pass.” *Biānjìng* 邊竟, equivalent to *biānjìng* 邊境, meaning “frontier, border.”
10. 大事 *dà shì*: lit. “big thing,” meaning “important matters.” It could specifically refer to military affairs.
11. 行作 *xíng zuò*: the term refers to *láozuò* 勞作, meaning “to do manual labour.”
12. 好事 *hǎo shì*: lit. “good things.” The term refers to activities of making friends, alliances, reconciliation, or establishing relationships.
13. 鳿謀 *jī móu*: *jī* 鳿 is equivalent to *jī* 羈, and is interpreted as *jì* 寄, meaning “to entrust.” The character *móu* 謀 here is equivalent to *méi* 媒, meaning matchmaking. The term *jīmóu* means “to entrust or ask somebody to be a matchmaker.”
14. 三閉 *sān bì*: lit. “three closed.” The term refers to the 3 transverse lines inside a rectangular box.

寬式隸定
Loose Transcription

此所謂戎曆日也。從朔日始數之，畫當一日。直一者，大徹。直周者，小徹。直周中三畫者，窮。入月一日、七日、十三日、十九日、廿五日，大徹。入月二日、六日、八日、十二日、十四日、十八日、廿日、廿四日、廿六日、卅日，小徹。入月三日、四日、五日、九日、十日、十一日、十五日、十六日、十七日、廿一日、廿二日、廿三日、廿七日、廿八日、廿九日，窮日。

凡大徹之日，利以遠行，絶邊境，攻擊。亡人不得。利以舉大事。

凡小徹之日，利以行作，爲好事，娶婦、嫁女，吉。是謂小徹，利以羈謀。

凡窮日，不利有爲毆。亡人得。是謂三閉。

白話文
Vernacular Chinese

這是所説的戎曆日。從朔日開始數，每畫相當於一日。對應一的，是大徹日。對應環繞的部分的，是小徹日。對應環繞部分中間三畫的，是窮日。入月的第一日、第七日、第十三日、第十九日、第二十五日，是大徹日。入月的第二日、第六日、第八日、第十二日、第十四日、第十八日、第二十日、第二十四日、第二十六日、第卅日，是小徹日。入月的第三日、第四日、第五日、第九日、第十日、第十一日、第十五日、第十六日、第十七日、第二十一日、第二十二日、第二十三日、第二十七日、第二十八日、第二十九日，是窮日。

凡是大徹日，利於遠行，過邊境，攻打別人。逃亡的人抓不住。利於舉行大事。

凡是小徹日，利於勞作，進行通使、會盟等促進友好之事，娶妻、嫁女，吉利。這叫做小徹，利於託人説媒。

凡是窮日，不利於做事。逃亡的人能夠抓住。這就是三閉日。

英文翻譯
English Translation

Here, the so-called “*rónglìrì*”, counting from the first day of the month, each stroke in the graph represents a day. The days corresponding to the stroke outside the box are days of *dàchèrì* (major auspicious days) ; the days corresponding to strokes at the periphery are days of *xiǎochèrì* (minor auspicious days) ; the days corresponding to strokes within boxes are days of *qióngrì* days of difficulty. Thus, each month, the first, seventh, thirteenth, nineteenth, and twenty-fifth day are *dàchèrì*. The second, sixth, eighth, twelfth, fourteenth, eighteenth, twentieth, twenty-fourth, twenty-sixth, and thirtieth day of the month are *xiǎochèrì*. The third, fourth, fifth, ninth, tenth, eleventh, fifteenth, sixteenth, seventeenth, twenty-first, twenty-second, twenty-third, twenty-seventh, twenty-eighth, and twenty-ninth day are *qióngrì*. On the days of *dàchèrì*, it will be good for traveling afar, going abroad, attacking an enemy. In the case of escapees, they will not be captured. Good time to execute important business. On the days of *xiǎochèrì*, it will be good for doing manual labor, establishing diplomatic and other relationships, forging alliances, marrying a wife, marrying off a daughter, and matchmaking. All will be auspicious. For the days of *qióngrì*, any activity will not be good. Even escapees will be captured. This is why these days are also called *sānbìrì*, the three days enclosed in the box.

練習
Practice

釋讀圖表 3、圖表 4 中睡虎地秦墓竹簡《日書》乙種 189—193 號簡、195 號簡的第二欄文字。

Read parts of Shuìhǔdì Qín tomb bamboo slips *Rìshū* B, slips No.189-193 and 195 in Tableau 3 and Tableau 4.

第五組　夢書
Group 5　Dream Book

簡介
Introduction

占夢，是一種常見於傳世古籍的行爲，根據夢的内容占卜吉凶至晚在周代就已存在。《漢書・藝文志》雜占類文獻見有《黄帝長柳占夢》《甘德長柳占夢》等占夢文獻，惜已失傳。上一組已經介紹了睡虎地秦墓竹簡《日書》乙種中的《夢》，王家臺秦簡中也有類似的夢占内容。這兩種秦簡有關夢占的敘述並不系統。嶽麓書院藏秦簡中則見有自題爲《夢書》(整理者稱爲《占夢書》) 的一篇文獻，共計48枚簡，是目前此類文獻的首次系統發現。《夢書》主要由兩部分構成，一部分記載了夢占理論，不分欄書寫，另一部分則分兩欄書寫，主要記載夢象及對應的占語。我們以下就舉例討論《夢書》的若干部分。要注意的是由於這批簡牘埋藏於地下的位置關係不明，夢象與占語部分一些簡牘的編聯順序還存在很大争議。謹慎起見，我們僅列舉幾組相對比較確定的編聯組。

To divine and interpret dreams is a common practice frequently seen in ancient texts. This practice has existed at least since the Zhōu Dynasty. Miscellaneous divination texts in the chapter of *Treatise on Literature* (*Yìwénzhì* 藝文志) in *Hànshū* 漢書 include the *Yellow Emperor's Long-Willow Method of Dream Divination* (*Huángdì cháng liǔ zhān mèng* 黄帝長柳占夢) and *Gān Dé's Long-Willow Method of Dream Divination* (*Gān Dé cháng liǔ zhān mèng* 甘德長柳占夢) and other similar texts, but unfortunately they have been lost. We have already introduced *Dreams* (*Mèng* 夢) in Shuìhǔdì Qín tomb 11 bamboo slips. Texts of similar type on dream divination can be seen in Qín bamboo slips unearthed at Wángjiātái. However, in both cases, the narratives about dream divination appear to be incomplete. In the Yuèlù Academy corpus of Qín slips, a document entitled *Dream Book* (*Mèngshū* 夢書) was re-named as *Book of Dream Divination* (*Zhānmèngshū* 占夢書) by the collator. It contains a total of 48 bamboo slips, representing the first discovery of a comprehensive and systematic document on dream divination. The *Book of Dream Divination* is composed of two parts: one records the theory of dream divination, written without separation into segments; the other part deals with dream images/events and corresponding occult interpretations, written pair-wise in two segments. We will use examples selected from the *Book of Dream Divination*. It should be noted that due to the uncertainty of the exact location and placement of these bamboo slips while buried underground, there is still some controversy about the sequence of bamboo slips that relate dream events and occult interpretations. Here, we only select examples where the correlation is certain.

篇目來源
Text Source

第 11 篇　占夢書（節選：《嶽麓書院藏秦簡（貳）》）
11. *Book of Dream Divination*（selected from *Yuèlù Academy Corpus of Qín Slips Ⅱ*）

參考文獻
References

陳松長主编：《嶽麓書院藏秦簡（壹—叁）釋文修訂本》，上海辭書出版社 2018 年。
荊州地區博物館：《江陵王家臺 15 號秦墓》，《文物》1995 年第 1 期。
廉超：《嶽麓書院藏秦簡〈夢書〉研究綜述》，《簡帛研究二〇一九》（秋冬卷），廣西師範大學出版社 2020 年。
吕亞虎：《秦簡中的夢幻占禳信仰初探》，《寶雞文理學院學報》2016 年第 6 期。
孫占宇、魯家亮：《放馬灘秦簡及嶽麓秦簡〈夢書〉研究》，武漢大學出版社 2017 年。
朱漢民、陳松長：《嶽麓書院藏秦簡（壹）》，上海辭書出版社 2010 年。

照片、隸定本
Photo, Transcription

圖表 1　嶽麓書院藏秦簡《占夢書》2—5
Tableau 1: Yuèlù Academy corpus of Qín slips, *Book of Dream Divination*, No.2-5
圖表 2　嶽麓書院藏秦簡《占夢書》1，48，9，10，15
Tableau 2: Yuèlù Academy corpus of Qín slips, *Book of Dream Divination*, No.1, 48, 9, 10, 15
圖表 3　嶽麓書院藏秦簡《占夢書》31，32，37，38，39
Tableau 3: Yuèlù Academy corpus of Qín slips, *Book of Dream Divination*, No.31, 32, 37, 38, 39

圖表 1　Tableau 1

《占夢書》5			《占夢書》4			《占夢書》3			《占夢書》2		
隸定	照片（下）	照片（上）	隸定	照片（下）	照片（上）	隸定	照片（下）	照片（上）	隸定	照片（下）	照片（上）
宮事吉庚辛夢攻山鑄鐘吉壬癸夢行川爲橋吉晦而夢三年至夜半夢者二年而至雞鳴夢者		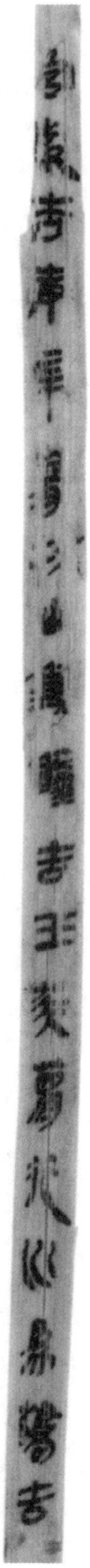	戊己夢語言也庚辛夢喜也壬癸夢生事也甲乙夢伐木吉丙丁夢失火高陽吉戊己		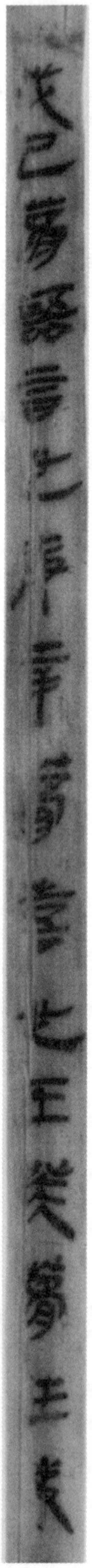	亓類毋失四時之所宜五分日参分日夕吉兇有節善羛有故甲乙夢開臧事也丙丁夢憂也			□□□□□□□始□□之時亟令夢先春曰發□夏曰陽秋曰閉冬曰臧占夢之道必順四時而豫	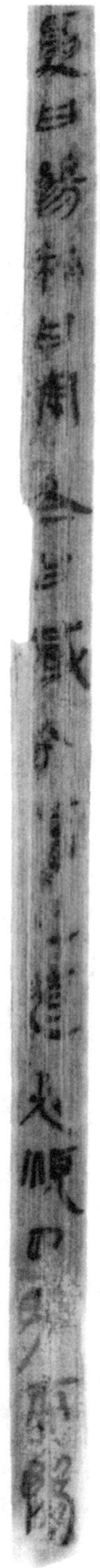	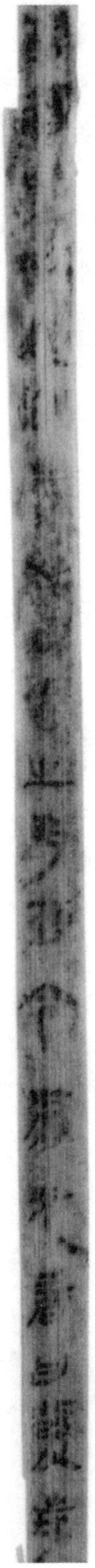

圖表 2　Tableau 2

《占夢書》15 第 1、2 欄		《占夢書》10 第 1、2 欄		《占夢書》9 第 1、2 欄		《占夢書》48		《占夢書》1		
隸定	照片	隸定	照片	隸定	照片	隸定	照片（上）	隸定	照片（下）	照片（上）
秋冬夢亡於上者吉亡於下者兇是謂□兇		夢亡下者吉		春夏夢亡上者兇		不占	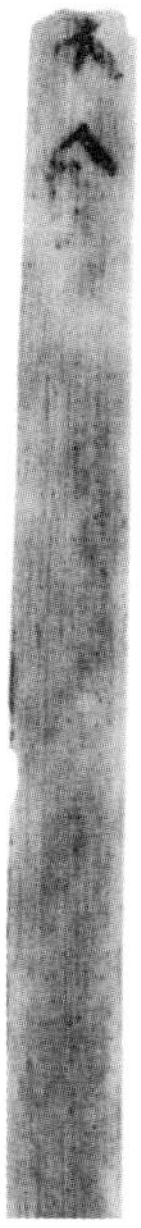	若晝夢亟發不得其日以來爲日不得亓時以來爲時醉飽而夢雨變氣不占晝言而莫夢之有	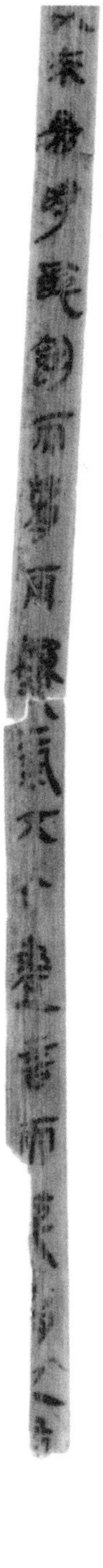	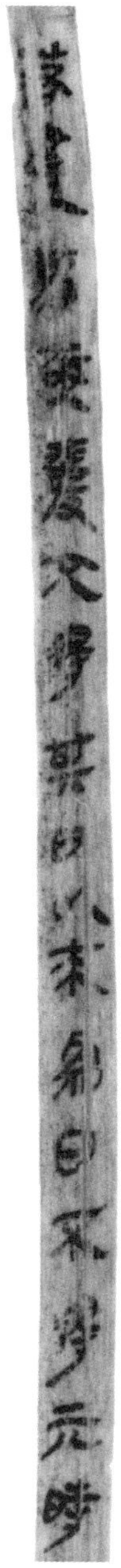
夢爲女子必有失也女子兇		夢身被枯妻若女必有死者丈夫吉		夢夫妻相反負者妻若夫必有死者						

圖表 3　Tableau 3

《占夢書》39 第 2 欄		《占夢書》38 第 2 欄		《占夢書》37 第 2 欄		《占夢書》32 第 1、2 欄		《占夢書》31 第 1、2 欄	
隸定	照片	隸定	照片	隸定	照片	隸定	照片	隸定	照片
夢見熊者見官長		夢見虎豹者見貴人		夢見衆羊有行千里		夢以泣灑人得亓亡子		夢以弱灑人得亓亡弩婢	
						夢見李爲復故吏		夢見桃爲有苛憂	

十一、占夢書
11. Book of Dream Divination

原文
Bamboo Script

第一節

□□□□□□□□始□□之時，亟令夢先①，春曰發□②，夏曰陽，秋曰閉，冬曰臧（藏）。占夢之道，必順四時而豫③02 亓（其）類，毋失四時之所宜，五分日④，參（三）分日夕⑤，吉兇有節，善羛（俄）⑥有故。甲乙⑦夢，開臧（藏）⑧事也；丙丁夢，憂也；03 戊己夢，語言⑨也；庚辛夢，喜也；壬癸夢，生事⑩也。甲乙夢伐木，吉；丙丁夢失火、高陽⑪，吉；戊己【夢】04 宮事⑫，吉；庚辛夢攻山、鑄鐘⑬，吉；壬癸夢行川、爲橋，吉。晦而夢三年至；夜半夢者二年而至；雞鳴夢者 05……⑭若晝夢亟發，不得其日，以來爲日；不得亓（其）時，以來爲時；醉飽而夢雨、變氣⑮，不占。晝言而莫（暮）夢之，有 01……不占。48

第二節

春夏夢亡上⑯者，兇。（09 上）夢亡下者，吉。（10 上）秋冬夢亡於上者，吉。亡於下者，兇。是謂□兇。（15 上）……夢夫妻相反負⑰者，妻若夫必有死者。（09 下）夢身被枯⑱，妻若女必有死者，丈夫吉。（10 下）夢爲女子，必有失也，女子兇。（15 下）

第三節

夢以弱（溺）灑人，得亓（其）亡䊸（奴）婢。（31 上）夢以泣灑人，得亓（其）亡子。（32 上）……

夢見桃，爲有苛憂⑲。（31 下）夢見李，爲復故吏⑳。（32 下）

第四節

夢見衆羊，有行千里。（37 下）夢見虎豹者，見貴人。（38 下）夢見熊者，見官長。（39 下）

注釋
Annotation

① 先：次序在前。雖前文有大量未釋字，但大體可以推斷此處指將要發生之事以夢爲先兆出現。

② 春曰發："發"後的未釋字整理者釋爲"時"，但字形與該篇其他"時"字字形不類，故

此處不釋。《潛夫論》載："春夢發生，夏夢高明，秋冬夢熟藏。此謂應時之夢也。"與簡文所載相近。春季萬物生長，故"發某"應爲發生義，是對春季事物的概括。後文的"陽""閉""臧（藏）"與季節對應，也是對夢象性質的概括。秋季萬物開始蕭條，"閉"有收藏義，故用來概括秋季的事物。冬季寒冷，萬物藏匿，故冬季事物用"藏"來概括。值得注意的是，《管子・禁藏》載："故春仁、夏忠、秋急、冬閉，順天之時，約地之宜，忠人之和。""閉"用來指冬季之事。《左傳・僖公五年》載："凡分、至、啟、閉，必書雲物。"杜預注："閉，立秋、立冬。"看來"閉"既可指秋季，也可指冬季。

③ 豫：與前文的"順"語義相近，也可釋爲順應。

④ 五分日：將白天分爲5段，睡虎地秦墓竹簡《日書》屢見這樣的劃分，如《吏》篇將白日分爲"朝""晏""晝""日虒""夕"，《禹須臾（二）》分爲"旦""莫食""日中""市日""莫市"。另《隋書・天文志》載："晝有朝，有禺，有中，有晡，有夕。"名稱大同小異，大體相當於今天的早晨、上午、中午、下午、傍晚。

⑤ 參分日夕："參"即"三"，"參分日夕"指將夜晚分爲3段，下文的"晦""夜半""雞鳴"即與此對應，分別是上半夜、午夜和下半夜。

⑥ 羛：即"義"，通"俄"，奸邪，與"善"意義相反。

⑦ 甲乙：天干日名，或以爲對應春季。五行文化本就有將季節、天干日等相對應的情況，這在《禮記・月令》等文獻中多有記載。但具體到占夢，主要關注的還是日、時，因此，我們認爲此處的"甲乙"等天干名稱還是理解爲日名更合理。

⑧ 開臧：臧，通"藏"。春季萬物復甦，相對於冬季的"藏"爲"開藏"。

⑨ 語言：口舌之事。

⑩ 生事：發生事端。

⑪ 失火、高陽："失火"如字解，"高陽"指位置高、陽光充足之處，這裏大概用作動詞，指居於"高陽"之處。

⑫ 宮事：營造房屋之事。

⑬ 攻山、鑄鐘：開山，鑄造鐘類樂器。

⑭ 此處有缺簡。

⑮ 變氣：奇異的雲氣。

⑯ 亡上：上，長輩，相對應的後文的"下"指晚輩，亡上，指長輩死亡。或以爲"亡上"指死在別人的上面。

⑰ 反負：背棄。

⑱ 柀枯：柀，一部分。柀枯，指身體偏癱。

⑲ 苛憂：苛，責備。苛憂，泛指憂愁之事。

⑳ 復故吏：吏，指身份。復故吏，回復以前的身份。

1. 先 *xiān*: "preceded," meaning the dream comes first as a portent for what may happen. There are several missing characters at the beginning of this sentence.
2. 春曰發 *chūn yuē fā*: the unidentified character after *fā* 發 is thought to be *shí* 時 , but the graph

appears to be different from the characters for *shí* that occur in all other places. The character *fā* 發 literally means "happening" and here refers to the growth of new life in the spring. There are similar records in *Comments of a Recluse*（*Qián fū lùn* 潛夫論）: "In spring dreams things happen; in summer dreams things high and bright; in autumn and winter dreams things mature and get stored."

3. 豫 *yù*: it is similar in semantics to *shùn* 順 , meaning to conform or conformity.
4. 五分日 *wǔ fēn rì*: dividing the daytime into 5 sections, roughly equivalent to morning, before noon, noon, afternoon, and evening. Such a division is commonly seen in the Qín and pre-Qín bamboo slips and in received ancient texts.
5. 參分日夕 *sān fēn rì xī*: *sān* 參 is equivalent to *sān* 三 , meaning three. The term *sān fēn rì xī* means to divide the night into 3 segments: before midnight, midnight and after midnight, equivalent to the following three terms: darkness（*huì* 晦）, midnight（*yèbàn* 夜半）, and cock crow（*jīmíng* 雞鳴）.
6. 羕 *yì*: archaic form of the character *yì* 義 . But here it reads as *è* equivalent to *è* 惡 , meaning evil, bad.
7. 甲乙 *jiǎ yǐ*: there are ten stems or heavenly stems（*gān* 干）and twelve branches or earthly branches（*zhī* 支）in the 60-day *gānzhī* system, the combination of one *gān* and one *zhī* in an orderly manner forms 60 pairs to denote each day in a 60-day cycle. Thus, day *jiǎyǐ* means the day containing *jiǎ* or *yǐ* stems.
8. 開臧 *kāi zāng*: lit. "to open the concealed." *zāng* 臧 , equivalent to *cáng* 藏 , concealed, hidden, stored. In spring, organisms start to open up, i.e., to grow, whereas in winter, organisms start to hide or conceal.
9. 語言 *yǔ yán*: lit. "matter of mouth and tongue," referring to disputes or quarrel.
10. 生事 *shēng shì*: lit. "to cause matters," meaning to cause trouble or create a disturbance.
11. 失火 *shī huǒ*, 高陽 *gāo yáng*: *shīhuǒ* 失火 to be on fire. *gāoyáng* 高陽 , lit. "high and sunny," meaning a place at high altitude with plenty of sunshine. Here, it is used as a verb, meaning to stay at a high place with ample sunshine.
12. 宫事 *gōng shì*: lit. "palace matters," referring to matters related to construction, like building houses.
13. 攻山 *gōng shān*, 鑄鐘 *zhù zhōng*: *gōngshān* 攻山 , lit. "to attack mountains," meaning to open up mountains for mining or for creating additional land. *Zhùzhōng* 鑄鐘 , lit. "casting bells," meaning matters related to casting bells and other bronze instruments.
14. There are missing slips here.
15. 變氣 *biàn qì*: lit. "change air," here refers to *yúnqì* 雲氣 , floating clouds. The term *biàn qì* means changing clouds.
16. 亡上 *wáng shàng*: *shàng* 上 refers to seniors, whereas *xià* 下 refers to juniors. The term *wáng shàng* means the death of elders.

17. 反負 *fǎn fù*: lit. “to turn over and carry on one’s back,” meaning betrayal, abandon.
18. 柀枯 *bǐ kū*: *bǐ* 柀 , partially; *kū* 枯 , paralysis. The term refers to hemiplegia, that is, the paralysis of one side of the body.
19. 苛憂 *kē yōu*: *kē* 苛 , scolding, condemnation; *yōu* 憂 , matters that cause worries, sorrow, or sadness.
20. 復故吏 *fù gù lì*: *lì* 吏 refers to a person’s status. The term *fù gù lì* indicates that the old status or position is restored.

寬式隸定
Loose Transcription

第一節

□□□□□□□始□□之時，亟令夢先，春曰發□，夏曰陽，秋曰閉，冬曰藏。占夢之道，必順四時而豫其類，毋失四時之所宜，五分日，三分日夕，吉兇有節，善俄有故。甲乙夢，開藏事也；丙丁夢，憂也；戊己夢，語言也；庚辛夢，喜也；壬癸夢，生事也。甲乙夢伐木，吉；丙丁夢失火、高陽，吉；戊己夢宮事，吉；庚辛夢攻山、鑄鐘，吉；壬癸夢行川、爲橋，吉。晦而夢三年至；夜半夢者二年而至；雞鳴夢者……若晝夢亟發，不得其日，以來爲日；不得其時，以來爲時；醉飽而夢雨、變氣，不占。晝言而暮夢之，有……不占。

第二節

春夏夢亡上者，兇。夢亡下者，吉。秋冬夢亡於上者，吉。亡於下者，兇。是謂□兇。……夢夫妻相反負者，妻若夫必有死者。夢身柀枯，妻若女必有死者，丈夫吉。夢爲女子，必有失也，女子兇。

第三節

夢以溺灑人，得其亡奴婢。夢以泣灑人，得其亡子。……
夢見桃，爲有苛憂。夢見李，爲復故吏。

第四節

夢見衆羊，有行千里。夢見虎豹者，見貴人。夢見熊者，見官長。

白話文
Vernacular Chinese

第一節

……屢次使夢先出現（征兆），春季稱爲發生，夏季稱爲陽，秋季稱爲閉，冬季稱爲藏。占測的方法，一定要順應四季及其類别，不要違背四季所適宜者，將白天分爲五段，將夜晚分爲三段，吉凶有法度，好壞有緣由。甲乙日做夢，打開藏匿之物的事；丙丁日做夢，有憂愁；戊己日做夢，有言語争端；庚辛日做夢，有喜事；壬癸日做夢，有事端。甲乙日夢到伐木，吉利；丙丁日夢到失火、居於高而向陽處，吉利；戊己日夢到營造房屋之事，吉利；庚辛日夢到採礦、鑄造鐘之事，吉利；壬癸日夢到行水、造橋，吉利。上半夜做夢，夢象所示三年後實現；午夜做夢，夢象所示兩年後實現；下半夜做夢，……白日夢屢次發生，不能知道其日期，以來占測之日爲日期；不能知道其時刻，以來占測之時爲時刻；酒醉而夢到下雨或雲氣變化，不占測。白日談論某事而晚上夢到它，有……，不占測。

第二節

春季、夏季夢到長輩死亡，凶。夢到晚輩死亡，吉利。秋季、冬季夢到長輩死亡，吉利。夢到晚輩死亡，凶。這叫做“某凶”。……夢到夫妻相背棄，妻子或丈夫一定有要死去的。夢到身體偏癱，妻子或女兒一定有要死去的，成年男子則吉利。夢到成爲女子，一定會有所失去，女子凶。

第三節

夢到用溺淋人，得到逃亡的奴婢。夢到流淚淋人，得到其失去的孩子。……

夢見桃樹，爲有譴責憂愁。夢見李樹，爲恢復舊有身份。

第四節

夢見很多羊，將出行千里。夢見虎豹，見到身份尊貴之人。夢見熊，見到官署長官。

英文翻譯
English Translation

Section One

... make (or let) dream appear to be an augury or omen. In spring time, dream about things to grow; in summer time, about things sunny and bright; in autumn time, about things closed out or mature; in winter time, about storage or hiding. The method of divination or occult telling must be carried out in accordance with the nature of the seasons. Do not miss the cue that each season offers. Divide the day into five sections and night into three sections. There are rules on what is good and what is bad, and there are causes for that. Dreams on the days of *jiǎ* and *yǐ* (according to the *gānzhī* system) are related to things about opening up from some hidden state; dreams on the days of *bǐng* and *dīng*, are related to things worrisome or sad; dreams on the days of *wù* and *jǐ*, are related to disputes or gossip; dreams on the days of *gēng* and *xīn* are related to things auspicious; dreams on the days of *rén* and *guǐ* are related to things of trouble. Dreams of logging on the days of *jiǎ* and *yǐ*, auspicious; dreams of a fire on the days of *bǐng* and *dīng*, while living in a high and sunny place, auspicious; dreams of building houses on the days of *wù* and *jǐ*, auspicious; dream of mining and casting bells on the days of *gēng* and *xīn*, auspicious; dreams of river trips and building bridges on the days of *rén* and *guǐ*, auspicious. Dreaming in the first half of the night, the dream will come true in three years as shown; dreaming at midnight, the dream will come true in two years as shown; dreaming in the second half of the night ... If dreams at daytime occur repeatedly, and thus there is uncertainty about the exact date, then use the date of visiting for divination; if you are not certain about the time of dreaming, use the time of visiting for divination. If you dream about rain or change in weather after you were drunken, no divination [should be made] . If you dream about something that you have discussed at daytime, ... no divination [should be made] .

Section Two

In the spring and summer, dreaming of death of elders is bad omen, dreaming of the death of a junior is auspicious. In the autumn and winter, dreaming of the death of elders is auspicious, dreaming of the death of a junior is bad omen. This is called ... bad omen. ... Dreaming of husband and wife betraying each other, either the wife or the husband will die. If you dream of hemiplegia, your wife or daughter will die, while auspicious for adult men. To dream of becoming a woman, you will definitely lose something, it is a bad omen for a woman.

Section Three

Dreaming of splashing urine on people is a portent for recovering escaped slaves. Dreaming of splashing people with tears is a portent for recovering his lost child. ... Dreaming of peach trees is an omen for having condemnation or something worrisome. Dreaming of plum trees is an omen for restoring your old status.

Section Four

Dreaming of a lot of sheep is an omen for a forthcoming long trip. Dreaming of tigers and leopards is an omen for meeting a noble man. Dreaming of a bear is an omen for meeting a high official.

練習
Practice

釋讀圖表 4 中的幾枚嶽麓書院藏秦簡《占夢書》簡。

Read the slips in Tableau 4 (selected from *Book of Dream Divination*).

圖表 4　Tableau 4

《占夢書》36	《占夢書》34	《占夢書》33

第六組　醫方
Group 6　Medical Recipes

簡介
Introduction

中國早期文獻中，很早就有一類文獻被稱作“經方”。《漢書·藝文志》載：“經方者，本草石之寒温，量疾病之淺深，假藥味之滋，因氣感之宜，辯五苦六辛，致水火之齊，以通閉解結，反之於平。及失其宜者，以熱益熱，以寒增寒，精氣内傷，不見於外，是所獨失也。”《藝文志》的“經方”目録中包括很多醫方文獻。

張仲景的《傷寒雜病論》一向被奉爲中國醫方之祖，因此，人們以往將漢末視爲醫方書誕生的時間。自 20 世紀末以來，國内陸續出土了較多的秦簡醫方文獻。秦簡中的醫方文獻，主要分佈在周家臺秦墓竹簡、里耶秦簡、北京大學藏秦簡等秦簡中。周家臺秦墓竹簡醫方簡在被整理者命名爲《病方及其他》的文獻中，主要包含病方、祝由術（是一種包含了祝咒、符禁以及各種動作、物品在内的用於疾患的巫術治病法）等。或載於一枚簡，或載於多枚簡，有 20 組左右。里耶秦簡中的醫方散見於不同的出土層，《里耶秦簡（壹）》中有 10 余組，《里耶秦簡（貳）》中有近 10 組。主要是巫術色彩不顯著的單方，多數並不完整。有一枚醫方簡編號爲 98，説明當時的醫方書所載醫方數量應該不少。北京大學藏秦簡中的醫方被整理者命名爲《病方》，主要包括典型的祝由術和巫術色彩不顯著的單方兩類。

秦簡醫方具有重要的價值。首先，可以進一步認識秦代的疾病。如“温病”“齲”“癰（腫）”“鼠（鼠瘻）”等病名，也見於《黄帝内經》，應是秦漢時期的常見疾病。其次，可以進一步認識秦代醫學的治療手段。不僅有服藥、針石、艾灸、藥物與熱熨綜合治療等療法，還有“行禹步”等巫術手段，而巫術治療的疾病，往往是心疾、齲齒、婦人早産等治療本身有一定難度的疾病。再次，可以進一步認識秦簡醫方的具體組成。如里耶秦簡 8-1221 號簡所載藥方由菥蓂果實、乾薑、菌桂等藥物組成，里耶秦簡 8-1057 號簡所載藥方由鼢鼠、長石、辛夷、甘草等藥物組成，這些多味藥物組成的藥方，爲東漢時的《金匱要略》等醫學文獻成熟的藥物配伍的形成起到了準備作用。再如醫方中多見以酒入藥，周家臺秦簡計有 25 例醫方，以酒入藥者有 6 例，這與《黄帝内經·湯液醪醴論》所述相合，也印證了《漢書·食貨志》所言“酒爲百藥之長”。最後，可以進一步認識中國古代哲學與醫學的互動。如秦簡醫方中多見“東首卧”“印（迎）屋左榮”“東向”等語，太陽升起的東方象徵着生長，或是五行學説對疾病治療方法的具體影響。

The term *jīngfāng* 經方 (classical recipes) appears first in *Hànshū* 漢書 , the official history of the Western Hàn Dynasty (206 BCE-8 CE). The chapter *Treatise on Literature* 藝文志 in *Hànshū* states: “The so-called *jīngfāng* are based on the nature of herbal and mineral ingredients. They are

圖 1　曲阜孔廟藏東漢扁鵲行醫畫像石

Figure 1　A stone relief from Confucius Temple in Qūfù dated to Eastern Hàn Dynasty showing Biǎnquè, the famous Chinese doctor, practiced medicine

（引自和中浚、吴鴻洲：《中華醫學文物圖集》49 頁）

categorized according to the severity of illness; take into consideration the taste of medicine in line with seasonal cycle and external conditions; differentiate five kinds of bitterness and six kinds of pungency; aim at achieving leveling of water and fire in order to open up obstructions and untie knots, so that ultimately the body returns to an equilibrium. If one does not conform to external conditions: adding heat to heat, cold to cold, then the internal essence and *qì* 氣 would be damaged, even without outward signs, and failure [to cure] would be assured." Based on this description, we can conclude that the term *jīngfāng* refers to medical prescriptions.

The Zhōujiātái Qín tomb 30 bamboo slips, Lǐyē Qín slips, and Peking University corpus of Qín bamboo slips all contain slips related to medical recipes. The slips of recipes among Zhōujiātái Qín tomb 30 bamboo slips have been assembled and published under the title *Prescription for Illness and Others* (*Bìngfāng jí qítā* 病方及其他), containing mostly prescriptions and the shamanistic healing (*zhùyóu* 祝由) formula. Slips of recipes from the Lǐyē site were discovered in different archaeological layers and are mostly incomplete. The slips of recipes in the Peking University corpus of Qín bamboo slips have been assembled and published under the title *Prescription for Illness* (*Bìngfāng* 病方). This publication contains both medical prescriptions and shamanistic healing formula.

All of these medical recipes are quite valuable: First, it allows us to gain understanding of common illnesses that occurred at the time of Qín. The name of diseases such as fever (*wēnbìng* 温病), caries (*qǔ* 齲), carbuncle (*yōng* 癰), *shǔ* 鼠 or fistula of tuberculous lyphadenitis (*shǔlòu* 鼠瘻) are also mentioned in the *Inner Canon of the Yellow Emperor* (*Huángdìnèijīng* 黄帝内經), indicating that they were quite common during the time of the Qín and Hàn Dynasties. Secondly, we can learn about the treatment methods commonly used in Qín medicine. These methods not only include medications, acupuncture, moxibustion and medications plus heat applications, but also shamanistic methods such as walking Yǔ steps (*xíng Yǔbù* 行禹步), which usually was used to treat intractable diseases like heart conditions, dental caries, or premature birth. Third, we can further understand the specific composition of medical prescriptions from the recipes listed in the bamboo slips. For example, one recipe from Lǐyē Qín slips (Lǐyē 8-1221) is composed of the fruit of the thlaspi arvens, dried ginger, cinnamon and other medicines. Another recipe (Lǐyē 8-1057) is composed of zokor, feldspar, flower bud of lily magnolia, licorice and other drugs. Such multi-component recipes are the precursor of more effective recipes as described in advanced medical treatises like the *Synopsis of Golden Chamber* (*Jīnguìyàolüè* 金匱要略) of the Eastern Hàn Dynasty. Another example is that grain wine is often used as medicine in medical prescriptions. Among the 25 recipes in bamboo slips from Qín tomb 30 at Zhōujiātái, 6 of them use grain wine. This is consistent with the description in the *Inner Canon of the Yellow Emperor*. And it also confirms what was said in the chapter "*Treatise on Food and Money*" in the *Hànshū* that "among the hundred medicines, grain wine ranks at the top". Lastly, we can further gain understanding of how medicine and philosophy are interwined with each other in ancient time. For example, words such as lying down [or sleeping] with your head to the East (*dōngshǒu wò* 東首卧), facing the eaves on the left side of the house (*yíng wū zuǒróng* 迎屋左榮), and facing east (*dōngxiàng* 東向) are often seen in Qín bamboo slips. The rising sun in the east symbolizes growth, hence those words were likely influenced by the philosophy of Five Elements (*Wǔxíng* 五行) theory.

篇目來源
Chapter Source

第 12 篇　已腸辟方（周家臺秦墓竹簡 309—310 號簡）

12. *A Recipe for Treating Dysentery* (Zhōujiātái Qín tomb 30 bamboo slips, slips 309-310)

第 13 篇　不癉病方（周家臺秦墓竹簡 313 號簡）

13. *A Recipe for Preventing Colds* (Zhōujiātái Qín tomb 30 bamboo slips, slip 313)

第 14 篇　長髮方（周家臺秦墓竹簡 314 號簡）

14. *A Recipe for Hair Growth* (Zhōujiātái Qín tomb 30 bamboo slips, slip 314)

第 15 篇　治暴心痛方（里耶秦簡 8-1221 號簡）

15. *A Recipe for Curing Sudden Heartburn* (Lǐyē Qín slips, slip 8-1221)

第 16 篇　祝心疾方（北京大學藏秦簡《病方》221 號簡）

16. *A Recipe for Treating Heartache* (Peking University corpus of Qín bamboo slips Prescription for Illness, slip 4-028)

第 17 篇　已癰方（北京大學藏秦簡《病方》211 號簡）

17. *A Recipe for Treating Carbuncle* (Peking University corpus of Qín bamboo slips Prescription for Illness, slip 4-248)

參考文獻
References

陳侃理：《北大秦簡中的方術書》，《文物》2012 年第 6 期。

陳偉主編:《秦簡牘合集釋文注釋修訂本(叁)》,武漢大學出版社 2016 年。
方勇、侯娜:《讀周家台秦簡醫方簡札記(二則)》,《魯東大學學報》2015 年第 3 期。
方勇、胡潤怡:《讀秦醫方簡札記二則》,《長春師範大學學報》2015 年第 7 期。
和中浚、吴鴻洲:《中華醫學文物圖集》,四川人民出版社 2001 年。
湖北省荊州市周梁玉橋遺址博物館:《關沮秦漢墓簡牘》,中華書局 2001 年。
紀婷婷、李志芳:《胡家草場漢簡醫方雜識兩則》,《江漢考古》2020 年第 1 期。
賈海燕、王秦江:《從出土材料看先秦秦漢醫學》,《中國社會科學報》2020 年 8 月 17 日第 4 版。
劉金華:《周家台秦簡醫方試析》,《甘肅中醫》2007 年第 6 期。
田天:《北大秦簡〈醫方雜抄〉初識》,《北京大學學報》2017 年第 5 期。
謝妍、沈澍農:《周家臺〈病方〉疾病名研究》,《南京中醫藥大學學報》2017 年第 4 期。
張雷:《秦漢簡牘醫方集注》,中華書局 2018 年。
周祖亮、方懿林:《簡帛醫藥文獻校釋》,學苑出版社 2014 年。

照片、隸定本
Photo, Transcription

圖表 1　周家臺秦墓竹簡 309,310,313,314
Tableau 1: Zhōujiātái Qín tomb 30 bamboo slips, slips 309, 310, 313, 314
圖表 2　里耶秦簡 8-1221,北京大學藏秦簡《病方》221,北京大學藏秦簡《病方》211
Tableau 2: Lǐyē Qín slips, slip 8-1221; Peking University corpus of Qín bamboo slips Prescription for Illness, slip 221, 211

圖表 1　Tableau 1

周家臺 314		周家臺 313		周家臺 310		周家臺 309	
隸定	照片	隸定	照片	隸定	照片	隸定	照片
•取新乳狗子盡之即沐取一匕以殽沐長髮		•以正月取桃橐矢少半升置淳酒中温歓之令人不單病		復益歓之鬻足以入之腸		•取肥牛膽盛黑叔中盛之而係縣陰所乾用之取十餘叔置鬻中而歓之已腸辟不已	

圖表 2　Tableau 2

北京大學藏《病方》211		北京大學藏《病方》221		里耶 8-1221	
隸定	照片	隸定	照片	隸定	照片
痍而内扁血不出者以女子月吏布水一桮濯之而歓		祝心疾唾之曰歜某父某母爲某不以時令某心甬毋期令某唾之		•七病暴心痛灼〃者治之析蓂實治二枯橿菌 桂治各一凡三物并和取三指冣到節二温醇酒	

十二、已腸辟方
12. A Recipe for Treating Dysentery

原文
Bamboo Script

取肥牛膽① 盛黑叔（菽），中② 盛之而係（繫）縣（懸）③ 陰所，乾。用之，取十餘叔（菽）置鬻（粥）中而歙（飲）之，已腸辟④。不已，復益歙（飲）之。鬻（粥）足以入之腸。⑤

注釋
Annotation

① 牛膽：《本草綱目》記載“牛膽”能“止下痢”。

② 中：或屬上讀，或釋爲滿，這裏暫且將其理解爲内，“中盛之”指用置於肥牛膽内的方式盛黑豆。

③ 係縣：係通“繫”，縣通“懸”，同義連用義爲懸掛。

④ 腸辟：又作“腸澼”，即痢疾。《醫宗金鑒》：“腸辟、滯下，古痢名。”

⑤ 治療“腸澼”的藥方，既見於上述周家臺秦墓竹簡醫方 309、310 號簡，也見於武威醫簡 82 號簡，前者僅言“腸辟”，後者言“腸辟卧血”，具體病候有所不同，周家臺秦簡醫方以牛膽所盛黑豆置粥中飲服治療腸澼，而武威醫簡以黄芩、石脂、龍骨、人參、薑、桂等藥物治療腸澼便血，可見秦漢時期對於腸澼這種疾病有了比較成熟的認識、分類和具體治療。

1. 牛膽 *niú dǎn*: ox gall. According to the *Compendium of Materia Medica*（*Běncǎo gāngmù* 本草綱目）, prescription of ox gall could stop diarrhea.
2. 中 *zhōng*: inside. Here, it means the black bean was put inside the gall.
3. 係縣 *xì xiàn*: The word *xì* 係 reads as *xì* 繫, the word *xiàn* 縣 reads as *xuán* 懸, they are synonymous, meaning to hang something up.
4. 腸辟 *cháng pì*: according to the *Golden Mirror of Medicine*（*Yīzōng jīnjiàn* 醫宗金鑒）, *chángpì* 腸辟 is the ancient term for dysentery.
5. The recipes for treating intestinal illnesses（*chángpì*）can be found in slips No.309 and 310 unearthed from tomb 30 at Zhōujiātái, as well as in slip No.82 of Wǔwēi medical slips; the former mentions only *chángpì*, the latter makes reference to intestinal illnesses with blood stool. As the specific symptoms are different, the prescription for *chángpì* in the slips unearthed from tomb 30 at Zhōujiātái uses black beans in porridge, whereas the Wǔwēi medical slip

uses scutellaria baicalensis, stone ester, dragon bones, ginseng, ginger, cinnamomum cassia for treating intestinal diarrhea and bleeding. Clearly, at the time of the Qín and Hàn Dynasties, people already had a good understanding of illnesses linked to the intestinal tract and offered classification and specific treatment.

寬式隸定
Loose Transcription

取肥牛膽盛黑菽，中盛之而繫懸陰所，乾。用之，取十餘菽置粥中而飲之，已腸辟。不已，復益飲之。粥足以入之腸。

白話文
Vernacular Chinese

取肥牛膽盛黑豆，置盛於其中然後懸掛到陰暗處，使之乾燥。用药，取十多個豆子放到粥中而飲服，（可以）治療痢疾。不能痊愈，再增加飲用次數。粥以足夠將黑豆送入腸中爲宜。

英文翻譯
English Translation

Take fat ox gallbladder to hold black beans, hang them in the dark to dry. When using them, put more than ten beans into the porridge and drink [the porridge] to treat dysentery. If still not well, drink more. Eat just enough porridge to help the black beans to descend into the intestines.

十三、不癉病方
13. A Recipe for Preventing Colds

原文
Bamboo Script

以正月①取桃橐（蠹）矢（屎）②少半升，置淳（醇）酒中，温，歙（飲）之，令人不單③（癉）病。

注釋
Annotation

① 正月：此月有重要的民俗意義，此時合藥，寓有破舊迎新之意，也是祈福、製藥的最佳時節。後世元日喝椒柏酒，服辟疫方“屠蘇酒”也是此意。

② 桃橐矢：橐通“蠹”，矢通“屎”，《本草綱目》卷41載：“桃蠹蟲……糞主治辟温疫，令不相染，爲末，水服，方寸匕。”《肘後備急方・治瘴氣疫癘温毒諸方》載：“斷温病令不相染著，斷髪仍使長七寸，盜著病人卧席下……又方，桃木中蟲矢末，服方寸匕”相類。桃在早期文化中具備辟邪殺鬼的特性，如桃符、桃木劍等被用於殺鬼祛邪。通過服用桃蛀蟲屎避免癉病，可能與桃的民俗文化有關。類似的記載還見於《神農本草經》：“桃蠹，殺鬼邪惡不祥。……桃蠹，食桃樹蟲也。”

③ 單：單通“癉”，秦簡常見，是一種熱病。《山海經・北山經》：“其中多鰼鰼之魚……食之不癉。”

1. 正月 *zhēng yuè*: lit. “standard month,” meaning the first month of the year. This is a month of great significance in folk culture. It is a good time to prepare for the new year and to get blessed. Thus, it is also a good time to prepare medicine to keep oneself healthy. Later, the custom of having pepper cypress wine and serving the anti-epidemic wine of *Túsū* on the first day of a year follows this tradition.
2. 桃橐矢 *táo tuó shǐ*: the word *tuó* 橐, equivalent to *dù* 蠹, refers to beetles. *Táotuó* 桃橐 means peach beetles. The character *shǐ* 矢 is equivalent to *shǐ* 屎, meaning dung. According to *Compendium of Materia Medica* (*Běncǎo gāngmù* 本草綱目), volume 41, peach beetle dung can be used to treat febrile disease.
3. 單 *dān*: the word *dān* 單 is equivalent to *dān* 癉, referring to the common fever. The term is frequently mentioned in Qín bamboo slips.

寬式隸定
Loose Transcription

以正月取桃蠹屎少半升，置醇酒中，温，飲之，令人不瘴病。

白話文
Vernacular Chinese

在正月取桃蛀蟲屎約三分之一升，放到醇酒中，稍稍加熱，喝掉它，使人不生瘴病。

英文翻譯
English Translation

In the first month of the year, take about one third of a *shēng* (i.e., about 70 cc) of peach tree borer (i.e., peach beetle) feces, put them in alcoholic wine, warm the alcoholic wine, and drink it so as to prevent getting a cold.

十四、長髮方
14. A Recipe for Hair Growth

原文
Bamboo Script

取新乳① 狗子，盡鬻（煮）之。即② 沐，取一匕以殽③ 沐，長髮。

注釋
Annotation

① 乳：生。
② 即：如果。
③ 殽：混合。

1. 乳 *rǔ*: born.
2. 即 *jí*: if.
3. 殽 *xiáo*: to mix.

寬式隸定
Loose Transcription

取新乳狗子，盡煮之。即沐，取一匕以殽沐，長髮。

白話文
Vernacular Chinese

取剛生下來的狗崽，整個煮熟。如洗頭，取一匕湯液混合水中用來洗頭，滋長頭髮。

英文翻譯
English Translation

Take a newly born, suckling dog and cook it. When bathing, take a spoon［of the liquid］, mix well with the bath water and wash your hair. This will help the hair grow.

十五、治暴心痛方
15. A Recipe for Curing Sudden Heartburn

原文
Bamboo Script

七①。病暴心痛②灼₌③（灼灼）者，治之：析（菥）蓂④實冶⑤二⑥，枯橿（薑）、菌Ⅰ桂⑦冶各一。凡三物并和，取三指冣（撮）到節二⑧，温醇酒⑨Ⅱ

注釋
Annotation

① 七：醫方的編號。
② 暴心痛：突然發作的心痛。
③ 灼₌：灼灼，炙熱貌。
④ 析蓂：即菥蓂，植物名。
⑤ 冶：搗碎，研末。
⑥ 二：與下文“各一”中的一均指配藥比例，二指佔四分之二。
⑦ 菌桂：植物名。具有“養精神、和顏色”的功效，常用爲藥引，也可用於治療心痛病症。
⑧ 三指冣到節二：散劑的計量方式，冣，通“撮”。
⑨ 里耶秦簡另見“治暴心痛方”：“治暴心痛方：令以迎屋左榮，以左手□取其木若草蔡長一尺，禹步三，折，□之病者心上。因以左足徐踵其心，男子七踵，女子二七踵。嘗試。勿禁。”（里耶秦簡 8-876，8-1376+8-1959）大意如下：“治療猝然心痛的醫方：使人面對着屋舍左邊屋簷，用左手摘取那裏的樹或草長一尺，用禹步的方式走三步，折斷，放在患者的心臟處上方。於是用左腳輕輕踩踏（患者的）心臟部位，男子踩踏七下，女子踩踏十四下。試行過。没有禁忌。”可與如下簡牘對讀：“病心者，禹步三，曰：‘皋！敢告泰山：泰山高也，人居之，□□之孟也，人席之，不智（知）而心疾，不智（知）而咸載。’即令病心者南首卧，而左足踐之二七。”（周家臺秦墓竹簡 337）“五十八。治心暴痛：屑椒（椒）覈（核）一升，以酒一杯畲（飲）之。其一曰：印（迎）屋左榮，以左手取其木若草蔡長尺，即禹步三，折，置病者心上，因以左足徐踵之，男七，女二七，已。已試。”（天回醫簡《治六十病和齊湯法》223，233）

1. 七 *qī*: the number seven, here the seventh piece of recipes.
2. 暴心痛 *bào xīn tòng*: heartburn or cardialgia that occurs suddenly.
3. 灼₌ *zhuó zhuó*: burning sensation.

4. 析蓂 *xī míng*: thlaspi arvens, an annual plant used in Traditional Chinese Medicine（TCM）.
5. 冶 *yě*: to grind.
6. 二 *èr*: two or two parts, two portions. Here, it refers to two quarters or two parts of a substance to be added to a medical recipe, whereas the next two items to be added（withered ginger and cinnamon）each will be one quarter.
7. 菌桂 *jūn guì*: cinnamon. According to TCM, cinnamon is useful as a guiding drug for enhancing the efficacy of a medicinal prescription, and is also used in treating heartburn.
8. 三指冣到節二 *sān zhǐ jù dào jié èr*: dosage of powders, roughly equivalent to two pinches. *Jù* 冣 is equivalent to *cuō* 撮.
9. In Lǐyē Qín Slips, there is a recipe for treating sudden heartburn（No.8-876, 8-1376+8-1959）. The recipe goes like this: "Make people face the eaves on the left side of the house, use your left hand to pick up the grass about one foot long, take three steps of Yǔ, break the grass, and smear it over the patient's heart. Then lightly step on the patient's heart with the left foot. Do this seven times for men and fourteen times for woman. Try it. There are no taboos." Another two recipes also mention similar treatment methods, one from Zhōujiātái Qín tomb 30 bamboo slips, No.337, and the other from the *Sixty Prescriptions*（*Zhì liùshí bìng héjì tāngfǎ* 治六十病和齊湯法）from Tiānhuí medical bamboo slips, No.223, 233.

寬式隸定
Loose Transcription

七。病暴心痛灼灼者，治之：菥蓂實冶二，枯薑、菌桂冶各一。凡三物并和，取三指撮到節二，温醇酒。

白話文
Vernacular Chinese

七。突然心痛而有灼熱感的，治療這種病：菥蓂子搗碎兩份，乾薑、菌桂搗碎各一份。總共三樣藥物混合，取三指撮到指節第二節的量，温熱醇酒……

英文翻譯
English Translation

Seventh. Treating sudden cardialgia with burning sensation: crush two portions of thlaspi arvens seeds, one portion each of withered ginger and cinnamon into fine powder. Mix the three ingredients. Take two pinches of the mixed powder with warm good wine.

十六、祝心疾方
16. A Recipe for Treating Heartache

原文
Bamboo Script

祝①心疾：唾之，曰：歜②，某父某母，爲某不以時，令某心甬（痛）毋期③，令某唾之。

注釋
Annotation

① 祝：詛咒。
② 歜：《説文解字》載："歜，盛氣怒也。"
③ 期：限度。

1. 祝 *zhù*: to curse, swear away.
2. 歜 *chù*: a voice that expresses great anger.
3. 期 *qī*: to limit.

寬式隸定
Loose Transcription

詛咒心疾：唾之，曰：歜，某父某母，爲某不以時，令某心痛毋期，令某唾之。

白話文
Vernacular Chinese

祝心痛病：吐唾沫，説：歜，我爸我媽，生我不按合宜的時間，使我心痛無限，使我爲之吐唾沫。

英文翻譯
English Translation

To swear away heartache: spit and then say the following: Grrr! My father, my mother, they gave birth to me at an inappropriate time, this makes my heart ache infinitely, and makes me spit for it.

十七、已癰方
17. A Recipe for Treating Carbuncle

原文
Bamboo Script

痍①而内屚（漏）②血不出者，以女子月吏（事）布③，水一桮（杯）濯之而歙。

注釋
Annotation

① 痍：創傷。
② 内屚：體内出血。
③ 月吏布：女子月經時墊於下體的布，用於防止經血沾染衣物。

1. 痍 *yí*: bruise or trauma.
2. 内屚 *nèi lòu*: internal bleeding, hemorrhage.
3. 月吏布 *yuè lì bù*: menstrual cloth.

寬式隸定
Loose Transcription

痍而内漏血不出者，以女子月事布，水一杯濯之而歙。

白話文
Vernacular Chinese

創傷而體内出血血淤積不出的，用女子的月事布，用水一杯清洗並喝下洗布水。

英文翻譯
English Translation

When suffering from internal bleeding and blood stasis due to trauma or bruising, take a woman's menstrual cloth and rinse it in a cup of water, then drink that water.

練習
Practice

釋讀圖表 3 中的兩組醫方。

Read the slips in Tableau 3.

圖表 3　Tableau 3

去黑子方							下氣方
周家臺 318 上	周家臺 317 下	周家臺 317 上	周家臺 316 下	周家臺 316 上	周家臺 315 下	周家臺 315 上	周家臺 312

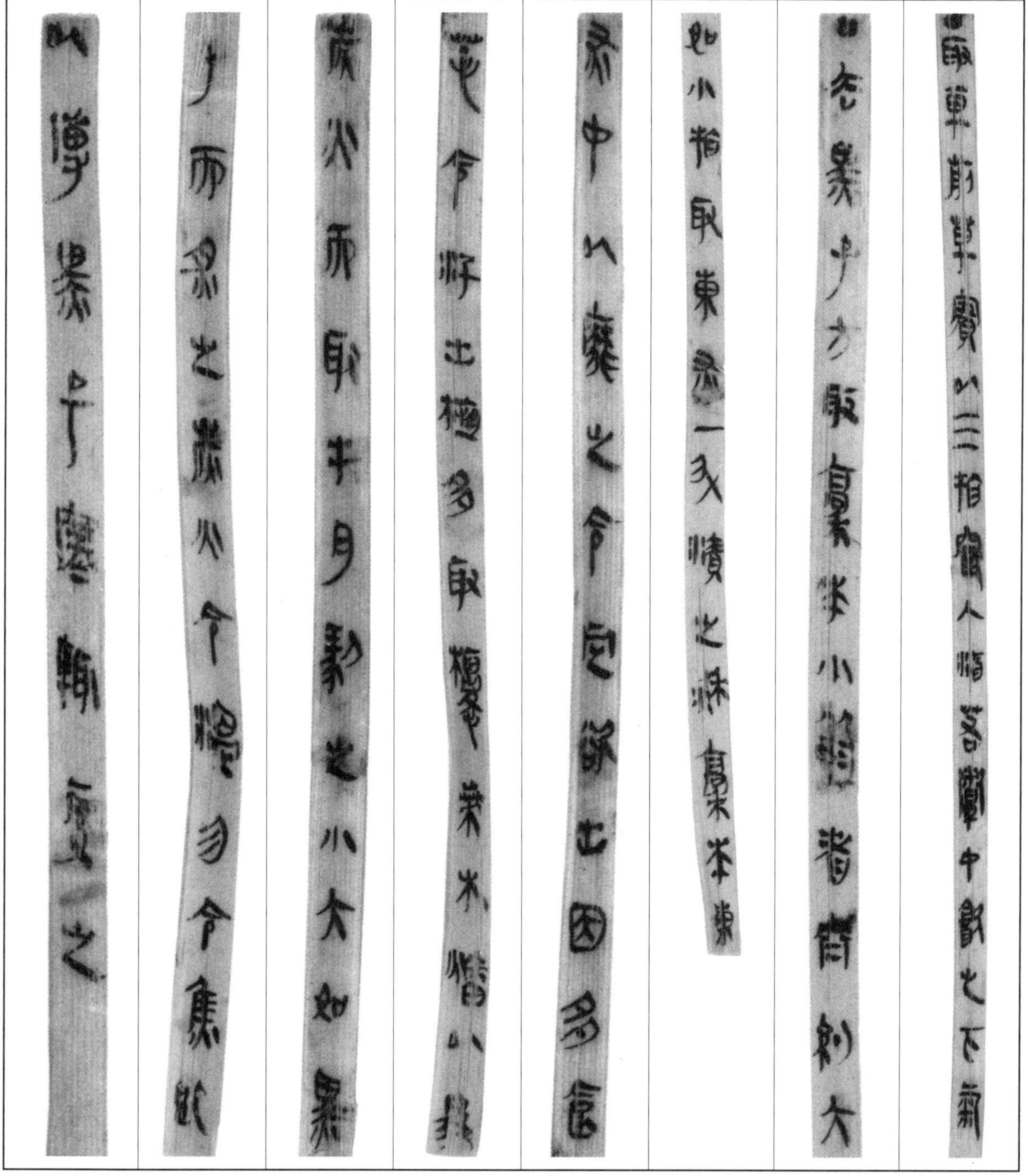

第七組　數書
Group 7　Book on Mathematics

簡介
Introduction

秦簡中已出現幾種與數學有關的文獻，包括里耶秦簡中的乘法口訣、嶽麓書院藏秦簡《數》、北京大學藏秦簡《算書》《田書》與乘法口訣等。嶽麓書院藏秦簡《數》有 200 多枚簡，包括描述算法的“術”和具體算題，《數》作爲篇題見於其中一枚簡的背面。北京大學藏秦簡中的數學文獻包括 4 卷竹簡和記載“九九術”乘法口訣的 1 枚木方。其中一種自名爲《田書》，羅列多種矩形土地的長寬和對應的面積。還有《算書》甲種、乙種、丙種等。《算書》甲種開篇是 800 字左右的有關數學起源和意義的議論性文字，被命名爲《魯久次問數于陳起》；之後是“九九術”表格；再後是“少廣術”（由已知長方形面積或長方體體積求其一邊之長的方法）；再後是“田”（有關土地面積、長、寬的算題）、“租禾”（有關繳納糧食作物田租的算題）、“租枲”（有關繳納麻類作物田租的算題）3 篇，每篇之前都有一枚單獨的標題簡；再後又是一些田畝、租稅算題；再後是各種算題的雜抄；最後是衡制換算。《算書》乙種、丙種則只羅列各種算題。

這些數學文獻具有重要的數學史意義，不僅有助於我們了解戰國至秦代中國的數學水平，也有助於進一步認識《九章算術》等傳世數學文獻的形成等問題。

Among Qín bamboo slips, there are several that deal with mathematics, including mnemonic formula of multiplication in Lǐyē Qín slips, *Mathematics*（*Shù* 數）in the Yuèlù Academy corpus of Qín slips, *Book on Arithmetic*（*Suànshū* 算書）, *Book on Fields*（*Tiánshū* 田書）and mnemonic formula of multiplication in the Peking University corpus of Qín manuscripts.

Mathematics in the Yuèlù Academy corpus of Qín slips contains more than 200 slips, including slips on methodology and practical problems. The title *Shù* was written on the back of one of the slips. The Peking University corpus of Qín slips contains four sets of bamboo slips, and one wood block with mnemonic formula of multiplications. Among the four sets, one was entitled *Book on Fields*（*Tiánshū*）, which deals with calculations of the area of farm land. The other three sets are named *Suànshū* Ⅰ, Ⅱ, and Ⅲ. *Suànshū* Ⅰ starts with a chapter on the origin and significance of mathematics, entitled *Lǔ Jiǔcì Asks Chén Qǐ about Shù*（*Lǔ Jiǔcì wèn shù yú Chén Qǐ* 魯久次問數于陳起）, followed by the so-called Method on Multiplications, and the Method of *Shǎoguǎng* 少　廣, which describes methods of calculating the length of a side from the area or volume of a rectangle surface or body. Another three chapters are:（i）farmland（*tián* 田）, dealing with calculating area, length and width of a field;（ii）crop taxation（*zūhé* 租禾）, dealing with calculating taxation of field grain crops; and（iii）hemp taxation（*zūxǐ* 租枲）, dealing with calculating taxation of hemp crops. Each chapter starts with a title slip, followed by questions and problems, and concludes with some miscellaneous notes on problems and some unit converting tables of measurements. *Suànshū*（算書）Ⅱ and Ⅲ compile all sorts of calculation problems.

Qín bamboo slips that deal with mathematics are highly significant in the history of mathematics. They demonstrate the level of mathematical skills at that time and enable us to understand how mathematical classics like *Nine Chapters of Arithmetic*（*Jiǔ zhāng suànshù* 九章算術）came about.

篇目來源
Text Source

第 18 篇　取禾程術（嶽麓書院藏秦簡《數》2 號簡）

18. *Method of Crop Measurement*（Yuèlù Academy corpus of Qín slips, *Shù*, slip No.2）

第 19 篇　誤券（嶽麓書院藏秦簡《數》12、13 號簡）

19. *The Incorrect Coupon*（Yuèlù Academy corpus of Qín slips, *Shù*, slips No.12, 13）

第 20 篇　周田術（嶽麓書院藏秦簡《數》52、65、66 號簡）

20. *Method for Calculating Circular Area*（Yuèlù Academy corpus of Qín slips, *Shù*, slips No.52, 65, 66）

第 21 篇　句股算題（嶽麓書院藏秦簡《數》213、214 號簡）

21. *Pythagorean Problem*（Yuèlù Academy corpus of Qín slips, *Shù*, slips No.213, 214）

參考文獻
References

陳松長主編:《嶽麓書院藏秦簡（壹—叁）釋文修訂本》，上海辭書出版社 2018 年。

日本“中國古算書研究會”著，[日] 大川俊隆、馬彪譯:《嶽麓書院藏秦簡〈數〉譯注稿（1）》，簡帛網，http://www.bsm.org.cn/show_article.php?id=1824，2013 年 1 月 30 日。

日本“中國古算書研究會”著，[日] 大川俊隆、馬彪譯:《嶽麓書院藏秦簡〈數〉譯注稿（2）》，簡帛網，http://www.bsm.org.cn/show_article.php?id=1845，2013 年 4 月 20 日。

肖燦:《嶽麓書院藏秦簡〈數〉研究》，湖南大學博士學位論文，2010 年。

朱漢民、陳松長主編:《嶽麓書院藏秦簡（貳）》，上海辭書出版社 2011 年。

照片、隸定本
Photo，Transcription

圖表 1　嶽麓書院藏秦簡《數》第 2、12、13、52、65 號簡

Tableau 1: Yuèlù Academy corpus of Qín slips, *Shù*, slips No.2, 12, 13, 52, 65

圖表 2　嶽麓書院藏秦簡《數》第 66、213、214、80、81 號簡

Tableau 2: Yuèlù Academy corpus of Qín slips, *Shù*, slips No.66, 213, 214, 80, 81

圖表 1　Tableau 1

嶽麓《數》65			嶽麓《數》52		嶽麓《數》13		嶽麓《數》12			嶽麓《數》2	
隸定	照片（下）	照片（上）	隸定	照片	隸定	照片	隸定	照片（下）	照片（上）	隸定	照片
周田述曰周乘周十二成一其一述曰半周半徑田即定徑乘周四成一半徑乘周二成一			田方十五步半步爲田一畝四分步一	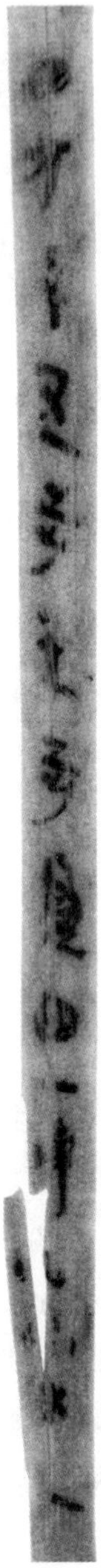	爲法除貣如法一步		禾兑田卌步五步一斗租八斗今誤券九斗問幾可步一斗得曰四步九分步四而一斗述曰兑田爲貣九斗			取禾程述以所已乾爲法以生者乘田步爲貣=如法一步	

圖表 2　Tableau 2

嶽麓《數》81 第 1、2、3 欄	嶽麓《數》80 第 1、2、3 欄	嶽麓《數》214		嶽麓《數》213			嶽麓《數》66	
照片	照片	隸定	照片	隸定	照片（下）	照片（上）	隸定	照片
		一寸爲法如法得一寸有以深益之即材徑也		□有園材薶地不智小大斲之入材一寸而得平一尺問材周大幾可即曰半平得五寸令相乘也以深			周田卅步爲田七十五步	

十八、取禾程術
18. Method of Crop Measurement

原文
Bamboo Script

取禾①程②述（術）③：④以所已乾⑤爲法⑥，以生者⑦乘田步⑧爲貣⑨（實）=（實，實）如法一步⑩。

注釋
Annotation

① 禾：泛指糧食作物。
② 程：計量標準。
③ 述：通“術”，方法。
④ 取禾程術：求取某種糧食作物的計量標準的方法。具體來講，即依據已知的土地面積與所收穫的某種糧食在數量上的對應關係，求取一定數量的其他類别的糧食對應多少土地面積的方法。可參照 4 號簡所載算題：“取程，禾田五步一斗，今乾之爲九升，問幾可（何）步一斗？曰：五步九分步五而一斗。”
⑤ 乾：曬乾。
⑥ 法：除數。
⑦ 生者：收割後未經曬乾的糧食作物。對應 4 號簡中的“一斗”。
⑧ 田步：“步”在《數》中作長度單位時，折合六尺一步。本簡中的“田步”是作面積單位使用的，即平方步，對應 4 號簡中的“五步”。
⑨ 貣：通“實”，被除數。
⑩ 貣如法一步：被除數中與除數相等的部分就是一步。這是對如何運算除法的解釋。

1. 禾 *hé*: general term for food crops.
2. 程 *chéng*: measurement standards.
3. 述 *shù*: used here as a homophone of *shù* 術 , meaning methodology, methods, techniques.
4. 取禾程術 *qǔ hé chéng shù*: the method of obtaining the measurement of certain food crops. Specifically, it calculates the land area required to produce a certain number of crops, based on the known relationship between land area and crop production. An example of such method is described on No.4 slip: “Given that a land area of five *bù* 步（unit of land area）yields one *dǒu* 斗（unit of volume）of undried crops, and this crop, once dried, yields nine *shēng* 升（unit of volume）, how many *bù* will yield one *dǒu* of dried crop? Answer: five and five ninths *bù*

will give you one *dǒu* of dried crop."

5. 乾 *gān*: dry.
6. 法 *fǎ*: divisor.
7. 生者 *shēng zhě*: undried crop, the crop directly harvested from the field.
8. 田步 *tián bù*: here *bù* is a unit of length corresponding to 6 *chǐ* 尺, about 140 cm. The term *tiánbù* 田步 refers to the area, equivalent to the square of *bù*.
9. ⿱君貝 *shí*: a variant of *shí* 實, meaning dividend or numerator to be divided.
10. ⿱君貝如法一步 *shí rú fǎ yī bù*: literally it means the identical portion in the numerator and divisor is considered as one or one *bù*. For example, 12 ÷ 4=3, where *shí*, the numerator 12 contains 3 portions of *fǎ* 法, the divisor 4, so it gives the answer of 3 or 3 *bù*.

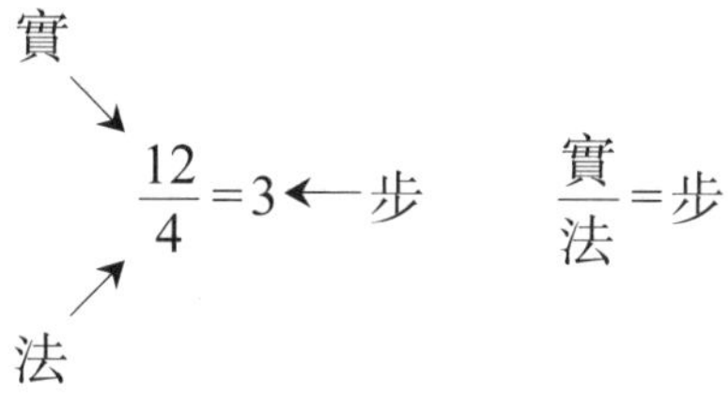

圖 1　取禾程術示意
Figure 1　Equation showing the calculation

寬式隸定
Loose Transcription

取禾程術：以所已乾爲法，以生者乘田步爲實，實如法一步。

白話文
Vernacular Chinese

求取（一定數量乾燥的）糧食作物所需土地面積的算法：用乾燥的糧食作物的數量作除數，用未乾的糧食作物數量乘以田的步數作爲被除數，被除數中與除數相等的部分即爲一步。

英文翻譯
English Translation

The algorithm for obtaining the land area that is required for producing (dried) crops: Use the amount of dried crops as the divisor, multiply the number of undried crops by the number of square *bù* as the dividend. The part of dividend that is equal to the divisor is one square *bù*.

十九、誤券
19. The Incorrect Coupon

原文
Bamboo Script

禾兑（税）田①卌②步，五步一斗，租八斗，今誤券③九斗，問幾可（何）步一斗？得曰：四步九分步四而一斗。述（術）曰：兑（税）田爲貇（實），九斗12爲法，除，貇（實）如法一步。13

注釋
Annotation

① 兑田：兑，通“税”。税田，納税之田，秦時在總田畝（《數》中稱爲“輿田”）數中按一定比例劃出一定的數量作爲納税之田。
② 卌：四十。
③ 誤券：券，券書，用作憑證的契據，往往有一定數量的刻齒，代表交易數，分爲兩半或三半，由雙方或多方各執其一。誤券，指製作了錯誤的券。

1. 兑田 *duì tián: duì* 兑, equivalent to *shuì* 税, meaning tax. *Shuìtián* 税田 means tax-paying fields, i.e., land on which tax needed to be paid based on the crop yield.
2. 卌 *xì*: forty.
3. 誤券 *wù quàn*: lit. “incorrect coupon.” Coupons, contracts, and deeds used as vouchers often have a certain number of notches, the notches representing the number of transactions. Such coupons are divided into two halves or three parts, one for each of the two or more parties involved in a transaction. Incorrect coupons refer to the wrong coupons made.

寬式隸定
Loose Transcription

禾税田卌步，五步一斗，租八斗，今誤券九斗，問幾何步一斗？得曰：四步九分步四而一斗。術曰：税田爲實，九斗爲法，除，實如法一步。

白話文
Vernacular Chinese

糧食作物的納税之田四十平方步，五平方步得一斗田租，田租爲八斗，現在錯誤製作了九斗的契券，請問折合多少平方步交納一斗？答案是：四又九分之四平方步交納一斗。方法是：用納稅之田的步數作爲被除數，九斗作爲除數，除，被除數中與除數相同的即爲一步。計算可以表示如下：$40 \div 9=4\frac{4}{9}$（平方步）

英文翻譯
English Translation

The taxable crop from a field of forty square *bù* is eight *dǒu*, where the rule is one *dǒu* of crops be taxed as land rent for five square *bù*. The tax voucher was erroneously made as nine *dǒu*. How many square *bù* are now equivalent to pay one *dǒu* of crops? The answer is: four and four ninths of a square *bù* pays one *dǒu*. The method is: Use the number of *bù* in the taxable field as the dividend, and nine *dǒu* as the divisor, and divide. The same portion of the dividend as the divisor is one *bù*. The calculation can be expressed as: $40 \div 9=4\frac{4}{9}$ (square *bù*)

二十、周田術
20. Method for Calculating Circular Area

原文
Bamboo Script

田方①十五步半步，爲田一畝②四分步一。52

周田③述（術）曰：周乘周，十二成一；其一述（術）曰，半周半徑，田即定④；徑乘周，四成一；半徑乘周，二成一。65

周田卅步⑤爲田七十五步。66

注釋
Annotation

① 方：計量面積的術語，後接數字指縱和橫的長度。
② 畝：1 畝相當於 240 平方步。
③ 周田：圓形田地。
④ 田即定：田地面積就確定了。
⑤ 卅步：這裏指圓形田地的周長。

1. 方 *fāng*: a term for area of a surface or land; numbers following this term refers to the length and width of the surface area.
2. 畝 *mǔ*: an area of 240 square *bù*.
3. 周田 *zhōu tián*: circular field or round field.
4. 田即定 *tián jí dìng*: the area of the field is fixed.
5. 卅步 *sà bù*: this refers to the perimeter of the circular field.

寬式隸定
Loose Transcription

田方十五步半步，爲田一畝四分步一。

周田術曰：周乘周，十二成一；其一術曰，半周半徑，田即定；徑乘周，四成一；半徑乘周，二成一。

周田卅步爲田七十五步。

白話文
Vernacular Chinese

田地四邊長爲十五步半步，折合田地一畝四分之一平方步。計算如下：

$$15\frac{1}{2} \times 15\frac{1}{2} = 240\frac{1}{4}\text{（平方步）}$$

求取圓形田地的面積的方法是：周長乘以周長，十二分之一就是田地面積；另一種方法是：一半的周長乘以半徑，田地面積就確定了；直徑乘以周長，四分之一就是田地面積；半徑乘以周長，二分之一就是田地面積。

圓形田地的周長爲三十步，折合田地面積七十五平方步。計算如下：

$$30 \times 30 \times \frac{1}{12} = 75\text{（平方步）}$$

英文翻譯
English Translation

The four sides of the field are fifteen and a half *bù*, the land area is equivalent to one *mǔ* and a quarter of square *bù*.

$$15\frac{1}{2} \times 15\frac{1}{2} = 240\frac{1}{4}\ (\text{square } bù)$$

The method to obtain the area of a circular field is: multiply the perimeter by the perimeter, and one twelfth of that is the field area; another method is to multiply half the perimeter by the radius to determine the area of the field; multiply the diameter by the circumference, and one quarter of the length is the field area; the radius is multiplied by the perimeter, and one half is the field area.

The circumference of the circular field is thirty *bù*, which is equivalent to seventy-five square *bù* of the field area.

$$30 \times 30 \times \frac{1}{12} = 75\ (\text{square } bù)$$

二十一、句股算題
21. Pythagorean Problem

原文
Bamboo Script

□有園（圓）材薶（埋）地，不智（知）小大，斲之，入材一寸而得平①一尺，問材周大幾可（何）？即曰，半平得五寸，令相乘也，以深213一寸爲法，如法得一寸，有（又）以深益②之，即材徑也。214

注釋
Annotation

① 平：橫截面的長度。
② 益：加。

1. 平 *píng*: length of cross section.
2. 益 *yì*: plus, to add.

寬式隸定
Loose Transcription

□有圓材埋地，不知大小，斲之，入材一寸而得平一尺，問材周大幾何？即曰，半平得五寸，令相乘也，以深一寸爲法，如法得一寸，又以深益之，即材徑也。

白話文
Vernacular Chinese

有圓木埋於地下，不知大小，用斧頭砍它，砍入木材厚度一寸而對應橫截面長度一尺，請問木材周長是多少？答曰：取橫截面長度的一半得數爲五寸，使之相乘，以砍入的厚度一寸作爲除數，等同於除數即得到一寸，又用厚度與之相加，就是木材的直徑。

$$\text{直徑}=\frac{5\times 5}{1}+1=26\text{ 寸}$$

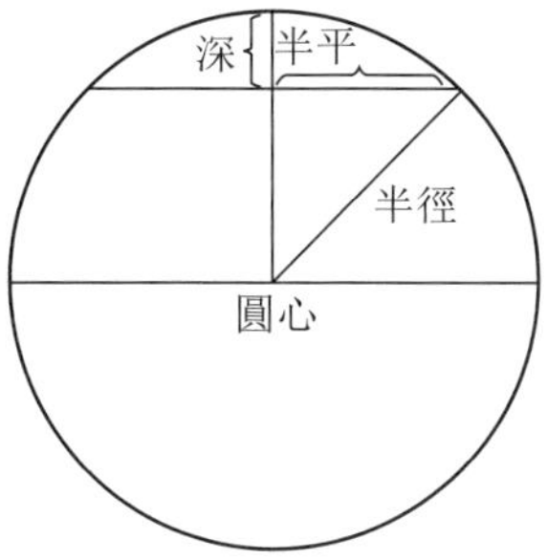

圖 2　句股算題示意

Figure 2　Diagram for solving Pythagorean problem

英文翻譯
English Translation

There is a round wood buried in the ground. I don't know its size. I cut it with an axe. The thickness of the wood is one *cùn* and the corresponding cross-sectional length is one *chǐ*. What is the circumference of the wood? Answer: Take half of the length of the cross section to get the number five *cùn*, multiply it, and use one *cùn* of the cut thickness as the divisor, which is equivalent to the divisor to get one *cùn*, and add the thickness to it to get the diameter of the wood.

$$\text{Diameter}=\frac{5\times 5}{1}+1=26\ (\textit{cùn})$$

練習
Practice

釋讀表 2 中的嶽麓書院藏秦簡《數》80、81 號簡。

Read the slips No.80 and 81from *Shù* in the Yuèlù Academy corpus of Qín slips in Tableau 2.

第八組　宦學讀本
Group 8　Exhortations for Officials

簡介
Introduction

秦簡中有一類特殊的文獻，主體部分大多分欄書寫，主要内容是告誡官吏作爲官吏的行事準則，或稱其爲宦學讀本，或稱其爲官箴。目前主要有四種，睡虎地秦墓竹簡《爲吏之道》、嶽麓書院藏秦簡《爲吏治官及黔首》、王家臺秦簡《政事之常》、北京大學藏秦簡《從政之經》。《爲吏之道》共51枚簡，簡長27.5釐米，寬0.6釐米，厚0.1釐米，主要分5欄或4欄書寫。《爲吏治官及黔首》共88枚簡，簡長約30釐米，大部分分3欄或4欄書寫。《從政之經》共46枚簡，簡長27.5—27.9釐米，主體分4欄書寫，少數不分欄書寫。《政事之常》共65枚簡，抄寫形製特殊，先繪製方形圖，將其分爲4圈，將文字分别寫在每個圈中，中間寫有"員（圓）以生枋（方），政事之常"，第2圈寫有"處如資（齋），言如盟……"等，第3、4圈是對第2圈内容的説明與注釋。

There is a special kind of literature in bamboo slips of Qín which deals with warnings and cautions to underlings on how to behave and act as officials. They can be called *Guānzhēn* 官箴 or *Exhortations for Officials*（*Huànxué dúběn* 宦學讀本）. To date, four different texts of such exhortations have been found:（1）*The Way of Being an Official*（*Wéilì zhī dào* 爲吏之道）from Shuìhǔdì Qín tomb 11 bamboo slips;（2）*Being Officials Governing Government Office and Commoners*（*Wéilì zhìguān jí qiánshǒu* 爲吏治官及黔首）from the Yuèlù Academy corpus of Qín slips;（3）*Regulations of Political Affairs*（*Zhèngshì zhī cháng* 政事之常）from the Wángjiātái Qín tomb 15 bamboo slips in Jiānglíng, Húběi Province; and（4）*Practice in Politics*（*Cóngzhèng zhī jīng* 從政之經）from the Peking University corpus of Qín bamboo slips. *The Way of Being an Official* consists of 51 bamboo slips, each slip with a length of 27.5 cm, a width of 0.6 cm and a thickness of 0.1 cm. They are mainly written in 5 or 4 rows. There are a total of 88 slips for the piece *Being Officials Governing Government Offices and Commoners* and each slip is about 30 cm long, and most of them are written in 3 or 4 rows. The piece of *Regulations of Political Affairs* consists of 46 bamboo slips, ranging in length from 27.5 to 27.9 cm. The main part is written in 4 rows, and a few are written without clear division into rows. There are a total of 65 bamboo slips in the piece of the *Regulations of Political Affairs*. The characters of this piece are arranged in an unusual manner: first, a square diagram was drawn, then divided into 4 circles, and the text was written in the circle.

篇目來源
Text　Source

第 22 篇　爲吏之道（節選：睡虎地秦墓竹簡 1—5 號）
22. *The Way of Being an Official*（selected from Shuìhǔdì Qín tomb 11 bamboo slips, slips No.1-5）

參考文獻
References

白于藍：《睡虎地秦簡〈爲吏之道〉校讀札記》，《江漢考古》2010 年第 3 期。
陳偉主編：《秦簡牘合集釋文注釋修訂本（壹）》，武漢大學出版社 2016 年。
方勇：《讀秦漢簡札記二則》，簡帛網，http://www.bsm.org.cn/show_article.php?id=1572，2011 年 10 月 28 日。
連劭名：《睡虎地秦簡〈爲吏之道〉與古代思想》，《江漢考古》2008 年第 4 期。
睡虎地秦墓竹簡整理小組：《睡虎地秦墓竹簡》，文物出版社 1990 年。
孫機：《漢代物質文化資料圖說（增訂本）》，上海古籍出版社 2011 年。
王輝：《簡帛爲臣居官類文獻考論》，上海古籍出版社 2022 年。
王明欽：《王家臺秦簡研究概述》，《新出簡帛研究》，文物出版社 2004 年。
魏德勝：《雲夢秦簡與〈說文〉的用字》，《簡帛語言文字研究》第 1 輯，巴蜀書社 2002 年。
朱鳳瀚：《北大藏秦簡〈從政之經〉述要》，《文物》2012 年第 6 期。
朱漢民、陳松長主編：《嶽麓書院藏秦簡（壹）》，上海辭書出版社 2010 年。

照片、隸定本
Photo，Transcription

圖表 1　睡虎地秦墓竹簡《爲吏之道》第 1—5 簡
Tableau 1: Shuìhǔdì Qín tomb 11 bamboo slips, *The Way of Being an Official*, slips No.1-5

圖表 1　Tableau 1

睡虎地《爲吏》5			睡虎地《爲吏》4			睡虎地《爲吏》3			睡虎地《爲吏》2			睡虎地《爲吏》1		
隸定	照片（下）	照片（上）	隸定	照片（下）	照片（上）	隸定	照片（下）	照片（上）	隸定	照片（下）	照片（上）	隸定	照片（下）	照片（上）
微密韱察 正行脩身過去福存 奊悍冤暴 與民有期 操邦柄慎度量來者有稽莫敢忘賢鄙			審悉毋私 毋賤貧 均繇賞罰 有嚴不治 民心將移乃難親			慎謹堅固 毋喜富 老弱獨轉 寬以治之 凡戾人表以身民將望表以戾真表若不正			必精絜正直 欲貴大甚賤不可得 孤寡窮困 惠以聚之 藉肖人聶心不敢徒語恐見惡			凡爲吏之道 欲富大甚貧不可得 毋=皋=可赦 敬而起之 凡治吏敢爲固謁私圖畫局陳畀以爲		

二十二、爲吏之道
20. The Way of Being an Official

原文
Bamboo Script

凡爲吏之道，必精絜（潔）① 正直，慎謹堅固 ②，審悉 ③ 毋（無）私，微密韱察 ④……

欲富大（太）甚，貧不可得。欲貴大（太）甚，賤不可得。毋喜富，毋惡貧，正行脩（修）身，過（禍）去福存……

毋＝皋（罪）＝（毋罪無罪）可赦。孤寡窮困，老弱獨轉 ⑤，均繇（徭）賞罰，㪍 ⑥ 悍寃暴 ⑦……

敬而起之，惠以聚之，寬以治之，有嚴不治。與民有期 ⑧……

凡治吏（事），敢爲固，謁 ⑨（遏）私圖，畫局陳𢍰（棋）以爲藉 ⑩。肖人 ⑪ 聶（慑）⑫ 心，不敢徒語 ⑬ 恐見惡。凡戾人 ⑭，表 ⑮ 以身，民將望表以戾 ⑯ 真，表若不正，民心將移乃難親。操邦柄，慎度量，來者有稽莫敢忘。賢鄙……

注釋
Annotation

① 精絜：即“精潔”。精粹純潔。
② 堅固：堅定。
③ 審悉：詳細了解。
④ 韱察：嶽麓書院藏《爲吏治官及黔首》中作“咸察”，作“咸察”文義更流暢，且與“無私”結構對稱。
⑤ 轉：遺棄者。
⑥ 㪍：勇猛强横。
⑦ 寃暴：暴虐。
⑧ 期：約定。
⑨ 謁：通“遏”，遏止。
⑩ 藉：憑藉。
⑪ 肖人：小人。
⑫ 聶：通“慑”，恐懼，使恐懼。
⑬ 徒語：說空話。
⑭ 戾人：戾，定。戾人，安定百姓。
⑮ 表：標木，這裏以標木爲喻說明治人者應以自身作爲表率。
⑯ 戾：至。

1. 精絜 *jīng jié*: same as *jīngjié* 精潔, meaning fine and pure.
2. 堅固 *jiān gù*: firm, determined.
3. 審悉 *shěn xī*: to review and examine in detail.
4. 鐵察 *xiān chá*: equivalent to *xiánchá* 咸察, meaning to investigate all facets.
5. 轉 *zhuǎn*: outcast.
6. 琴 *háo*: brave, bullyish and tyrannical.
7. 冤暴 *yuān bào*: tyrannical.
8. 期 *qī*: to appoint.
9. 謁 *yè*: equivalent to *è* 遏, meaning to restrain, to stop.
10. 藉 *jiè*: by virtue of, dependent on.
11. 肖人 *xiào rén*: equivalent to *xiǎorén* 小人, lit. "little man," meaning villain.
12. 聶 *niè*: equivalent to *shè* 懾, meaning to fear, to make others fear.
13. 徒語 *tú yǔ*: to speak empty words.
14. 戾人 *lì rén: lì* 戾, meaning to stabilize; *lìrén* 戾人, meaning to stabilize the people.
15. 表 *biǎo: biāomù* 標木, lit. "standard wood." Here it means that those who govern others should model with correct behavior.
16. 戾 *lì*: to arrive.

寬式隸定

Loose Transcription

凡爲吏之道，必精潔正直，慎謹堅固，審悉無私，微密鐵察……

欲富太甚，貧不可得。欲貴太甚，賤不可得。毋喜富，毋惡貧，正行修身，禍去福存……

毋罪無罪可赦。孤寡窮困，老弱獨轉，均傜賞罰，琴悍冤暴……

敬而起之，惠以聚之，寬以治之，有嚴不治。與民有期……

凡治事，敢爲固，遏私圖，畫局陳棋以爲藉。肖人懾心，不敢徒語恐見惡。凡戾人，表以身，民將望表以戾真，表若不正，民心將移乃難親。操邦柄，慎度量，來者有稽莫敢忘。賢鄙……

白話文

Vernacular Chinese

作爲官吏的準則，一定要清白正直，謹慎堅定，詳察無私，精微周密都能夠明察……

喜好富有太過分，貧窮而得不到富有。喜好尊貴太過分，卑賤而得不到尊貴。不要偏爱富有，不要厭惡貧窮，端正行爲，修養身心，災禍就會離開，福氣就會存留……

不要給無罪者或可赦免者定罪。孤兒、喪失配偶者、窮困者，年老者、體弱者、被遺棄者，均調徭役及賞罰，强横暴虐……

尊敬（百姓）而發動他們，以恩惠使他們聚集，以寬仁使他們安定，嚴苛則不安定。與民有會面……

處理政事，敢於固守本職、專一做事，遏制私念，像規劃棋盤陳設棋子一樣。使小人有恐懼之心，不敢説空話怕被厭惡。安定百姓要以身作則，百姓將看着表率以達到真，表率如不正，民心將改變而難以親附。掌管國家的權柄，謹慎考量，將來之事要仔細思考上述内容，不要遺忘。

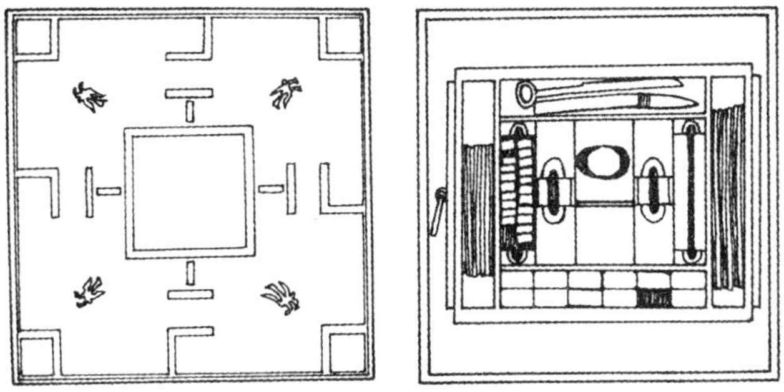

圖 1　馬王堆漢墓中的棋盤及博具

Figure 1　Chessboard and Gaming Equipment unearthed from the Mǎwángduī Hàn tomb

（引自孫機:《漢代物質文化資料圖説（增訂本）》453 頁）

英文翻譯

English Translation

The way to be a good official: one should be incorruptible and just, discreet and firm, knowledgeable and selfless, meticulous and observant...

Do not try too much to be rich, or you will be poor and never be rich. Do not try too hard to attain noble position, or you will stay lowly and not to attain that position. Do not favor wealth, and do not detest poverty, cultivate your body and mind, and behave upright, misfortune will go away and fortune will remain...

Do not punish or convict the innocent or those who may be forgiven. For orphans, the widows and widowers, the poor, the elderly, the infirm and the outcast, do ensure equalization of corvee labor as well as of rewards and punishments. For the bullyish and the tyrannical...

Respect people when mobilizing them, show grace and favor when gathering them, put people at ease by treating them leniently and benevolently, treating people in a harsh and severe manner only causes uneasiness. When meeting with the people...

When handling administrative and bureaucratic affairs, stick to your own duties and responsibilities, concentrate on the matters at hand, and curb any selfish thoughts, and plan things methodically like planning a chessboard game. Instill fear into the heart of villains so that they don't dare speak empty words for fear of being loathed. Stabilize people by your own example. People look at your example to behave correctly. Otherwise, people will change their mind and will not follow you. An official holds the authority of the state, [he] should be careful in any of his deliberations. [He] should carefully consider the above content for future affairs and not forget them.

練習
Practice

釋讀圖表 2 中的幾枚《爲吏治官及黔首》簡。

Read the slips from the piece of *Being Officials Governing Underlings and Commoners* in Tableau 2.

圖表 2　Tableau 2

《治官》32 第 1、2、3 欄	《治官》31 第 1、2、3 欄	《治官》30 第 1、2、3 欄	《治官》29 第 1、2、3 欄	《治官》28 第 1、2、3 欄	《治官》27 第 1、2、3 欄

第九組　私人信件
Group 9　Personal Letters

簡介
Introduction

先秦以及秦代簡帛文獻中的私人信件並不多，主要見於睡虎地 4 號秦墓中的兩枚木牘及里耶秦簡。從這些私人信件中可以窺見當時人寫信的習用語和格式慣例，也可知曉一些重要的歷史、語言文化信息。

Only a few of personal letters have been discovered in the Qín bamboo and silk collections, most of them were in wood slips recovered from Shuìhǔdì tomb 4 and Lǐyē Qín slips. They are invaluable documents, providing a unique windows and first-hand information with regard to written styles, languages and certain customs at that time.

篇目來源
Text Source

第 23 篇　黑夫信件（睡虎地 4 號秦墓 11 號木牘）
23. *Letter from Hēifū*（Shuìhǔdì Qín tomb 4 wood slips, No.11）

參考文獻
References

陳偉主編:《秦簡牘合集釋文注釋修訂本（貳）》，武漢大學出版社 2016 年。
湖北孝感地區第二期亦工亦農文物考古訓練班:《湖北雲夢睡虎地十一座秦墓發掘簡報》，《文物》1976 年第 9 期。
黃盛璋:《雲夢秦墓兩封家信中有關歷史地理的問題》，《文物》1980 年第 8 期。
黃盛璋:《雲夢秦墓出土的兩封家信與歷史地理問題》，《歷史地理論集》，人民出版社 1982 年。
馬怡:《居延簡〈宣與幼孫少婦書〉——漢代邊吏的私人通信》，《南都學壇》2010 年第 3 期。
任攀:《秦簡語詞札記三則》，《出土文獻研究》第 20 輯，中西書局 2021 年。
湯餘惠:《戰國銘文選》，吉林大學出版社 1993 年。
楊芬:《出土秦漢書信匯校集注》，武漢大學博士學位論文，2010 年。
［韓］尹在碩:《睡虎地秦簡〈日書〉所見“室”的結構與戰國末期秦的家族類型》，《中國史研究》1995 年第 3 期。
《雲夢睡虎地秦墓》編寫組:《雲夢睡虎地秦墓》，文物出版社 1981 年。

照片、隸定本
Photo, Transcription

圖表 1，2　睡虎地 4 號秦墓 11 號木牘正面，反面

Tableau 1, 2: Front and back view, Shuìhǔdì Qín tomb 4 wood slips, No.11

圖表 1　Tableau 1

11 号木牘隸定	11 号木牘下	11 号木牘上
二月辛巳黑夫驚敢再拜問中母毋恙也黑夫驚毋恙也前日黑夫與驚別今復會矣 黑夫寄乞就書曰遺黑夫錢毋操夏衣來今書節到母視安陸絲布賤可以爲禪 帬襦者母必爲之令與錢偕來其絲布貴徒操錢來黑夫自以布此 黑夫等直佐淮陽攻反城久傷未可智也顯母遺黑夫用勿少書到 皆爲報報〃必言相家爵來未來告黑夫其未來狀聞王得苟得	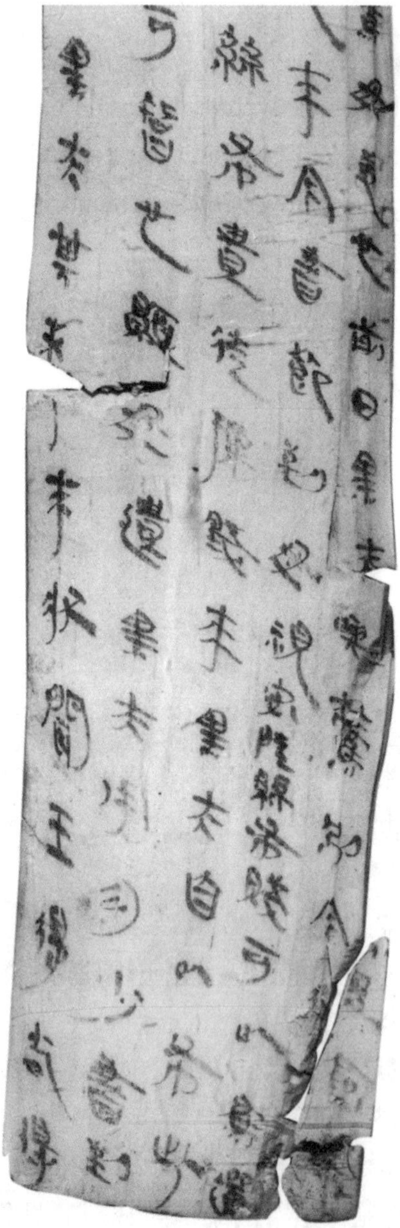	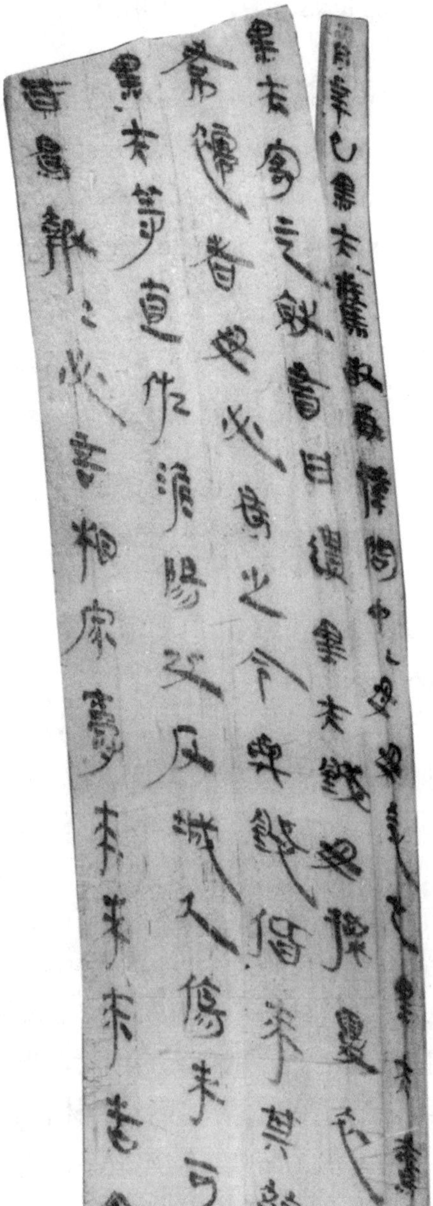

圖表 2　Tableau 2

11 号木牘背面隸定	11 号木牘背面下	11 号木牘背面上
毋恙也辭相家爵不也書衣之南軍毋王得不也 爲黑夫驚多問姑姊康樂季須故術長姑外內毋恙也 爲黑夫驚多問東室季須苟得毋恙也 爲黑夫驚多問嬰氾季吏可如定不定 爲黑夫驚多問夕陽呂嬰匽里閻諍丈人得毋恙也嬰諍皆毋恙也毋矣 驚多問新負㛸得毋恙也新負勉力視瞻丈人毋與□□□垣柏未智歸時新負勉力也		

二十三、黑夫信件
23. Letter from Hēifū

原文
Bamboo Script

二月辛巳，黑夫①、驚②敢再拜問中③、母毋恙④也？黑夫、驚毋恙也。前日黑夫與驚別，今復會矣。Ⅰ黑夫寄⑤乞就⑥書曰：遺黑夫錢，毋操夏衣來。今書節（即）到，母視安陸絲布賤可以爲禪⑦Ⅱ帬（裙）、襦⑧者，母必爲之，令與錢偕來。其絲布貴，徒操錢來，黑夫自以布此。Ⅲ黑夫等直佐⑨淮陽⑩，攻反城久，傷未可智（知）也。巔（願）母遺黑夫用勿少。書到，Ⅳ皆爲報＝（報。報）必言相家爵⑪來未來，告黑夫其未來狀。聞王得⑫苟得Ⅴ（正面）毋恙也？辭相家爵不也？書衣之南軍，毋……王得不也？Ⅰ爲黑夫、驚多問姑姊⑬、康樂⑭季須（嬃）⑮、故術長姑外内……毋恙也？Ⅱ爲黑夫、驚多問東室⑯季須（嬃）苟得毋恙也？Ⅲ爲黑夫、驚多問嬰汜季吏（事）可（何）如？定不定？Ⅳ爲黑夫、驚多問夕陽⑰呂嬰、𨛭里閻諍丈人⑱得毋恙也？嬰、諍皆毋恙也，毋錢用、衣矣。Ⅴ驚多問新負（婦）⑲、妴⑳得毋恙也？新負（婦）勉力視瞻丈人，毋與□□□。垣柏㉑未智（知）歸時。新負（婦）勉力也。Ⅵ背面

注釋
Annotation

① 黑夫：人名。
② 驚：人名。
③ 中：人名，黑夫和驚的哥哥。
④ 毋恙：毋通“無”，無恙字面義爲没有憂慮、疾病，這裏指一切都好。
⑤ 寄：委託。
⑥ 乞就：人名。
⑦ 禪：單層的衣服。
⑧ 襦：短衣、短襖。
⑨ 直佐：擔任佐這一職務。
⑩ 淮陽：郡名。
⑪ 相家爵：或認爲是人名，或認爲是立功受爵，或認爲指輔助家用的军功爵。
⑫ 王得：人名。
⑬ 姑姊：父親的姐姐。
⑭ 康樂：或認爲是對姑姊慰問的内容，或認爲是人名，我們懷疑這裏的康樂是里名，是季須的居所。下文的故術疑也指居所，不知是里名或是其他。

⑮ 須：即嬃，姐姐。
⑯ 東室：東屋，指房子裏東面的居室。
⑰ 夕陽：里名。
⑱ 丈人：老人。
⑲ 新負：負通“婦”，新婦是尊者對卑者的妻子的稱呼，因中、母都是黑夫的尊長，故信裏稱妻子爲新婦。
⑳ 𡟰：驚的孩子。
㉑ 垣柏：人名。

1. 黑夫 *hēi fū*: name of the first writer.
2. 驚 *jīng*: name of the second writer.
3. 中 *zhōng*: name of the elder brother of Hēifū and Jīng.
4. 毋恙 *wú yàng*: *wú* 毋 , equivalent to *wú* 無 , lit. “no worry or no illness,” meaning everything is fine.
5. 寄 *jì*: entrust.
6. 乞就 *qǐ jiù*: a personal name.
7. 褌 *dān*: single-layer clothes.
8. 襦 *rú*: short coat, short jacket.
9. 直佐 *zhí zuǒ*: a military position acting as *zuǒ* 佐 , lieutenant or assistant, in the army.
10. 淮陽 *huái yáng*: name of commandery.
11. 相家爵 *xiàng jiā jué*: name of a person or title of nobility awarded to family members.
12. 王得 *wáng dé*: name of a person.
13. 姑姊 *gū zǐ*: aunt.
14. 康樂 *kāng lè*: name of a village or neighborhood where one of the author’s sister lived.
15. 須 *xū*: a variant of *xū* 嬃 , meaning sister.
16. 東室 *dōng shì*: room at the east of the house.
17. 夕陽 *xī yáng*: name of a village or neighborhood.
18. 丈人 *zhàng rén*: old gentleman.
19. 新負 *xīn fù: fù* 負 , equivalent to *fù* 婦 , meaning wife or woman. *Xīnfù* 新婦 is the term used by elders referring to the wife of a junior.
20. 𡟰 *yuàn*: name of Jīng child.
21. 垣柏 *yuán bǎi*: a personal name.

寬式隸定
Loose Transcription

二月辛巳，黑夫、驚敢再拜問中、母毋恙也？黑夫、驚毋恙也。前日黑夫與驚別，今復會矣。黑夫寄乞就書曰：遺黑夫錢，毋操夏衣來。今書即到，母視安陸絲布賤可以爲禪裙、襦者，母必爲之，令與錢偕來。其絲布貴，徒操錢來，黑夫自以布此。黑夫等直佐淮陽，攻反城久，傷未可知也。願母遺黑夫用勿少。書到，皆爲報。報必言相家爵來未來，告黑夫其未來狀。聞王得苟得毋恙也？辭相家爵不也？書衣之南軍，毋……王得不也？爲黑夫、驚多問姑姊、康樂季嬃、故術長姑外內……毋恙也？爲黑夫、驚多問東室季嬃苟得毋恙也？爲黑夫、驚多問嬰汜季事何如？定不定？爲黑夫、驚多問夕陽呂嬰、匽里閻諍丈人得毋恙也？嬰、諍皆毋恙也，毋錢用、衣矣。驚多問新婦、妴得毋恙也？新婦勉力視瞻丈人，毋與□□□。垣柏未知歸時。新婦勉力也。

白話文
Vernacular Chinese

二月辛巳，黑夫、驚斗膽再拜問候中、母親一切都好吧？黑夫、驚一切都好。之前黑夫與驚分別，現在又相會了。黑夫委託乞就的信裏說：給黑夫錢，不要持夏日的衣服來。現在信若到達，母親看安陸縣絲布便宜可以用來做單層裙、衣的，母親一定買一些，將其與錢一起寄來。絲布如果太貴，只寄錢來即可，黑夫自己在此處用來買布。黑夫等在淮陽擔任佐，攻打反叛的城池很長時間，是否會受傷還不知道。希望母親給黑夫的錢不要少。信到了，一同回復。回復時一定要告知因軍功獲得的爵位來還是沒來，告知黑夫它未來的原因。聽說王得一切安好與否？是否向官府訴訟爵位之事？書與衣物到南軍，不要……王得？爲黑夫、驚問候姑媽、康樂里的姐姐、故術長姑一家等人……一切安好吧？爲黑夫、驚問候東屋的姐姐一切安好吧？爲黑夫、驚問候嬰汜季的事情怎麼樣？是否已經確定？爲黑夫、驚問候夕陽里的呂嬰、匽里的閻諍兩家的老人一切安好吧？嬰、諍都一切安好，只是沒有錢、衣服。驚問候妻子、妴一切安好吧？妻子努力照顧丈人，不要與□□□。垣柏不知回家的時間。妻子努力啊。

英文翻譯
English Translation

On the day *xīnsì* of the second month, Hēifū and Jīng dare to greet Zhōng and Mother: everything is well? After being apart for several days, Hēifū and Jīng are now together again. Hēifū has previously entrusted Qǐjiù to send a letter stating: "Gave Hēifū money, no need to bring summer clothing." Now that the letter must have arrived, Mom, please check whether the price of silk and cloth for making pants and clothes is cheap in Ānlù County, if so, do buy some and send them together with money. If they are expensive, then just send money. I will buy cloth here. Hēifū and others are stationed at Huáiyáng as lieutenant. We are to attack the enemy city, it may take a long time and we are not sure whether we may get injured during the fight. So, we wish Mom send enough money. Please do answer our letters. When you answer, make sure to let us know whether the title obtained through military merit has arrived or not, and if not the cause of it. Have you heard that Wáng Dé is well or not? Has he appealed to the government about the title?... Extend our greetings to aunt, sister at Kānglè Village as well as to Aunt Zhǎng and her family at Gùshù... is everything good? Please give our greetings to the sister at East room, [trust that] everything is well? Ask for us how is the situation of Yīng Fánjì? Is it certain? Please send greetings to father-in-laws of Lǚ Yīng in Xīyáng Village and of Yán Zhèng in Lòu Village, [trust that] everything is well? Yīng and Zhèng are well here, except they don't have enough money and clothes. Jīng sends greetings to his wife and his kid Yuàn, wishes that everything is well. May the wife take good care of father-in-law, do not.... Yuánbǎi does not know the date of his return. So, may the wife exert herself and do her best.

練習
Practice

整理黑夫信件中的稱謂語與書信常用格式語。
List salutations and greetings used in this letter.

第十組　王室或皇室文書
Group 10　The Royal Documents

簡介
Introduction

王室或皇室文書，指戰國時期諸侯王發佈的文書與秦代皇帝發佈的文書。目前所見戰國時期的王室文書主要是命書，秦代則改稱爲詔書、制書。里耶秦簡 8-461 號簡記載："王譴曰制譴。以王令曰以皇帝詔。承命曰承制。"《史記・秦始皇本紀》："命爲'制'，令爲'詔'。"都記載了這一文書名稱的變化。比較典型的皇室文書如秦始皇統一度量衡的詔書："廿六年皇帝盡并（併）兼天下諸侯，黔首大安，立號爲皇帝，乃詔丞相狀、綰，灋度量，則不壹、歉疑者皆明壹之。"（二十六年，皇帝統一天下，百姓安心，立號稱皇帝，於是詔令丞相狀和綰，統一度量，如有不一致和不準確的都使他們一致。）屢次見於銅方升、銅橢量、銅權等標準器及銅詔版等文物上。如圖 1 "兩詔銅橢量" 就見有這一詔書。

另如益陽兔子山 J9③1 簡中的秦二世元年十月甲午詔書，具體内容如下：

> 天下失始皇帝，皆遽恐悲哀甚，朕奉遺詔，今宗廟吏及箸以明至治大功德者具矣；律令當除定者畢矣；以元年與黔首更始，盡爲解除故罪，令皆已下矣。朕將自撫天下吏、黔首。其具行事，毋以繇（徭）賦擾黔首，毋以細物苛劾縣吏。亟佈。

大意爲：天下失去了始皇帝，都恐惧悲哀得很，我奉始皇帝的遺詔（繼位），現在處理宗廟事務的官員以及著述以彰顯始皇帝英明偉大功德的工作（已經）完備，律令應當廢除、確定的（已經）完畢。在元年和百姓重新開始新政，全部免除百姓以前的罪過，相關命令都已經頒佈，我將親自撫慰天下官吏、百姓。備辦巡行之事，不要用徭役、軍賦煩擾百姓，不要因小事嚴格追究縣吏的過失。快速公佈。

我們這裏選了一種關於更修爲《田律》的命書，該文書見於四川青川郝家坪秦墓 16 號木牘，文書年代爲秦武王二年（309 BCE）。另外選了秦令中引用的兩種制書，這些秦令選自《嶽麓書院藏秦簡（伍）》，都是秦始皇時代的材料。

The royal documents mentioned here include documents issued by kings of Qín state during the Warring States Period（475-221 BCE）and the Emperors of Qín Dynasty（221-206 BCE）. So far, the unearthed royal documents during the Warring States Period are mainly comprised of *mìngshū* 命書（royal commanding orders）, which were later renamed as imperial orders（*zhàoshū* 詔書）and imperial edicts（*zhìshū* 制書）during the Qín Dynasty. Slip No.8-461 unearthed from Lǐyē records

圖 1　兩詔銅橢量

Figure 1　Two edicts inscribed on a bronze measurement standard

（引自周天游:《秦漢雄風》16 頁）

the following: "[From now on, the term] 'king's condemnation' is hereby called 'imperially-issued condemnation', 'the king's order' is hereby called 'imperial order (*zhào* 詔)'. 'Receiving an order' is called 'receiving an imperially-issued order (*zhì* 制)'." Changes of the same kind are mentioned in the *Basic Annals of the First Emperor of Qín* in Sīmǎ Qiān's *Records of the Grand Historian*: "*Mìng* 命 is replaced by *zhì* 制 and *lìng* 令 is replaced by *zhào* 詔 ."

An example of a typical royal document is the edict of the First Emperor of Qín concerning the standardization of measurements: "In the 26th regnal year, the emperor conquered all lords and kings under the heaven, the world is peaceful now as I am enthroned as the emperor. I ordered the Chief Ministers Zhuàng 狀 and Wǎn 綰 to standardize the measurements, to eliminate any inconsistency and dubious ones." Indeed, this particular edict was inscribed and is frequently seen in many unearthed bronze vessels and standards.

Another example of a royal document is the proclamation of succession of the Second Emperor of Qín (Tùzǐshān bamboo slips, No.J9③1) : "When the world lost the First Emperor of Qín, people were terrified and grief stricken. I received the [former emperor's] posthumous edict [that confirms me as his successor] , now the officials dealing with the affairs of the ancestral temple and history writing which eulogizing [First Emperor's] wise governance and merits and virtues work are complete. And the work of determining which laws and statutes should be abolished and which ones should be kept is also complete. Starting now in my first year of reign, I will renew [the covenant] with the black-headed ones (i.e., common people of Qín) and will declare an amnesty for all past offenses. All of these orders have already been issued. Henceforth I will comfort the world and take care of officials and black-headed ones. Prepare for the Emperor's Tour. Do not let the black-headed ones be overburdened with corvee labor, and do not let county officials be impeached over trivial matters. This announcement is for immediate release."

Here, we select a statute on matters related to agriculture as an example of a royal document. The slip was unearthed from Qín tomb 50 at Hǎojiāpíng, Qīngchuān, Sìchuān. The text dates from 309 BCE. The other two documents, selected from *Yuèlù Academy Corpus of Qín Slips V*, are both imperial edicts named *zhìshū*, both date from the reign of the First Emperor of Qín (221-210 BCE) .

篇目來源
Text Source

第 24 篇　更修爲《田律》命書（青川郝家坪秦墓 16 號木牘）

24. *Decree on Revision of Statutes on Agriculture* (wood slip in Qín tomb 50 at Hǎojiāpíng, Qīngchuān, Sìchuān, No.16)

第 25 篇　新地吏勿廢制書（《嶽麓書院藏秦簡（伍）》53—55 號簡）

25. *Decree on Officials of New Occupied Area Must Not Be Dismissed* (*Yuèlù Academy Corpus of Qín Slips V*, Slips No.53-55)

第 26 篇　舉留獄上之制書（《嶽麓書院藏秦簡（伍）》59—61 號簡）

26. *Decree on Reporting Detained Cases* (*Yuèlù Academy Corpus of Qín Slips V*, Slips No.59-61)

參考文獻
References

陳松長主編:《嶽麓秦簡藏秦簡（伍）》，上海辭書出版社 2017 年。

陳偉主編:《秦簡牘合集釋文注釋修訂本（肆）》，武漢大學出版社 2016 年。

陳偉主編:《秦簡牘校讀及所見制度考察》，武漢大學出版社 2017 年。

陳偉:《〈嶽麓書院藏秦簡（伍）〉校讀（續三）》，簡帛網，http://www.bsm.org.cn/show_article.php?id=3030，2018 年 3 月 21 日。

代國璽:《説“制詔御史”》,《史學月刊》2017 年第 7 期。

胡平生:《青川秦墓木牘“爲田律”所反映的田畝制度》,《文史》第 19 輯，中華書局

1983 年。
黄文傑：《秦至漢初簡帛文字研究》，商務印書館 2008 年。
任攀：《秦簡語詞札記三則》，《出土文獻研究》第 20 輯，中西書局 2021 年。
湯餘惠：《戰國銘文選》，吉林大學出版社 1993 年。
陶磊：《讀〈嶽麓書院藏秦簡（伍）〉札記》，簡帛網，http://www.bsm.org.cn/show_article.php?id=3184，2018 年 7 月 1 日。
王四維：《秦郡“執法”考——兼論秦郡制的發展》，《社會科學》2019 年第 11 期。
張金光：《論青川秦牘中的爲田制度》，《文史哲》1985 年第 6 期。
周天游：《秦漢雄風》，浙江人民美術出版社 1999 年。
朱錦程：《嶽麓秦簡所見秦上請制度》，簡帛網，http://www.bsm.org.cn/show_article.php?id=2693，2016 年 12 月 30 日。

照片、隸定本
Photo，*Transcription*

圖表 1　四川青川郝家坪 50 號秦墓 16 號木牘
Tableau 1: wood slip in Qín tomb 50 at Hǎojiāpíng, Qīngchuān, Sìchuān, No.16
圖表 2 《嶽麓書院藏秦簡（伍）》53—55 號簡與 59 號簡
Tableau 2: *Yuèlù Academy Corpus of Qín Slips V*, No.53-55, 59
圖表 3 《嶽麓書院藏秦簡（伍）》60—61 號簡與 185 號簡；
《嶽麓書院藏秦簡（肆）》344、345 號簡
Tableau 3: *Yuèlù Academy Corpus of Qín Slips Ⅴ*, No.60-61, 185;
Yuèlù Academy Corpus of Qín Slips Ⅳ , No.344, 345

圖表 1 Tableau 1

下半部圖版	上半部圖版	隸定	青川 16 號木牘圖版
	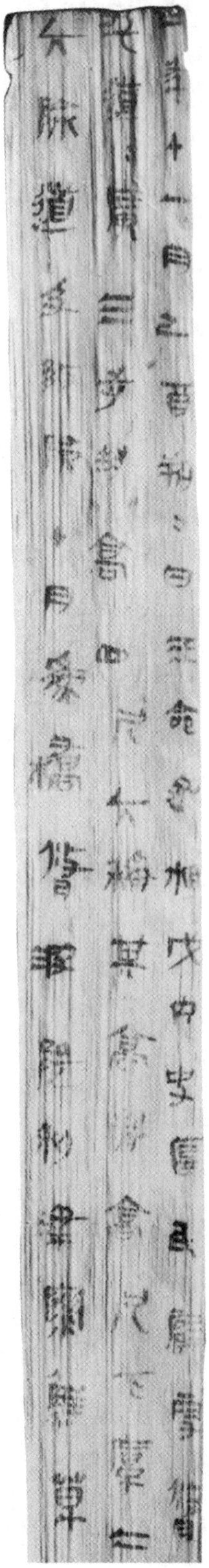	二年十一月己酉朔〃日王命丞相戊内史匽氏臂更脩爲田律田廣一步袤八則爲畛畮二畛一百道百畮爲頃一千道〃廣三步封高四尺大稱其高捋高尺下厚二尺以秋八月脩封捋正彊畔及發千百之大草九月大除道及阪險十月爲橋脩波隄利津梁鮮草雖非除道之時而有陷敗不可行輒爲之章手	

圖表 2　Tableau 2

嶽麓伍 59		嶽麓伍 55		嶽麓伍 54		嶽麓伍 53	
隸定	照片	隸定	照片	隸定	照片	隸定	照片
制詔御史聞獄多留或至數歲不決令無辠者久毄而有辠者久留甚不善其舉留獄上		巳後此等勿言　廿六		廢官令以故秩爲新地吏四歲而勿廢請論慶制書曰諸當廢而爲新地吏勿廢者即非廢		定陰忠言律曰顯夫〓有辠當廢以上勿擅斷必請之今南郡司馬慶故爲冤句令詐課當	

圖表 3　Tableau 3

<table>
<tr><th>嶽麓肆 345</th><th colspan="2">嶽麓肆 344</th><th colspan="2">嶽麓伍 185</th><th colspan="2">嶽麓伍 61</th><th colspan="2">嶽麓伍 60</th></tr>
<tr><td>照片（上）</td><td>照片（下）</td><td>照片（上）</td><td>照片（下）</td><td>照片（上）</td><td>隸定</td><td>照片</td><td>隸定</td><td>照片</td></tr>
<tr><td></td><td></td><td></td><td></td><td></td><td>冣偕上御史御史奏之其執灋不將計而郡守丞將計者亦上之制曰可　卌六</td><td></td><td>之御史請至計令執灋上冣者各牒書上其餘獄不決者一牒署不決歲月日及毄者人數爲</td><td></td></tr>
</table>

二十四、更修爲《田律》命書
24. Decree on Revision of Statutes on Agriculture

原文
Bamboo Script

二年十一月己酉朔＝（朔朔）日，王命丞相戊（茂）①、内史②匽氏③、臂④更脩（修）爲《田律》⑤：田廣一步⑥，袤八則⑦，爲畛⑧畮（畝）⑨，二畛一百（陌）道。百畮（畝）爲頃，一千（阡）道⑩＝（道。道）廣三步。封⑪高四尺，大稱其高。捋（埒）⑫高尺，下厚二尺。以秋八月，脩（修）封捋（埒），正彊（疆）畔，及發⑬千（阡）百（陌）之大草。九月，大除道及阪險⑭。十月爲橋，脩（修）波隄（堤），利津𨻶（隧）鮮草⑮。雖非除道之時，而有陷敗不可行，輒爲之。章手⑯。

注釋
Annotation

① 戊：人名，即甘茂。
② 内史：官職名稱，是秦國國都地區的長官。
③ 匽氏：人名，另見於出土的秦國兵器。
④ 臂：人名。
⑤ 田律：作爲律名屢見於秦漢文獻。或認爲《爲田律》是律名。
⑥ 步：指左右腳各邁一次的長度。《司馬法》："六尺爲步，步百爲畝。"《禮記・王制》："古者以周尺八尺爲步，今以周尺六尺四寸爲步。" 秦國1尺大約23.1釐米，1步大約140釐米。
⑦ 則：長度單位，1則爲30步。
⑧ 畛：具有固定面積的人爲設置的耕田區域。或認爲是田間道路、界限、壟畝、田埂等。
⑨ 畮：通"畝"。秦以寬1步、長240步爲1畝，這在出土秦漢《數書》中也有類似記載。約當461平方米。
⑩ 陌道，阡道：田地邊緣的小道。
⑪ 封：作爲田界標誌的土堆。
⑫ 捋：通"埒"，封與封之間的矮墻。
⑬ 發：除草。
⑭ 阪險：阪，崎嶇不平，"阪""險"連用，泛指道路險要之處。
⑮ 鮮草：諸家説法不一，或認爲是衍文，或認爲指新鮮緑草，或認爲義爲除草，或認爲讀爲棧造，指棧道與浮橋。
⑯ 章手：章，人名；手，手寫。秦時公文往往署明書寫者。

1. 戊 *wù*: equivalent to *mào* 茂 . This is the personal name of the Prime Minister Gān Mào 甘茂 .
2. 内史 *nèi shǐ*: a title of an official, roughly equivalent to Minister of Capital.
3. 匽氏 *yǎn shì*: personal name, also appears on some unearthed Qín weapons.
4. 臂 *bì*: personal name.
5. 田律 *tián lǜ*: Statutes on Agriculture.
6. 步 *bù*: unit of length, equivalent to about 140 cm, approximately 6 Qín *chǐ* 尺 .
7. 則 *zé*: unit of length. 1 *zé* 則 is equivalent to 30 steps.
8. 畛 *zhěn*: a unit of farming field.
9. 畮 *mǔ*: a variant of *mǔ* 畝 . 1 *mǔ* is equivalent to about 461 square meters.
10. 陌道 *mò dào*, 阡道 *qiān dào*: small road path along the farming fields.
11. 封 *fēng*: mound made as landmark or border marker.
12. 埒 *lǚ*: equivalent to *liè* 埒 , low walls between the mounds.
13. 發 *bá*: weeding.
14. 阪險 *bǎn xiǎn: bǎn* 阪 , rugged road, *xiǎn* 險 , dangerous road; together, *bǎnxiǎn* refers to rugged and difficult places or roads.
15. 鮮草 *xiān cǎo*: precise meaning here is unclear. Here are some possible interpretations: (i) fresh grass; (ii) weeding; (iii) plank road and pontoon bridge; (iv) extra word that should be deleted.
16. 章手 *zhāng shǒu: zhāng* 章 , a personal name; *shǒu* 手 , lit. "handwriting," used as a standard way for scribes to sign the official documents in Qín Dynasty.

寬式隸定
Loose Transcription

二年十一月己酉朔朔日，王命丞相茂、内史匽氏、臂更修爲《田律》：田廣一步，袤八則，爲畛畝，二畛一陌道。百畝爲頃，一阡道。道廣三步。封高四尺，大稱其高。埒高尺，下厚二尺。以秋八月，修封埒，正疆畔，及發阡陌之大草。九月，大除道及阪險。十月爲橋，修波堤，利津隧鮮草。雖非除道之時，而有陷敗不可行，輒爲之。章手。

白話文
Vernacular Chinese

（秦武王）二年十一月己酉日，王命令丞相茂、内史匽氏、臂重新修訂《田律》：田寬一步、長八則（二百四十步）作爲畛畝，每兩畛有一條陌道。百畝爲頃，一條阡道。道寬三步。（作爲地界的）封土堆高四尺，大小與其高度相應。（作爲地界的）矮墻高一尺，下部厚二尺。在秋天八月，修封土堆和矮墻，校訂地界，除掉陌道上的大草。九月，大規模修治道路及道路險要處。十月造橋，修堤壩，疏通水道。即使不是修治道路的時候，有塌陷不能行走之處，就要修治。章手寫。

英文翻譯
English Translation

On the day *jǐyǒu* of the eleventh month, the second year of King Wǔ of Qín（309 BCE）, the King ordered the Chief Minister Mào and Ministers of capital Yǎnshì and Bì to revise the Statutes on Agriculture: The field that is one step wide and eight *zé* long（two hundred and forty *bù*）equals the size of one *mǔ*. Between two pieces of zhěn there is to be a road called *mòdào*. One hundred *mǔ* makes one *qǐng* with a road called *qiāndào*, three *bù* wide. The mound［as a land boundary］is four feet high, its size being commensurate with its height. The low wall is one foot high and two feet thick at the bottom. In autumn at about the eighth month, repair the mounds and low walls［as the boundary of the land］, inspect the boundary of the land, and remove the grass weed on the *mòdào*. In the ninth month, a large-scale repair of roads and dangerous roads will be carried out. In the tenth month, bridges will be built, dams will be repaired, and waterways will be cleared. At other times, if any road collapses or becomes impassable, repair it. Handwritten by Zhāng.

二十五、新地吏勿廢制書
25. Decree on Officials of New Occupied Area Must Not Be Dismissed

原文
Bamboo Script

定陰〈陶〉①忠言，律曰：顯夫₌（大夫）②有辠（罪）當廢以上勿擅斷，必請之。今南郡③司馬慶故爲冤句④令，詐（詐）課⑤，當廢官⑥，令以故秩爲新地⑦吏四歲而勿廢，請論慶。制書曰：諸當廢而爲新地吏勿廢者，即非廢。巳（已）後此等勿言。廿六

注釋
Annotation

① 定陰：陰，“陶”字的誤寫。定陶，縣名，秦屬東郡。
② 顯大夫：睡虎地秦墓竹簡記載：“可（何）謂宦者顯大夫？宦及智（知）於王，及六百石吏以上，皆爲顯大夫。”
③ 南郡：郡名。
④ 冤句：縣名，秦屬東郡。
⑤ 課：考核官吏並評定優劣。
⑥ 廢官：是一種針對官吏的特殊刑罰，將犯有過失的官吏免職後永不再録用。
⑦ 新地：秦新佔領的土地。是否爲新地應該有個劃分的時間界限，如南郡不屬新地，定陶、冤句則屬新地。

1. 定陰 *dìng yīn*: name of a county, also called Dìngtáo 定陶 , belongs to East Commandery.
2. 顯大夫 *xiǎn dà fū*: a title higher than *dàfū* 大夫 . *Xiǎn dàfū* 顯大夫 are officials attending to or known to the King, or with annual salary higher than 600 *dàn* 石 .
3. 南郡 *nán jùn*: commandery or commandery name; lit. “South Commandery.”
4. 冤句 *yuān qú*: county name, belongs to East Commandery.
5. 課 *kè*: to evaluate the performance of officials and assign the grades.
6. 廢官 *fèi guān*: removal from the office, a penalty in Qín Kingdom. Once removed from the office, the person can never be re-appointed.
7. 新地 *xīn dì*: a term referring to newly acquired land. For a territory to be considered as *xīndì* 新地 , there is probably a timeline; for example, South Commandery is not a new land, while Dìngtáo 定陶 and Yuānqú 冤句 still are.

寬式隸定
Loose Transcription

定陶忠言，律曰：顯大夫有罪當廢以上勿擅斷，必請之。今南郡司馬慶故爲冤句令，詐課，當廢官，令以故秩爲新地吏四歲而勿廢，請論慶。制書曰：諸當廢而爲新地吏勿廢者，即非廢。已後此等勿言。廿六

白話文
Vernacular Chinese

定陶縣令忠報告，律說：顯大夫（皇帝的侍從、爲王所知的人以及俸禄在六百石以上的官吏）如果犯了應當廢除官職以上的罪，（其上級）不要擅自判決，一定要請示。現在的南郡司馬慶以前是冤句縣令，在考核官吏時有欺騙行爲，應當廢除官職，使其按以前的秩級做新取得的郡縣的官吏四年而不廢除官職，請求判決慶。制書説：應當廢除官職而去做新取得的郡縣的官吏不廢除官職，就不廢除。以後這樣的情況不要再匯報。第二十六號

英文翻譯
English Translation

Magistrate Zhōng of Dìngtáo County reports: According to the Law: Honorable officials who have committed crimes deserving to be dismissed from their official positions should not be sentenced without authorization. Instruction has to be requested [for sentencing] . Now there is the case of Major (Sīmǎ) Qìng serving in the South Commandery, who was formerly Magistrate of Yuānqú County, who committed a crime of deception. [According to the law] , he should be removed from his position. [We recommend that] he should be moved to the newly conquered land and keep his [old] salary grade for four years. [We] request a judgment on Qìng. The Decree stated: A situation where an official should be dismissed but instead is now appointed [at the same level] in a newly conquered territory is no longer being dismissed, therefore is tantamount to non-dismissal. Do not ever report similar situations in the future. No.26.

二十六、舉留獄上之制書
26. Decree on Reporting Detained Cases

原文
Bamboo Script

制詔御史①：聞獄②多留③或至數歲不決，令無辠（罪）者久毄（繫）而有辠（罪）者久留，甚不善，其舉留獄上之。御史請：至計，令執灋④上冣（最）⑤者，各牒書⑥上其餘獄不決者，一牒署不決歲月日及毄（繫）者人數，爲冣（最），偕上御₌史₌（御史，御史）奏之，其執灋不將計而郡守、丞將計者，亦上之。制曰：可。卅六

注釋
Annotation

① 制詔御史：制詔指制作詔書。御史是“侍御史”的省稱。漢代的侍御史既是御史大夫的屬官，又是御史中丞的屬官，在殿中給事。秦代不明。“制詔御史”作爲文書用語，表明該詔令由皇帝口述，由侍御史書寫或抄録並製作成規範文書。有學者認爲“制詔御史”指“皇帝告御史”。

② 獄：案件。

③ 留：滯留。

④ 執灋：這裏的執灋指郡執灋，是秩級爲二千石的郡中長吏，擁有單獨的官署，其官署稱“府”，府中有丞、都吏，府外還設有若干屬官。不僅是監察官員，還擁有司法審判、黜免官吏、調發徒隸、管理徭役、分配錢款和循行案舉等多種權力。應該是一種過渡官職，後來不設。

⑤ 冣：即“最”，匯總。

⑥ 牒書：以簡札書寫。

1. 制詔御史 *zhì zhào yù shǐ*: title of an official, “Royal Scribe” (or “Imperial Counselor”) who is responsible for recording the imperial edicts. *Zhìzhào* 制詔 , literally means “[The Emperor] makes an imperial edict and the Royal Scribe records it as such.” This term became an imperial procedure for the Emperor to make formal announcements and edicts, which become part of royal archives. Some scholars believe that it refers to the Emperor informing the Royal Scribe.
2. 獄 *yù*: lit. “jail, prison,” here it means cases.
3. 留 *liú*: lit. “to keep, stay or lag behind.”
4. 執灋 *zhí fǎ*: title of an official in law enforcement. Here it refers to the chief official of a commandery, with a salary grade of two-thousand *dàn* 石 . The office of *zhífǎ* 執灋 is called *fǔ*

府 , which is staffed with several levels of administrative officials and equipped with additional offices. The office of *zhífǎ* not only could supervise other officials, but also was given a multitude of authorities, including judicial power, dismissal of officials, transfer of forced labor, management of servitude, distribution of money, etc. This position appears to have been only a provisional arrangement in the early days of the First Emperor of Qín.

5. 冣 *jù*: equivalent to *zuì* 最 , meaning to collect, to combine or to summarize, also meaning to aggregated registers or records.
6. 牒書 *dié shū*: documents written on wood or bamboo slips.

寬式隸定
Loose Transcription

制詔御史：聞獄多留或至數歲不決，令無罪者久繫而有罪者久留，甚不善，其舉留獄上之。御史請：至計，令執灋上最者，各牒書上其餘獄不決者，一牒署不決歲月日及繫者人數，爲最，偕上御史，御史奏之，其執灋不將計而郡守、丞將計者，亦上之。制曰：可。卅六

白話文
Vernacular Chinese

制詔御史：聽説案件多有滯留，有的達到幾年不判決，使無罪的人長時間拘繫而有罪的人長時間滯留不判決，很不好，選取滯留的案件上呈它們。御史請示：等到上計時，命令執灋上呈匯總的記録，各用簡札書寫上呈其剩餘的不判決的案件，一枚簡札書寫不判決的年月日及拘繫的人數，匯總，一起上呈御史，御史上奏它們，執灋不主持上計而郡的太守、丞主持上計的，也上呈它們。皇帝命令説：同意。第三十六號

英文翻譯
English Translation

An imperial decision instructed the Imperial Counselor: I have heard that [judgement in] many cases were delayed, sometimes for several years. In this way, innocent people are kept for a long time and the criminals also stay long. This is wrong. Make a list of those which are still being detained. The Imperial Counselor petitioned: [best method to deal with this issue:] When making a statistical project, order the *zhífǎ* to submit a complete list of delayed cases. List the remaining undecided cases. List the total number of detainees and the time (down to the day) that the case was sitting in the file in one slip. Submit all of them to the Imperial Counselor. The Imperial Counselor will bring them to the Emperor. If the *zhífǎ* is not the minister of making the statistical project, Commandery Governors or Assistant Magistrates who are authorized to take charge of the matters may submit them too. The decree states: Acceptable. No.36.

練習
Practice

釋讀圖表 3 中《嶽麓書院藏秦簡（伍）》185 號簡、《嶽麓書院藏秦簡（肆）》344 與 345 號簡中的文字。

Read slip No.185 from *Yuèlù Academy Corpus of Qín Slips* Ⅴ and slips No.344 and 345 from *Yuèlù Academy Corpus of Qín Slips* Ⅳ in Tableau 3.

第十一組　機構往來文書
Group 11　Documents of Bureaucratic Agencies

簡介
Introduction

日本學者冨谷至先生有本著作叫作《文書行政的漢帝國》，指出簡牘這種書寫材料成就了漢代的文書行政，而漢王朝集權帝制的確立與鞏固很大程度上也歸因於文書行政的貫徹實行。對於戰國晚期的秦國及秦王朝來説，文書及文書行政的意義同樣重大。除了王室文書，中央機構與地方郡縣之間、不同郡縣之間的往來文書都爲我們呈現了這一點。秦的機構往來文書在里耶秦簡中有集中體現。依照文書遞送的機構與方向，可以將其分爲上行、下行和平行三種不同類型的文書。上行文書是呈送給上級機構的文書，下行文書是發送給下級機構的文書，平行文書是同等級機構之間的往來文書。值得注意的是，一則文書有時會抄録之前一封或多封相關文書的内容，下文所列舉的兩則文書都有這樣的特點。

The Japanese scholar Tomiya Itaru has pointed out in his book *Document Administration in the Hàn Empire* (*Wénshū xíngzhèng de Hàn dìguó* 文書行政的漢帝國) that the writing materials such as bamboo slips helped to establish the document administration and consolidate the centralized authority over the vast empire of the Hàn Dynasty. Such assessment can also be applied to the Qín Kingdom at the end of the Warring States Period and Qín Dynasty. In addition to royal documents, the documents exchanged between central government agencies and local countries, and between different counties, all support the notion of huge document administration. Active document exchange among government agencies at the local level can be vividly seen in the Lǐyē Qín slips. According to the organization and direction of document delivery, it can be divided into three types of documents: ascending, descending and parallel. Ascending documents are documents submitted from lower-level to higher-level institutions; descending documents are documents sent from higher-level to lower-level institutions; and parallel documents are documents exchanged between institutions at the same level. It is worth noting that the content of one or more previous related documents is embedded in a later document, as is the case with the two examples in this group.

篇目來源
Text Source

第 27 篇　遷陵守丞敬告司空主書（里耶秦簡 8-63）

27. *Official Dispatch from Acting Assistant Magistrate of Qiānlíng Named Jìng to Minister of*

Convict Labor（Lǐyē Qín slips, No.8-63）
第 28 篇　遷陵守丞敦狐卻書（里耶秦簡 8-135）
28. *Official Dispatch on Rejection of Application from Acting Assistant Magistrate of Qiānlíng Named Dūnhú*（Lǐyē Qín slips, No.8-135）

參考文獻
References

陳劍:《讀秦漢簡札記三篇》,《出土文獻與古文字研究》第 4 輯，上海古籍出版社 2011 年。
陳偉主編:《里耶秦簡牘校釋（壹）》，武漢大學出版社 2012 年。
湖南省文物考古研究所:《里耶秦簡（壹）》，文物出版社 2012 年。
黄浩波:《里耶秦簡牘所見“計”文書及相關問題研究》，見楊振紅、鄔文玲主編:《簡帛研究二〇一六》(春夏卷)，廣西師範大學出版社 2016 年。
馬怡:《里耶秦簡選校》，見中國社會科學院歷史研究所學刊編委會編:《中國社會科學院歷史研究所學刊》第 4 集，商務印書館 2007 年。
王焕林:《里耶秦簡校詁》，中國文聯出版社 2007 年。
王偉:《里耶秦簡“付計”文書義解》,《魯東大學學報》(哲學社會科學版）2015 年第 5 期。
楊振紅、王安宇:《秦漢訴訟制度中的“覆”及相關問題》,《史學月刊》2017 年第 12 期。
張春龍、[日]大川俊隆、[日]籾山明:《里耶秦簡刻齒簡研究——兼論嶽麓秦簡〈數〉中的未解讀簡》,《文物》2015 年第 3 期。

照片、隸定本
Photo，Transcription

圖表 1　里耶秦簡 8-63
Tableau 1: Lǐyē Qín slips, No.8-63
圖表 2　里耶秦簡 8-135
Tableau 2: Lǐyē Qín slips, No.8-135

圖表 1　Tableau 1

里耶 8-63 背		里耶 8-63	
隸定	照片	隸定	照片
十月辛卯旦朐忍索秦士五狀以來慶半　兵手	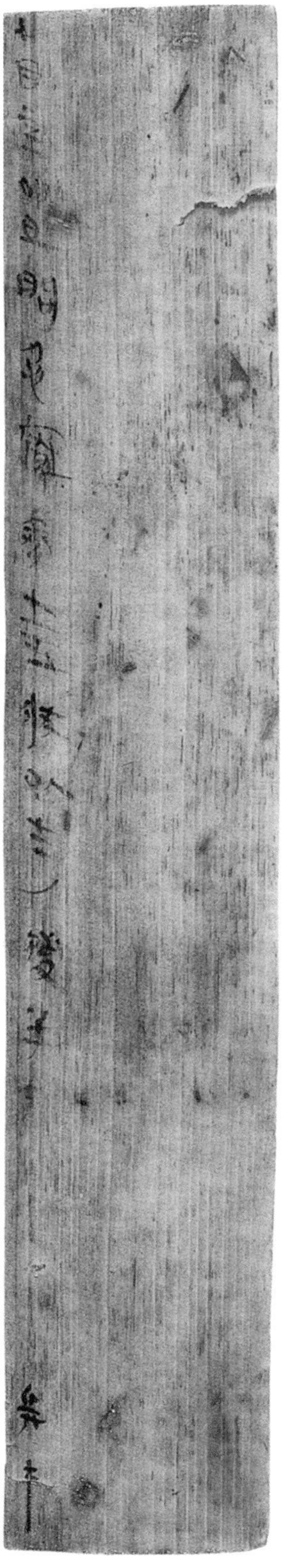	廿六年三月午朔癸卯左公田丁敢言之佐州里煩故爲公田吏徙屬事荅不備分 負各十五石少半斗值錢三百一十四煩冗佐署遷陵今上責校券二謁告遷陵 令官計者定以錢三百一十四受旬陽左公田錢計問可計付署計年爲報敢言之 三月辛亥旬陽丞滂敢告遷陵丞主寫移〃券可爲報敢告主兼手 廿七年十月庚子遷陵守丞敬告司空主以律令從事言麕手即走申行司空	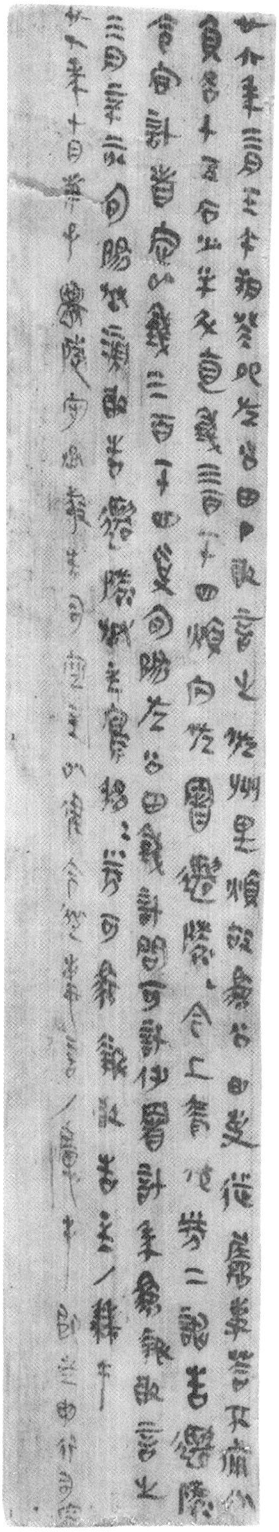

圖表 2　Tableau 2

里耶 8-135 背		里耶 8-135	
隸定	照片	隸定	照片
月戊寅走己巳以來廳半　□手	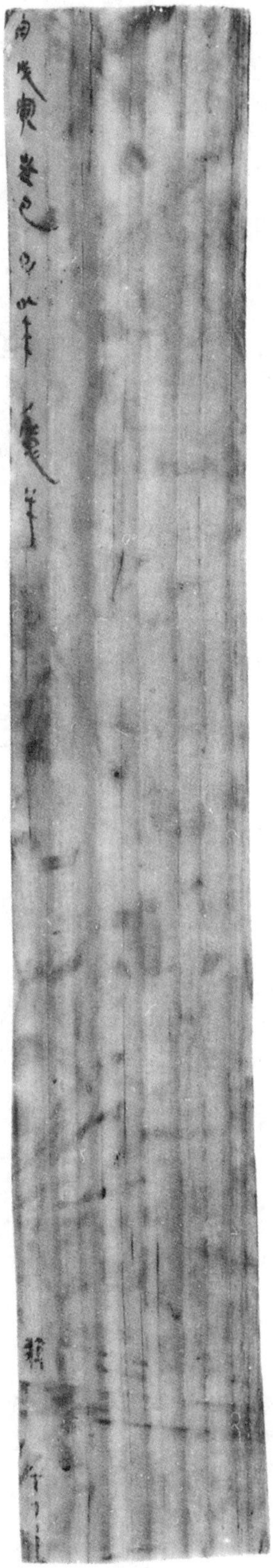	廿六年八月庚戌朔丙子司空守樛敢言前日言競陵漢陰狼假遷陵公船一袤三丈三尺名曰□ 以求故荆積瓦未歸船狼屬司馬昌官謁告昌官令狼歸船報曰狼有逮在覆獄巳卒史 衰義所今寫校券一牒上謁言巳卒史衰義所問狼船存所其亡之爲責券移遷陵弗□□屬 謁報敢言之九月庚辰遷陵守丞敦狐卻之司空自以二月叚狼船何故弗蚤辟至今而 誧曰謁問覆獄卒史衰義衰義事已不智所居其聽書從事廳手即令走壬行司空	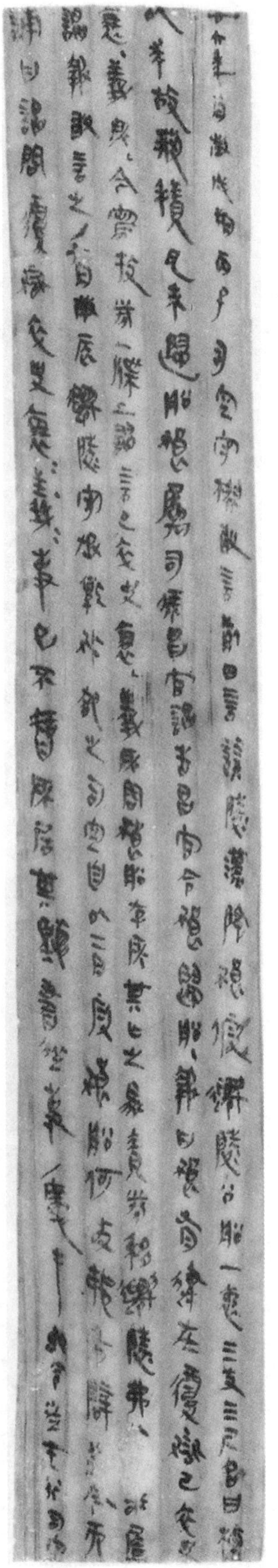

二十七、遷陵守丞敬告司空主書
27. Official Dispatch from Acting Assistant Magistrate of Qiānlíng Named Jìng to Minister of Convict Labor

原文
Bamboo Script

廿六年三月壬午朔癸卯，左公田丁①敢言之：佐州里煩②故爲公田吏，徙屬。事荅③不備④，分Ⅰ負⑤各十五石少半斗，直⑥錢三百一十四。煩冗佐署遷陵。今上責【校】券⑦二，謁告遷陵Ⅱ令官計者⑧定⑨以錢三百一十四，受旬陽⑩左公田錢計，問可（何）計付，署⑪計年⑫爲報。敢言之。Ⅲ

三月辛亥，旬陽丞滂敢告遷陵丞主：寫移₌（移，移）券，可（何）爲報。敢告主。/兼手。Ⅳ

廿七年十月庚子，遷陵守丞敬告司空主⑬：以律令從事，言。/慶手。即走申行司空。Ⅴ 8-63

十月辛卯旦，朐忍⑭索（索）秦⑮士五（伍）狀以來。/慶半。兵手。8-63 背

注釋
Annotation

① 左公田丁：丁，人名，旬陽縣左公田的負責人。秦簡常見“機構+人名”的格式，用來稱指某機構的負責人。

② 州里煩：州里，里名。煩，人名。

③ 事荅：事，治理。荅，小豆。“事荅”即管理種植小豆的事宜。

④ 不備：不足數。

⑤ 分負：負，賠償。分負，分攤賠償的金額。

⑥ 直：通“值”，價值，代價。

⑦ 校券：用於核驗的券。

⑧ 官計者：指製作計的官署。

⑨ 定：完成。

⑩ 旬陽：縣名。

⑪ 署：寫明。

⑫ 計年：計的年度。

⑬ 司空主：指司空主管官員。

⑭ 朐忍：縣名。

⑮ 索秦：里名。

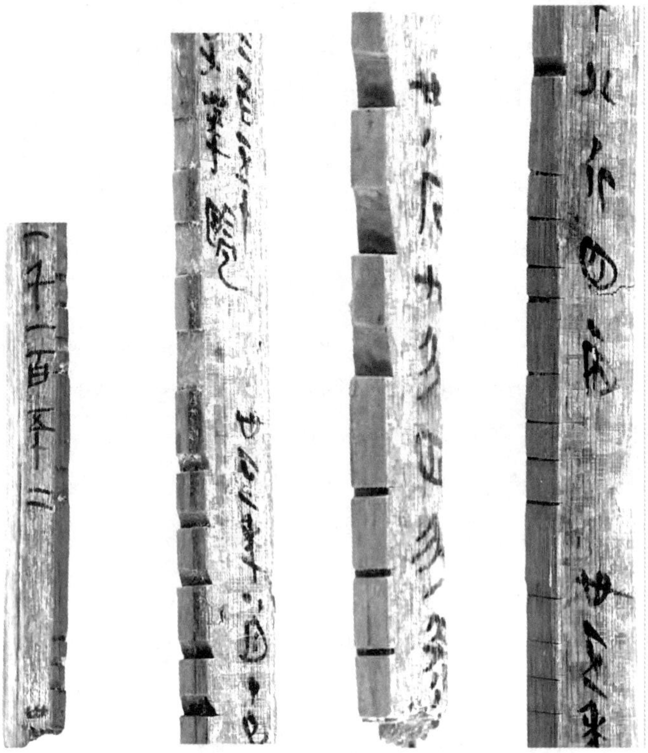

圖 1　里耶秦簡中的券及其刻齒

Figure 1　Tallies and their engraved teeth in Lǐyē Qín bamboo slips

（引自張春龍等：《里耶秦簡刻齒簡研究》57、58 頁）

1. 左公田丁 *zuǒ gōng tián dīng*: Dīng 丁 , personal name; *Zuǒ gōngtián* 左公田 , one of the directors of state-owned farmland of Xúnyáng County. It was customary in the Qín Dynasty to put the name of a goverment agency in front of the person overseeing or directing that agency.
2. 州里煩 *zhōu lǐ fán*: Zhōulǐ 州里 is the name of a village, and Fán 煩 is a personal name.
3. 事荅 *shì dá: shì* 事 , here used as a verb to mean to do things, to manage; *dá* 荅 , small beans or red beans; *shì dá* 事荅 means to manage the crops of red beans.
4. 不備 *bù bèi*: not sufficient, meaning not to reach the target.
5. 分負 *fēn fù: fù* 負 , compensation; *fēn fù* 分負 , to share the amount of compensation.
6. 直 *zhí*: equivalent to *zhí* 值 , meaning value, price.
7. 校券 *jiào quàn*: to check tallies.
8. 官計者 *guān jì zhě*: referring to the office that accounting（*jì* 計）.
9. 定 *dìng*: set, done, finished.
10. 旬陽 *xún yáng*: name of a county.
11. 署 *shǔ*: to sign, to detail.
12. 計年 *jì nián*: year of accounting.
13. 司空主 *sī kōng zhǔ*: director or master of the official office in charge of convict works.

14. 朐忍 *qú rěn*: name of a county.
15. 索秦 *suǒ qín*: name of a village.

寬式隸定
Loose Transcription

廿六年三月壬午朔癸卯，左公田丁敢言之：佐州里煩故爲公田吏，徙屬。事荅不備，分負各十五石少半斗，值錢三百一十四。煩冗佐署遷陵。今上責校券二，謁告遷陵令官計者定以錢三百一十四，受旬陽左公田錢計，問何計付，署計年爲報。敢言之。

三月辛亥，旬陽丞滂敢告遷陵丞主：寫移，移券，何爲報。敢告主。兼手。

廿七年十月庚子，遷陵守丞敬告司空主：以律令從事，言。應手。即走申行司空。

十月辛卯旦，朐忍索秦士伍狀以來。慶半。兵手。

白話文
Vernacular Chinese

始皇二十六年三月癸卯日，左公田嗇夫丁斗膽陳述：田佐州里人煩以前是公田的官吏，變動了任職的地方。他管理小豆種植未達到產量，分攤各賠償十五石三分之一斗，價值三百一十四錢。煩在遷陵縣從事冗佐的工作。現在上呈索取債務的校券兩枚，請求旬陽縣負責人告知遷陵縣命令從事計的官署用錢三百一十四作爲內容完成計，接受旬陽縣左公田的錢計，詢問錢計交付哪個官署，寫明計的年份回復。斗膽陳述。

三月辛亥日，旬陽縣丞滂斗膽告知遷陵縣丞：抄寫文書移送，移送校券，相關問題答案是什麼請回復。斗膽告知您。兼手寫。

始皇二十七年十月庚子日，遷陵縣代理縣丞敬告知司空的負責人，按照法律條文辦理此事，並匯報。應手寫。立即命令名爲申的走傳遞此文書到司空。

十月辛卯日旦時，朐忍縣索秦里名爲狀的士伍帶來。慶拆閱。兵手寫。

英文翻譯
English Translation

In the twenty-sixth year of the First Emperor, on the *guǐmǎo* day of the third month, Bailiff of Left Public Farmland (*zuǒ gōngtián*)[of Xúnyáng County] who is named Dīng dared to report: An assistant named Fán of Zhōulǐ Village used to be an assistant in the Office of Public Farmland (*gōngtián*) and was relocated. [He] was assigned to be in charge of adzuki bean crops, but [he] did not meet the [production] target. [His] share of making up the shortage was fifteen *dàn* and one third of *dǒu*, equivalent to 314 Qín coins. Fán is now working as Assistant who has a long service for government (*rǒngzuǒ*) at Qiānlíng County. Now [I] present two checking tallies for claiming the debt, to the office in charge of accounting (*jì*) in Qiānlíng County, that the amount of 314 Qín coins should be moved to Qiānlíng County. Please inform us which accounting office is responsible and [specify] the accounting year. I dare to report.

On the *xīnhài* day of the third month, Assistant Magistrate of Xúnyáng named Pāng dares to inform the Assistant Magistrate of Qiānlíng: Copy the document and transfer it, transfer checking tallies, ask which office handles the account and the accounting year. Replied here, dare to let you know. Handwritten by Jiān.

In the twenty-seventh year of the First Emperor, on the *gēngzǐ* day of the tenth month, Acting Assistant Magistrate of Qiānlíng County informed the person in charge of the Convict Labor Office to handle the matter in accordance with the legal provisions and report it. Handwritten by Kāng. Immediately order the person named Shēn to deliver this document to the Convict Labor Office.

On the *xīnmǎo* day of the tenth month, at daybreak, Qúrěn County, Suǒqín Village, a commoner (*Shìwǔ*: an ordinary person without titles of nobility) named Zhuàng brought it in. Qìng opened the official dispatch and read it. Handwritten by Bīng.

二十八、遷陵守丞敦狐卻書
28. Official Dispatch on Rejection of Application from Acting Assistant Magistrate of Qiānlíng Named Dūnhú

原文
Bamboo Script

廿六年八月庚戌朔丙子，司空守樛敢言：前日①言競陵②漢陰③狼假遷陵公船一，袤④三丈三尺，名曰□，Ⅰ以求故荆⑤積瓦⑥，未歸船。狼屬司馬昌官⑦。謁告昌官，令狼歸船。報曰：狼有逮⑧在覆獄⑨巴卒史⑩Ⅱ衰、義所。今寫校券一牒上，謁言巴卒史衰、義所，問狼船存所。其⑪亡之，爲責（債）券移遷陵，弗□□屬。Ⅲ謁報。敢言之。/【九】月庚辰，遷陵守丞敦狐卻之：司空自以二月叚（假）狼船，何故弗蚤⑫（早）辟⑬，至今而Ⅳ誧⑭（甫）曰謁問覆獄卒史衰₌義₌（衰、義。衰、義）事巳（已），不智（知）所居，其聽書從事。/ 慶手。即令走壬行司空。Ⅴ 8-135

【八】月戊寅走己巳⑮以來。/ 慶半。□手。8-135 背

注釋
Annotation

① 前日：往日。
② 競陵：即竟陵，縣名。
③ 漢陰：里名。
④ 袤：指縱長。
⑤ 故荆：以前的楚國。
⑥ 積瓦：儲藏的陶器。
⑦ 昌官：昌，人名。官，官府。
⑧ 有逮：被逮捕。
⑨ 覆獄：秦漢時期訴訟程式中的“覆”是指上級機關主理或由上級機關指定某機構（或使者）主理的訴訟審判，主理的程式包括立案、偵查、審判、覆核、監督等各個環節。
⑩ 巴卒史：巴郡卒史。
⑪ 其：指事之詞，此，是。或説爲假設連詞，如果，假使。
⑫ 蚤：通“早”。
⑬ 辟：召回。
⑭ 誧：通“甫”，方始。
⑮ 己巳：人名。

1. 前日 *qián rì*: past days.
2. 競陵 *jìng líng*: county name.
3. 漢陰 *hàn yīn*: name of a village（*lǐ* 里）.
4. 袤 *mào*: longitudinal or vertical length.
5. 故荆 *gù jīng*: the former state of Chǔ 楚 .
6. 積瓦 *jī wǎ*: stored pottery.
7. 昌官 *chāng guān*: chāng 昌 , personal name Chāng; *guān* 官 , office, official government.
8. 有逮 *yǒu dài*: arrested.
9. 覆獄 *fù yù*: during the time of Qín and Hàn, litigation and trials that were presided over by a higher authority or designated by a higher authority（or an envoy）are called *fù* 覆 . The litigation/trial process involves steps such as case filing, investigation, trial, review and supervision.
10. 巴卒史 *bā zú shǐ*: Accessory Scribes（that is, low level officials）of Bā 巴 Commandery.
11. 其 *qí*: indicative word, meaning this; or as suppositive conjunction, meaning if, assuming.
12. 蚤 *zǎo*: equivalent to *zǎo* 早 , early.
13. 辟 *pì*: recall.
14. 誧 *bū*: equivalent to *fǔ* 甫 , just start, just begin.
15. 己巳 *jǐ sì*: personal name.

寬式隸定
Loose Transcription

廿六年八月庚戌朔丙子，司空守樛敢言：前日言競陵漢陰狼假遷陵公船一，袤三丈三尺，名曰□，以求故荆積瓦，未歸船。狼屬司馬昌官。謁告昌官，令狼歸船。報曰：狼有逮在覆獄巴卒史衰、義所。今寫校券一牒上，謁言巴卒史衰、義所，問狼船存所。其亡之，爲債券移遷陵，弗□□屬。謁報。敢言之。九月庚辰，遷陵守丞敦狐卻之：司空自以二月假狼船，何故弗早辟，至今而甫曰謁問覆獄卒史衰、義。衰、義事已，不知所居，其聽書從事。慶手。即令走壬行司空。

八月戊寅走己巳以來。慶半。□手。

白話文
Vernacular Chinese

始皇二十六年八月丙子日，名爲樛的代理司空嗇夫斗膽陳述：之前陳述過名爲狼的競陵縣漢陰里人從遷陵縣借了一艘公船，船長三丈三尺，船的名字叫做……，用來求取之前楚國的儲藏陶器，没有把船還回來。狼歸屬於司馬昌的官署。請求縣廷告知昌的官署，命令狼歸還公船。回復説：狼被逮捕，現在在覆核案件的名爲衰和義的巴郡卒史處。現在抄寫校券於一枚簡牘呈上，請求縣廷向覆核案件的巴卒史衰和義處陳説，詢問狼公船所在的地方。如果公船丟失了，製作債券移交給遷陵縣，未丟失的話告知船現在歸屬誰。請求縣廷回復。斗膽陳述。

九月庚辰日，遷陵縣代理縣丞敦狐退回：司空自從二月借給狼公船，爲什麼不早些召回，現在才開始請求縣廷詢問覆核案件的卒史衰和義。衰和義的事務結束了，不知道狼所處的地方，按照文書辦理此事。慶手寫。立即命令名爲壬的走傳遞文書到司空。

八月戊寅日名爲己巳的走帶來。慶拆閱。某手寫。

英文翻譯
Translation

On the *bǐngzǐ* day (the twenty-seventh day) of the eighth month, the twenty-sixth regnal year of the First Emperor of Qín, Jiū, the Acting Bailiff of Convict Labor boldly stated: [We have] previously reported that Láng, a man of Hànyīn Village, Jìnglíng County borrowed a government boat of the size of three *zhàng* and three *chǐ* (about 7.6 meters) , known as ..., from Qiānlíng County in order to transport potteries collected from the former state of Chǔ. The boat was never returned. Láng now works under the office of Chāng, whose official position is Major (Sīmǎ). [We have requested you] to inform Chāng's office to order Láng to return the boat. [Country government] replied: Láng has already been arrested [for other matters] and is in the office of Shuāi and Yì who are Accessory Scribes (*zúshǐ*) of Bā Commandery. Now [we are] submitting a checking tally to request you to contact Shuāi and Yì to enquire from Láng the whereabouts of the boat. If [the boat] is lost, the office of Shuāi and Yì are to issue a debt voucher to Qiānlíng County. If [the boat is] not lost, then who currently owns it? [We] request [your] response and [we] dare to report as such.

On the *gēngchén* day of the nineth month, Acting Assistant Magistrate of Qiānlíng named Dūnhú rejected [the request] : Minister of Convict Labor lent the public boat to Láng in the second month, why has the boat not been recalled earlier? Why did you wait till now to request us to inquire from Shuāi and Yì [about Láng and the boat] ? The tenure of Shuāi and Yì has expired. [We] don't know where Láng is. The matter will have to be handled according to the documents. Handwritten by Kāng. Immediately ordered a messenger named Rén to pass the documents to the Convict Labor Office.

On the *wùyín* day of the eighth month, a messenger named Jǐsì brought this [document] in. Kāng opened and read it. Handwritten by so-and-so.

練習
Practice

釋讀圖表 3 中的里耶秦簡 8-154 號簡。

Read Lǐyē Qín slips, No.8-154 in Figure 3.

圖表 3　Tableau 3

里耶 8-154 背	里耶 8-154

第十二組　律令
Group 12　Statutes and Decrees

簡介
Introduction

在秦代，律與令是既相互關聯又有區別的兩種法律文獻。目前，在睡虎地秦墓竹簡、龍崗秦墓竹簡、嶽麓書院藏秦簡等多批次的簡牘文獻中都可見到律令文獻。據統計，睡虎地秦墓竹簡《秦律十八種》中有19種秦律：田律、厩苑律、倉律、金布律、關市律、工律、工人程、均工、興律、徭律、司空律、軍爵律、置吏律、效律、傳食律、行書律、内史雜律、尉雜律、屬邦律。睡虎地秦墓竹簡《秦律雜抄》中另見律名：除吏律、游士律、除弟子律、中勞律、藏律、公車司馬獵律、牛羊課、傅律、敦表律、捕盜律、戍律。嶽麓書院藏秦簡所見秦律除以上種類，還可見到如下律名：奔警律、尉卒律、賊律、具律、獄校律、雜律、索律等。秦令则可見：内史郡二千石官共令、廷内史郡二千石官共令、四謁者令、四司空卒令、卜祝酌及它祠令、尉郡卒令、縣官田令等。秦令的行文有一些標記特征，如部分以"令曰"起首、部分以"某某言"起首、大都帶有序號等。

In the Qín Dynasty, statutes (*lǜ* 律) and decrees (*lìng* 令) were two different but interrelated types of legal documents. So far, such legal documents have been found in Shuìhǔdì Qín tomb 11 bamboo slips, bamboo slips unearthed from Qín tomb 6 at Lónggǎng, and the Yuèlù Academy corpus of Qín slips. In the *Eighteen Kinds of Qín Laws* (*Qín lǜ shí bā zhǒng* 秦律十八種) unearthed from Shuìhǔdì, there are 19 kinds of statutes: Statutes on Agriculture (*tiánlǜ* 田律), Statutes on Stables and Royal Park (*jiùyuàn lǜ* 厩苑律), Statutes on Warehouses (*cānglǜ* 倉律), Statutes on Finance (*jīnbù lǜ* 金布律), Statutes on Passes and Markets (*guānshì lǜ* 關市律), Statutes on Government Service (*yáolǜ* 徭律), Statutes on the Establishment of Officials (*zhìlì lǜ* 置吏律), Statutes on Checking (*xiàolǜ* 效律), Statutes on Food Rations at Conveyance Stations (*chuánshí lǜ* 傳食律), Statutes on the Forwarding of Documents (*xíngshū lǜ* 行書律), etc. In the *Qín Statute Miscellany* (*Qínlǜ záchāo* 秦律雜抄) unearthed from Shuìhǔdì, we can also see names of other statutes including Statutes on Staff Appointment (*chúlì lǜ* 除吏律), Statutes on Enrollment (*fùlǜ* 傅律), etc. There are other statutes in the Yuèlù Academy corpus of Qín slips: Statutes on Emergency Troops (*bēnjǐng lǜ* 奔警律), Statutes of the Commandant and Accessory (*wèizú lǜ* 尉卒律), Statutes on Assault (*zéilǜ* 賊律), Statutes on the Composition of Judgments (*jùlǜ* 具律), etc. Qín decrees or orders recorded in bamboo slips include *Decrees to Officials with A Salary of 2000 Dàn in Capital Area and Commandery* (*Nèishǐ jùn èrqiān dàn guān gònglìng* 内史郡二千石官共令), etc. The Qín decrees have certain common features, such as: some begin with "the order said", some begin with "someone stated", and most of them are numbered.

篇目來源
Text Source

第 29 篇　田律（睡虎地秦墓竹簡《秦律十八種》4—7 號簡）

29. *Statutes on Agriculture*（Shuìhǔdì Qín tomb 11 bamboo slips, *Eighteen Kinds of Qín Laws*, No.4-7）

第 30 篇　除吏律（睡虎地秦墓竹簡《秦律雜抄》1—4 號簡）

30. *Statutes on Staff Appointment*（Shuìhǔdì Qín tomb 11 bamboo slips, *Qín Statute Miscellany*, No.1-4）

第 31 篇　寄長令（《嶽麓書院藏秦簡（伍）》73—75 號簡）

31. *Orders on Adoption*（*Yuèlù Academy Corpus of Qín Slips V*, No.73-75）

第 32 篇　屏匿令（《嶽麓書院藏秦簡（伍）》218，219 號簡）

32. *Orders on Criminal Concealment*（*Yuèlù Academy Corpus of Qín Slips V*, No.218, 219）

參考文獻
References

陳松長主編:《嶽麓書院藏秦簡（伍）》，上海辭書出版社 2017 年。

陳偉主編:《秦簡牘合集釋文注釋修訂本（壹）》，武漢大學出版社 2016 年。

陳偉:《論嶽麓秦簡法律文獻的史料價值》,《武漢大學學報》2019 年第 2 期。

李學勤:《簡帛佚籍與學術史》，江西教育出版社 2007 年。

睡虎地秦墓竹簡整理小組:《睡虎地秦墓竹簡》，文物出版社 1990 年。

趙平安:《也談睡虎地秦簡“夜草爲灰”》,《中原文化研究》2018 年第 6 期。

照片、隸定本
Photo，Transcription

圖表 1　睡虎地秦墓竹簡《秦律十八種》4—7 號簡

Tableau 1: Shuìhǔdì Qín tomb 11 bamboo slips, *Eighteen Kinds of Qín Laws*, No.4-7

圖表 2　睡虎地秦墓竹簡《秦律雜抄》1—4 號簡

Tableau 2: Shuìhǔdì Qín tomb 11 bamboo slips, *Qín Statute Miscellany*, No.1-4

圖表 3　《嶽麓書院藏秦簡（伍）》73—75 號簡，218、219 號簡

Tableau 3: *Yuèlù Academy Corpus of Qín Slips V*, No.73-75, 218, 219

圖表 1　Tableau 1

睡虎地《秦律十八種》7			睡虎地《秦律十八種》6			睡虎地《秦律十八種》5			睡虎地《秦律十八種》4		
隸定	照片（下）	照片（上）	隸定	照片（下）	照片（上）	隸定	照片（下）	照片（上）	隸定	照片（下）	照片（上）
之河禁所殺犬皆完入公其它禁苑殺者食其肉而入皮　田律		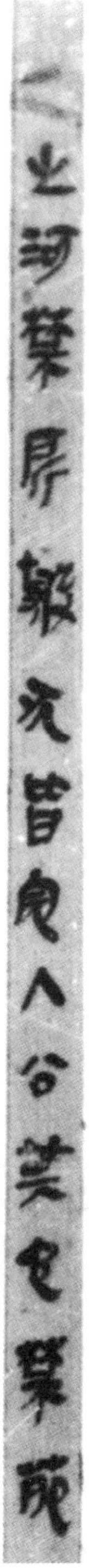	時毋敢將犬以之田百姓犬入禁苑中而不追獸及捕獸者勿敢殺其追獸及捕獸者殺			毒魚鱉置穽罔到七月而縱之唯不幸死而伐綰享者是不用時邑之紤皂及它禁苑者麛			春二月毋敢伐材木山林及雍隄水不夏月毋敢熱草爲灰取生荔麛鷇毋□□□□□□		

圖表 2　Tableau 2

睡虎地《秦律雜抄》4		睡虎地《秦律雜抄》3			睡虎地《秦律雜抄》2			睡虎地《秦律雜抄》1		
隸定	照片	隸定	照片（下）	照片（上）	隸定	照片（下）	照片（上）	隸定	照片（下）	照片（上）
除吏律		貲二甲免嗇夫任之駕騶除四歲不能駕御貲教者一盾免賞四歲繇戍	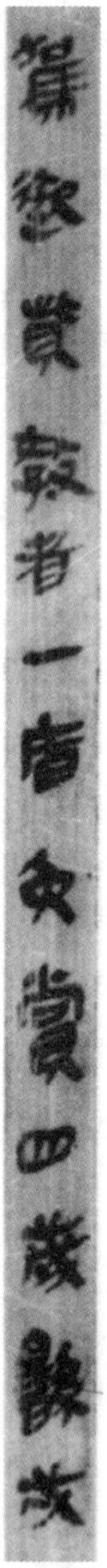		甲除士吏發弩嗇夫不如律及發弩射不中尉貲二甲發弩嗇夫射不中			任灋官者爲吏貲二甲有興除守嗇夫叚佐居守者上造以上不從令貲二		

圖表 3　Tableau 3

嶽麓伍 219		嶽麓伍 218		嶽麓伍 75		嶽麓伍 74		嶽麓伍 73	
隸定	照片	隸定	照片	隸定	照片	隸定	照片	隸定	照片
所屏匿辠論之有駕其辠一等　廷丁廿一		令曰諸有案行縣者縣官敢屏匿其所案行事及壅塞止辤者皆耐之所屏匿辠當䙴若耐以上以其		父母親所盈八歲輒輸之如令琅邪郡比　十三		別傳輸之恐行死議令寄長其父母及親所勿庸別輸丞相議年未盈八歲者令寄長其		泰山守言新黔首不更昌等夫妻盜耐爲鬼新白粲子當爲收柀有嬰兒未可事不能自食	

二十九、田律
29. Statutes on Agriculture

原文
Bamboo Script

春二月，毋敢伐材木山林及雍（壅）隄①水不②〈泉〉。夏月，毋敢㚈（爇）③草爲灰，取生④荔麛⑤𪏽（卵）㲉⑥，毋□□□□□□□毒魚鱉，置穽罔（網），到七月而縱⑦之。唯不幸死而伐綰（棺）享（椁）者，是不用時。邑之紤（近）皂⑧及它禁苑者，麛時⑨毋敢將犬以之田。百姓犬入禁苑中而不追獸及捕獸者，勿敢殺；其追獸及捕獸者，殺之。河（呵）禁⑩所殺犬，皆完入公；其它禁苑殺者，食其肉而入皮。田律

注釋
Annotation

① 雍隄：雍，通“壅”，堵塞。隄，築壩。
② 不：5 號簡相鄰位置是“不”，此處大概是看錯了列，將“泉”誤抄爲“不”。
③ 㚈：通“爇”，燒。
④ 生：活的。
⑤ 荔麛：荔，疑與幼獸義近。麛，幼獸。荔麛，泛指幼獸。
⑥ 𪏽㲉：𪏽，即“卵”。㲉，幼鳥。
⑦ 縱：開放限制。
⑧ 皂：特指王室的牧養馬牛的苑囿。
⑨ 麛時：幼獸繁殖時。
⑩ 河禁：河，通“呵”，呵斥。呵禁，指設置了警戒的苑囿。

1. 雍隄 *yōng dī*: *yōng* 雍, blocking; *dī* 隄, embankment, to build dykes and dams.
2. 不 *bù*: this character is a scribal error, it should be *quán* 泉, as the adjacent position of slip No.5 is *bù* 不, and the scribe obviously copied from the wrong column and mistakenly wrote *quán* as *bù*.
3. 㚈 *rè*: equivalent to the character *ruò* 爇, meaning to burn, to heat.
4. 生 *shēng*: alive, living.
5. 荔麛 *lì mí*: *lì* 荔, means young animals; *mí* 麛, young animals; the term *lìmí* refers to all young animals.
6. 𪏽㲉 *luǎn kòu*: *luǎn* 𪏽, equivalent to *luǎn* 卵, eggs; *kòu* 㲉, young birds.
7. 縱 *zòng*: to open up or relax restrictions.
8. 皂 *zào*: refers specifically to the royal pasture and ranch for keeping horses, cattle and other

animals.

9. 麛時 *mí shí*: breeding season, especially for young animals.
10. 河禁 *hé jìn*: *hé* 河 , used here as *hē* 呵 , meaning to scold, to forbid; *hējìn* 呵禁 refers to the guarded ranch and pasture.

寬式隸定
Loose Transcription

春二月，毋敢伐材木山林及雍隄水泉。夏月，毋敢爇草爲灰，取生荔麛卵鷇，毋□□□□□□□毒魚鱉，置穽網，到七月而縱之。唯不幸死而伐棺椁者，是不用時。邑之近皂及它禁苑者，麛時毋敢將犬以之田。百姓犬入禁苑中而不追獸及捕獸者，勿敢殺；其追獸及捕獸者，殺之。呵禁所殺犬，皆完入公；其它禁苑殺者，食其肉而入皮。田律

白話文
Vernacular Chinese

春季二月，不要在山林中砍伐木材和在水泉處堵塞築堤。夏季，不要燒草爲灰，取活的幼獸、鳥卵，不要……毒殺魚鱉，設置陷阱和獵網，到七月開禁。只有有人不幸死亡而需伐製棺椁的，可以不按時令來做事。城邑近于蓄養牛馬的苑囿及其他王室禁苑的，春季動物繁殖時不要帶獵犬田獵。百姓的狗進入王室禁苑中而不追逐野獸及獵捕野獸的，不要殺害，其中追逐野獸及獵捕野獸的，殺掉它們。設置警戒的禁苑所殺的狗，都完整納入公家，其他禁苑殺的狗，吃掉肉而納入狗皮給公家。田律

英文翻譯
English Translation

In the second month of spring, [one is] not allowed to cut timber in the forests or block watercourses. In the summer, [one is] not allowed to burn weeds to make ashes, to collect living young animals, eggs or fledglings. One should not... poison fish or tortoises or arrange pitfalls and nets. In the seventh month, [these prohibitions] are lifted. Only when someone has met an unfortunate death, people may cut timber for the inner and outer coffins, in spite of season's restrictions. People who live in the town near the royal pasture and ranch for keeping horses and cattle and the other kind of royal park, were forbidden to take hunting dogs to hunt when animals breed. When dogs of the commoners enter the royal Forbidden Garden without chasing and catching animals, [one] should not kill them; those that pursue and catch animals are to be killed. Dogs killed by the wardens in the guarded Forbidden Garden are to be handed over to the authorities intact; those that are killed in other forbidden ranches may be eaten, but the skin is to be handed over. Statutes on Agriculture

三十、除吏律
30. Statutes on Staff Appointment

原文
Bamboo Script

任①灋官②者爲吏③，貲④二甲⑤。有興⑥，除⑦守⑧嗇夫⑨、叚（假）⑩佐居守者，上造⑪以上不從令，貲二甲。除士吏⑫、發弩嗇夫⑬不如律，及發弩射不中⑭，尉⑮貲二甲。發弩嗇夫射不中，貲二甲，免⑯，嗇夫任⑰之。駕騶⑱除四歲，不能駕御，貲教者⑲一盾⑳；免，賞（償）㉑四歲繇（徭）戍㉒。除吏律㉓

注釋
Annotation

① 任：保舉。
② 灋官：灋，通“廢”，廢官指官吏免職並不再録用。
③ 吏：一般指中低層官吏。
④ 貲：罰款。
⑤ 二甲：罰款繳納的應該是錢，而非實物。秦律中一甲相當于秦幣 1344 錢，故“貲二甲”指罰款 2688 錢。
⑥ 興：派遣做某事。如戰事、公共建設。
⑦ 除：任命。
⑧ 守：代理。
⑨ 嗇夫：秦時政府機構的負責人往往被稱爲嗇夫，如倉有倉嗇夫，縣有縣嗇夫，鄉有鄉嗇夫，等級並不相同。
⑩ 叚：通“假”，臨時擔任某項事務的負責人。
⑪ 上造：爵位名，秦軍功爵裏的第二級。秦有二十等爵，由低到高爲：公士，上造，走馬（簪裊），不更，大夫，官大夫，公大夫，公乘，五大夫，左庶長，右庶長，左更，中更，右更，少上造，大良造，駟車庶長，大庶長，關内侯（倫侯），徹侯（列侯）。
⑫ 士吏：官職名稱，低級武官，在縣内是尉的屬吏。
⑬ 發弩嗇夫：官職名稱，縣尉的屬吏，主管發弩的訓練及指揮。
⑭ 射不中：射箭不能達到一定的標准。
⑮ 尉：縣尉。
⑯ 免：免職。
⑰ 任：承擔連帶責任。
⑱ 駕騶：騶，掌管養馬並管駕車的人。駕騶，泛指駕車者。

⑲ 教者：教駕騶學習駕車的人。

⑳ 一盾：秦律中一盾相當于 384 錢。

㉑ 賞：通“償”，償還。

㉒ 繇戍：繇，通“徭”。徭戍指戍守的義務，秦時成年公民在達到一定歲數前每年都有一定時間的戍守任務，如果駕騶駕車合格相當於服了徭戍，但如未合格，則要補償 4 年時間的徭戍。

㉓ 除吏律：律名，關於任命官吏的律文的合稱。

1. 任 *rèn*: to recommend.
2. 灋官 *fǎ guān*: *fǎ* 灋 , equivalent to *fèi* 廢 . lit. “abandoned official,” referring to people who were dismissed from the office.
3. 吏 *lì*: refers to middle and low-level officials, junior officials.
4. 貲 *zī*: to fine or to be fined.
5. 二甲 *èr jiǎ*: lit. “two pieces of armor.” One piece of armor is equivalent to 1344 Qín coins.
6. 興 *xīng*: to dispatch for certain public affairs, such as war or construction work.
7. 除 *chú*: to appoint.
8. 守 *shǒu*: acting on behalf of.
9. 嗇夫 *sè fū*: the person in charge of a certain agency in the Qín Dynasty. For example, the one in charge of a warehouse is called *cāng sèfū* 倉嗇夫 , i.e., Bailiff of the Granary; *xiāng sèfū* 鄉嗇夫 , Bailiff of the District; *xiàn sèfū* 縣嗇夫 , Bailiff of the County.
10. 叚 *jiǎ*: equivalent to 假 *jiǎ,* referring to someone temporarily serving in an official position, acting.
11. 上造 *shàng zào*: the rank title of Qín meritorious service, the second level out of 20 levels.
12. 士吏 *shì lì*: Sergeant Major, name of an official title, someone who is a subordinate of the County Commandant.
13. 發弩嗇夫 *fā nǔ sè fū*: official title, a subordinate of a County Commandant who is in charge of the training and command of the archers.
14. 射不中 *shè bù zhòng*: lit. “fail to shoot the goal,” meaning the archers fail the test to meet certain standards.
15. 尉 *wèi*: Commandant, in charge of military affairs in the county.
16. 免 *miǎn*: to exempt. Here it means to dismiss from official duty.
17. 任 *rèn*: the word may mean to take joint liability and responsibility.
18. 駕騶 *jià zōu*: *jià* 駕 , to drive; *zōu* 騶 , the person in charge of raising horses and driving carts; the term *jiàzōu* refers to horse cart drivers.
19. 教者 *jiào zhě*: means the trainer who teaches how to drive horse carts.
20. 一盾 *yī dùn*: lit. “one piece of shield.” According to Qín law, one piece of shield was equivalent to 384 Qín coins.

21. 賞 *shǎng*: equivalent to *cháng* 償 , meaning to compensate, to repay.
22. 繇戍 *yáo shù*: the word *yáo* 繇 is equivalent to *yáo* 徭 ; *yáoshù* refers to the military duty that Qín adults had to fulfill once a year for a certain amount of time.
23. 除吏律 *chú lì lǜ*: the collective name of the laws regulating the appointment of officials.

寬式隸定
Loose Transcription

任廢官者爲吏，貲二甲。有興，除守嗇夫、假佐居守者，上造以上不從令，貲二甲。除士吏、發弩嗇夫不如律，及發弩射不中，尉貲二甲。發弩嗇夫射不中，貲二甲，免，嗇夫任之。駕騶除四歲，不能駕御，貲教者一盾；免，償四歲徭戍。除吏律

白話文
Vernacular Chinese

保舉免除官職不能再任用者爲官吏，罰二甲。有派遣，任命有上造以上爵位者爲代理嗇夫以及代理佐在官署主持工作，不按律令接受任命的，罰二甲。不按照律法任命士吏、發弩嗇夫，以及發弩射箭不能達到標准，罰尉二甲。發弩嗇夫射箭不能達到標准，罰二甲，免職，嗇夫承擔連帶責任。任命駕車者四年後，不能駕馭，處罰教駕車的人一盾；免除駕車者的職務，駕車者還要補償四年的徭役戍守責任。除吏律

英文翻譯
English Translation

If [Chief Official of the County] recommends anyone who has been dismissed from the public office as junior officials, he will be fined with two pieces of armor. In the event of dispatchment due to outside public duties [e.g., war, public construction or other undertakings] , the office vacancies will be filled by those at the level above the *Shàngzào* rank, in the capacity as acting Bailiff or acting Assistant. If not following this rule, [the one who is appointed] will be fined with two pieces of armor. [A County Commandant] who does not follow the rule to appoint Sergeant Major and Bailiff of the Crossbowmen, or if the archer fails the test, [the County Commandant] will be fined with two pieces of armor. Bailiff of the Crossbowmen who fails the test will be punished with two pieces of armor and fired. [The County Chief] should take a joint liability and responsibility. Four years after been appointed as the horse cart driver for superiors, and the driver is still not competent, the horse cart trainer will be fined with a piece of shield, the driver will be fired and charged and punished with four years of corvee labor and military servitude. Statutes on Staff Appointment

三十一、寄長令
31. Orders on Adoption

原文
Bamboo Script

泰山守①言：新黔首②不更昌等夫妻盜，耐爲鬼新（薪）白粲③，子當爲收④，柀（頗）⑤有嬰兒未可事⑥，不能自食，别傳輸之，恐行死。議⑦：令寄長⑧其父母及親所，勿庸别輸。丞相議：年未盈八歲者令寄長其父母、親所，盈八歲輒輸之如令。琅邪（琊）郡⑨比⑩。十三⑪

注釋
Annotation

① 泰山守：泰山郡太守。
② 新黔首：泰山郡本爲齊國故地，雖已納入秦國的版圖，但爲區别於秦故地，稱其百姓爲新黔首。
③ 耐爲鬼新白粲：新，通"薪"。耐爲鬼薪白粲爲複合刑，耐針對身體而言，鬼薪白粲則針對從事勞役的類别而言。耐爲鬼薪是對於男性的刑罰，耐爲白粲是對於女性的刑罰。
④ 收：没入官府。
⑤ 柀：通"頗"，部分。
⑥ 嬰兒未可事：嬰兒指初生嬰兒或幼童，未可事指不能從事勞動。
⑦ 議：經過討論形成審判意見。
⑧ 寄長：寄，託付。長，撫育。
⑨ 琅邪郡：即瑯琊郡。
⑩ 比：等同。
⑪ 十三：本則令文的序號。

1. 泰山守 *tài shān shǒu*: Governor or Chief of Tàishān Commandery.
2. 新黔首 *xīn qián shǒu*: lit. "new black head," refers to new common people. Because most common people wore a black scarf or had a darker complexion, common people were called "black heads" or "black-headed ones" in Qín. Tàishān Commandery belonged to the state of Qí. Although it had already been incorporated into the territory of Qín, the land was called new, in order to distinguish it from the original homeland of the Qín state. The people of the newly acquired land were called "new black-headed people", meaning new citizens.

3. 耐爲鬼新白粲 *nài wéi guǐ xīn bái càn*: *xīn* 新，equivalent to *xīn* 薪；*nài* 耐 refers to a type of punishment applied to the body of convicts, having their beard removed; *guǐxīn* 鬼薪 *and báicàn* 白粲 refer to types of punishment. *Guǐxīn* are male convicts who were often given the task of gathering firewood for the spirits; *báicàn are* female convicts were often given the task of sifting white rice.
4. 收 *shōu*: meaning taken over by government.
5. 柀 *bǐ*: equivalent to *pō* 頗 , meaning part.
6. 嬰兒未可事 *yīng'ér wèi kě shì*: *yīng'ér* 嬰兒 , new-born of baby or babies; *wèi kě shì* 未可事 , cannot do labor work.
7. 議 *yì*: to deliver a legal opinion, to propose a judgement.
8. 寄長 *jì zhǎng*: *jì* 寄 , to entrust, to adopt; *zhǎng* 長 , to raise, to nurture.
9. 琅邪郡 *láng xié jùn*: name of a commandery, also called Lángyá 瑯琊 Commandery.
10. 比 *bǐ*: equivalent.
11. 十三 *shí sān*: thirteen, the serial number of this order.

寬式隸定
Loose Transcription

泰山守言：新黔首不更昌等夫妻盜，耐爲鬼薪白粲，子當爲收，頗有嬰兒未可事，不能自食，別傳輸之，恐行死。議：令寄長其父母及親所，勿庸別輸。丞相議：年未盈八歲者令寄長其父母、親所，盈八歲輒輸之如令。琅琊郡比。十三

白話文
Vernacular Chinese

泰山郡太守報告：新黔首名爲昌的不更等夫妻共爲盜賊，耐以爲鬼薪白粲，孩子應該被收入官府，其中有嬰兒不能從事，不能夠自己養活自己，另外移送他們，恐怕在路中死亡。討論後形成意見：使他寄養在父母及親屬之處，不用移送到他處。丞相討論後形成意見：年紀未滿八歲的使他寄養在父母或親屬之處，滿八歲就按照法令移送他。瑯琊郡等同。序號十三

英文翻譯
English Translation

Governor of Tàishān Commandery reported: New citizens with merit rank of *Bùgēng* (“Service-Rotation Exempt”) like Chāng and his wife committed theft and robbery. They were condemned with “*nài wéi guǐxīn báicàn*”, punishing by removing beard and hardwork of collecting fire wood, and sifting rice. [By law] their children should be taken into government custody [as laborers or slaves] , but some are too young to do labor work and cannot earn their own livelihood. They should not be sent away, otherwise they may perish on the road. Judgement: Order them to be adopted by their parents and relatives, do not send them away. Judgement by the Chief Minister: Children [of criminals] under the age of eight years old, shall be adopted by their parents and relatives. [Children] over eight will be transferred according to the law. [This order] is equally applicable to Lángyá Commandery. Thirteenth

三十二、屏匿令
32. Orders on Criminal Concealment

原文
Bamboo Script

令曰：諸有案行①縣₌官₌（縣官，縣官）敢屏匿②其所案行事及壅塞③止辤（辭）④者，皆耐之。所屏匿辠當⑤遷（遷）⑥若耐以上，以其所屏匿辠論之，有（又）駕（加）其辠一等。廷丁廿一⑦

注釋
Annotation

① 案行：巡視。
② 屏匿：屏，隱藏，隱蔽。匿，隱藏。同義連用，泛指隱藏。
③ 壅塞：特指阻塞巡視者與被調查對象或舉報者的交流渠道。
④ 止辤：制止言辭。
⑤ 當：對應。
⑥ 遷：通“遷”，刑罰名。
⑦ 廷丁廿一：廷，指令的整理機構，“丁”與“廿一”分別用天干及數字對應序號。

1. 案行 *àn xíng*: to patrol.
2. 屏匿 *píng nì*: *píng* 屏 , to hide, to screen; *nì* 匿 , to hide, to conceal; *píngnì,* used synonymously, to hide, to conceal.
3. 壅塞 *yōng sè*: lit. “blocking.” Here, the term specifically refers to the blocking of the channels between the inspectors and investigation targets by concealing facts or blocking the whistleblowers.
4. 止辤 *zhǐ cí*: to stop or to suppress words.
5. 當 *dāng*: corresponding, to correspond.
6. 遷 *qiān*: equivalent to *qiān* 遷 , a form of punishment: banishment.
7. 廷丁廿一 *tíng dīng niàn yī*: *tíng* 廷 , the organization or office that organizes or archives the orders. *Dīng* 丁 , the fourth heavenly stem (*tiāngān* 天干) is used together with number 21 (*niànyī* 廿一) here as a serial number for this order.

寬式隸定
Loose Transcription

令曰：諸有案行縣官，縣官敢屏匿其所案行事及壅塞止辭者，皆耐之。所屏匿罪當遷

若耐以上，以其所屏匿罪論之，又加其罪一等。廷丁廿一

白話文
Vernacular Chinese

令說：有巡視縣政府的，縣政府敢隱藏所巡視事務及阻塞交流渠道制止言辭的，都處以耐刑。所隱藏的罪行爲遷罪或耐罪以上，按照他所隱藏的罪行定罪，並加罪一等。廷丁類廿一號

英文翻譯
English Translation

The order said: During routine inspections of the County Administration, if the County Office dares to hide facts from the inspection team or attempts to block or suppress the information or communication channels, [County Officials] will be subject to the penalty named *nài* (beard removal). If the crime committed hidden corresponds to banishment or even more serious than *nài,* [they] will be convicted accordingly with an additional level of severity. Arranged by *tíng,* Group *Dīng,* twenty-first

練習
Practice

釋讀圖表 4 中的幾枚簡。
Read slips in Tableau 4.

圖表 4　Tableau 4

嶽麓伍 32	嶽麓伍 31		嶽麓伍 30		《秦律雜抄》6		《秦律雜抄》5	
上	下	上	下	上	下	上	下	上

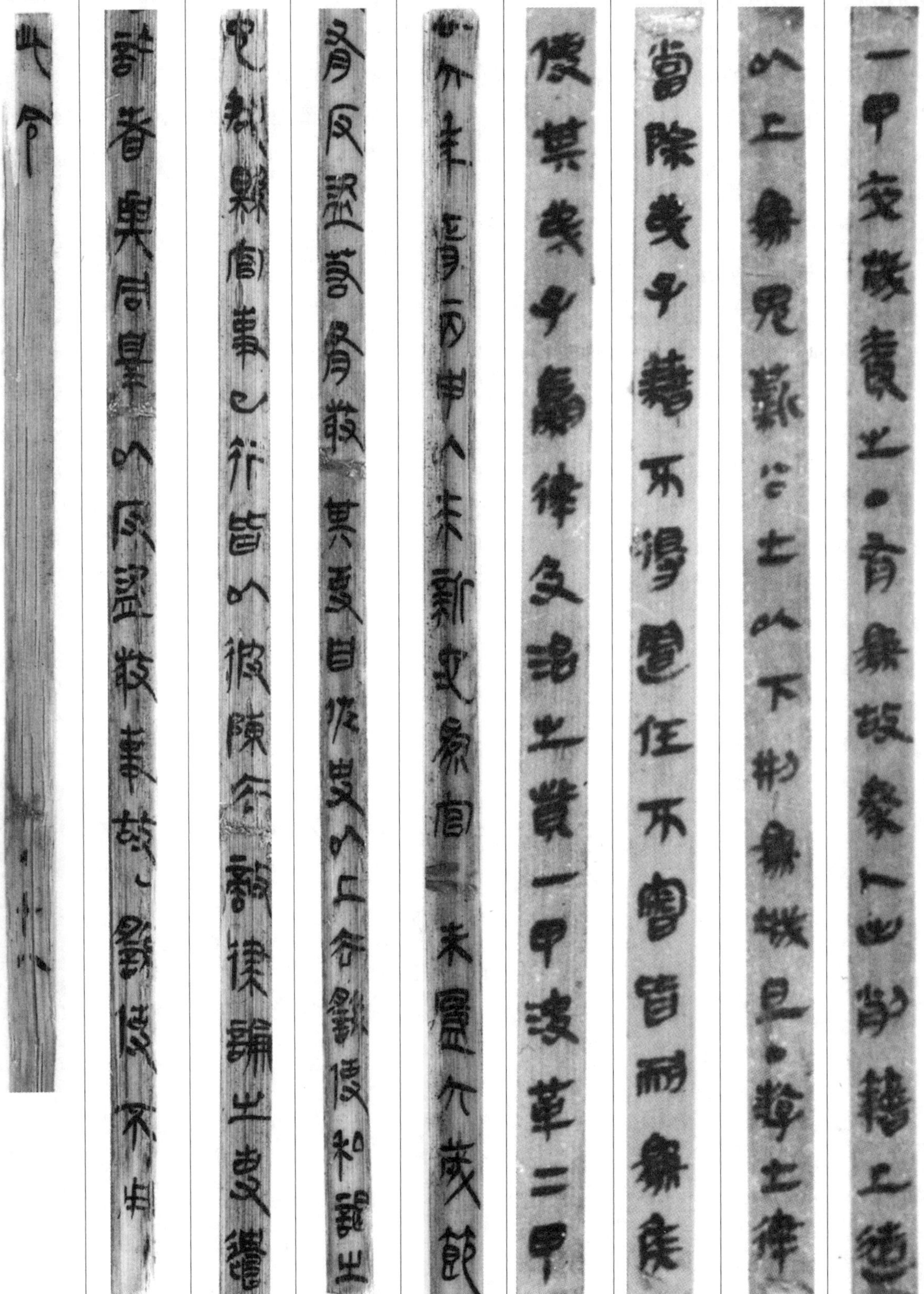

第十三組　式
Group 13　Model Formats

簡介
Introduction

秦簡所稱“式”作爲一種文書，取其範例、格式義，既有處理事務的記録模式，又有文書書寫記録格式。其核心功能是讓處理事務的官吏有所參考模仿，以保證文書的規範化以及有效地處理事務。最早見到的“式”是睡虎地秦墓竹簡中的《封診式》，應用於司法領域。在里耶秦簡中，可以看到其他類型的“式”。如里耶秦簡 8-94 號簡提及“群志式”，“志”是一種文書，“群志式”是集結多種“志”的格式之範本。再如里耶秦簡 9-1857 號簡記載有“受乘馬式”“受僕式”等有關接受人或物的“式”。

Shì 式 in the Qín Dynasty refers to particular models and formats of official documents. They were used as standard forms to document all bureaucratic matters so as to ensure more efficient processing of official functions. The earliest model forms discovered so far are *Models for Sealing and Physical Examinations* (*Fēngzhěn shì* 封診式), unearthed from Qín tomb 11 at Shuìhǔdì. Here, *fēng* 封 means to seal, seize, or closedown, and *zhěn* 診 means to detect, to investigate; both are standard forensic techniques. The model forms for sealing and physical examinations dealt with legal matters, particularly forensics. In Lǐyē Qín slips, there are other types of model formats. For example, slip No.8-94 mentions *qúnzhì shì* 群志式， that is a collection of the model formats about a special kind of document named *zhì* 志 . Slip No.9-1857 records various types of model formats dealing with receiving horses or personnel, called model formats of receiving riding horses (*shòuchéngmǎ shì* 受乘馬式) and model formats of receiving servants (*shòupú shì* 受僕式).

篇目來源
Text Source

第 33 篇　賊死（睡虎地秦墓竹簡《封診式》55—62 號簡）

33. *A Murder Case* (Shuìhǔdì Qín tomb 11 bamboo slips, *Models for Sealing and Physical Examinations,* No.55-62)

參考文獻
References

陳公柔:《先秦兩漢考古學論叢》，文物出版社 2005 年。
陳偉:《秦簡牘合集釋文注釋修訂本（壹）》，武漢大學出版社 2016 年。

黄鳳春:《楚器名物研究》,湖北教育出版社 2012 年。
劉釗:《讀秦簡字詞札記》,《簡帛研究》第 2 輯,法律出版社 1996 年。
陸倫章:《我國刑事檢驗制度歷史悠久——從出土秦簡〈賊死〉篇談起》,《法學雜誌》1982 年第 10 期。
單育辰:《秦簡“柀”字釋義》,《江漢考古》2007 年第 4 期。
睡虎地秦墓竹簡整理小組:《睡虎地秦墓竹簡》,文物出版社 1990 年。

照片、隸定本
Photo, Transcription

圖表 1　睡虎地秦墓竹簡《封診式》55—59 號簡

Tableau 1: Shuìhǔdì Qín tomb 11 bamboo slips, *Models for Sealing and Physical Examinations,* No.55-59

圖表 2　睡虎地秦墓竹簡《封診式》60—62,21,22 號簡

Tableau 2: Shuìhǔdì Qín tomb 11 bamboo slips, *Models for Sealing and Physical Examinations,* No.60-62, 21, 22

圖表 1　Tableau 1

封診式 59			封診式 58			封診式 57			封診式 56			封診式 55		
隸定	照片(下)	照片(上)	隸定	照片(下)	照片(上)	隸定	照片(下)	照片(上)	隸定	照片(下)	照片(上)	隸定	照片(下)	照片(上)
□污血男子西有鬃秦綦履一兩去男子其一奇六步一十步以履=男子利焉地堅不可智		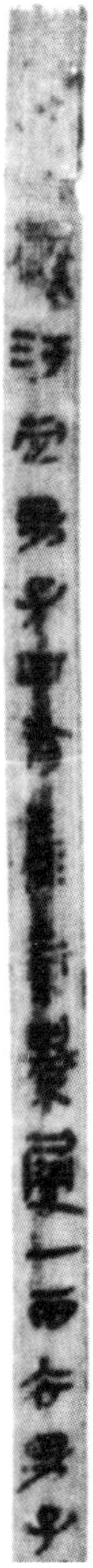	不可爲廣袤它完衣布禪帬襦各一其襦北直痏者以刃夬二所應痏襦北及中衽			北二所皆從頭北袤各四寸相耎廣各一寸皆臽中類斧腦角出皆血出柀污頭北及地皆			診令史某爰書與牢隸臣某即甲診男子死在某室南首正偃某頭左角刃痏一所			賊死　爰書某亭求盜甲告曰署中某所有賊死結髮不智可男子一人來告即令=史某往		

圖表 2 Tableau 2

封診式 22		封診式 21		封診式 62		封診式 61			封診式 60		
照片（下）	照片（上）	照片（下）	照片（上）	隸定	照片（上）	隸定	照片（下）	照片（上）	隸定	照片（下）	照片（上）
	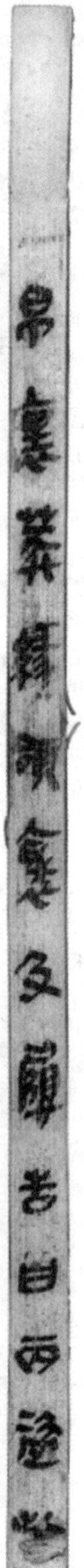	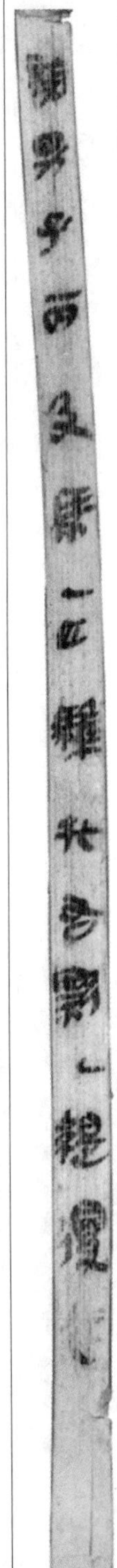		亭人及丙智男子可日死聞誂寇者不毆		步到某里士五丙田舍二百步令甲以布帬剡貍男子某所侍令以襦履詣廷訊甲			賊迹男子丁壯析色長七尺一寸髮長二尺其腹有久故瘢二所男子死所到某亭百	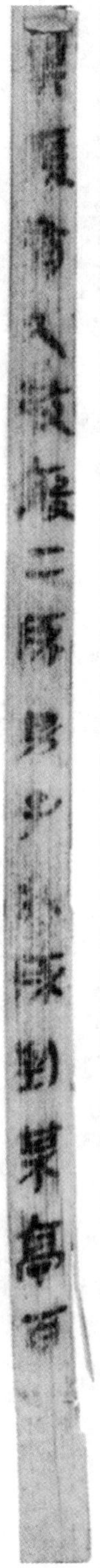	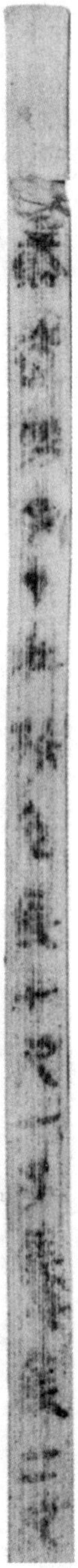

三十三、賊死
33. A Murder Case

原文
Bamboo Script

賊死　爰書①：某亭②求盜③甲告曰："署④中某所有賊死⑤、結髮⑥、不智（知）可（何）男子一人，來告。"即令₌（令令）史某往診。令史某爰書：與牢隸臣⑦某即甲診。男子死（屍）在某室，南首⑧，正偃。某頭左角⑨刃痏⑩一所，北（背）二所，皆從（縱）頭北（背），袤各四寸，相耎（濡），廣各一寸，皆臽（陷）中，類斧。腦、角、出（頔）⑪皆血出，柀（頗）污頭、北（背）及地，皆不可爲廣袤。它完。衣布禪帬、襦各一。其襦北（背）直痏者，以刃夬（決）二所，應痏。襦北（背）及中衽□污血。男子西有鬃秦綦⑫履一兩，去男子其一奇⑬六步，一十步。以履₌（履履）男子，利焉。地堅，不可智（知）賊迹。男子丁壯，析（皙）色，長七尺一寸，髮長二尺。其腹有久故瘢二所。男子死所⑭到某亭百步，到某里士五（伍）丙田舍二百步。令甲以布帬劉貍（埋）男子某所，侍（待）令⑮。以襦、履詣廷。訊甲⑯亭人及丙智（知）男子可（何）日死、聞誂（號）寇者不殴。

注釋
Annotation

① 爰書：一種文書名稱，指書面陳述，可以記録多種内容。在本文書中，後一爰書由令史某整理而成，是該令史對此案件檢驗、調查的記録，前一爰書則由縣廷進一步整理而成，包含後一爰書，增加了案件由誰報告、報告内容及縣廷應對該報告的措施的情況。

② 亭：治安機構。秦時將一縣分爲若干亭，分别管理轄區治安。

③ 求盜：身份名稱。亭所轄從事緝捕盜賊等工作的工作人員。

④ 署：管轄地域。

⑤ 賊死：殺死。

⑥ 結髮：梳髮髻，這裏可看作成年的標誌。

⑦ 牢隸臣：身份名稱。在監牢從事一定事務性工作的男性罪犯。

⑧ 南首：朝向南方。或認爲這裏指房子的南方。

⑨ 角：額角。

⑩ 痏：創傷。

⑪ 出：通"頔"，眼眶下部，顴骨。

⑫ 綦：青黑色。

⑬ 奇：大約。
⑭ 死所：死亡的地方。或將“死”讀爲“尸”。
⑮ 侍令：侍，通“待”，待令，等待命令。或認爲“侍”應讀爲本字，“侍令”是覆命文書中的結語之辭。
⑯ 或在“甲”字後斷讀頓號。

1. 爰書 *yuán shū*: term for a particular kind of document, referring to a transcript of an oral report. Here, the first one was made by County Government and the second was made by Prefectural Clerk X. The complete document, including these two transcripts, was then compiled by the County Government with additional information on who reported what and what had been done with this case.
2. 亭 *tíng*: a law enforcement agency, similar to police station. Each county was subdivided into several *tíng* 亭 in the Qín Dynasty.
3. 求盜 *qiú dào*: lit. “seeking robbers,” a title of a person in charge of apprehending criminals, or officers working in the *tíng,* responsible for inspecting and policing criminal matters.
4. 署 *shǔ*: territory under jurisdiction.
5. 賊死 *zéi sǐ*: to kill.
6. 結髮 *jié fà*: to bind one’s hair, signifying adulthood in ancient times.
7. 牢隸臣 *láo lì chén*: prison bondsman, a male prisoner who served certain circumscribed functions in prison.
8. 南首 *nán shǒu*: lit. “south head,” meaning facing south. It may also refer to the south of the house here.
9. 角 *jiǎo*: frontal eminence.
10. 痏 *wěi*: wound.
11. 出 *chū*: equivalent to *zhuō* 頔 , infraorbital region, zygomatic bone.
12. 綦 *qí*: livid.
13. 奇 *jī*: about.
14. 死所 *sǐ suǒ*: the place of death.
15. 侍令 *shì lìng*: *shì* 侍 , equivalent to *dài* 待 ; *dàilìng* 待令 , meaning waiting for a command.
16. Some scholars suggest that a full stop be put after the word “*jiǎ*” .

寬式隸定

Loose Transcription

爰書：某亭求盜甲告曰：“署中某所有賊死、結髮、不知何男子一人，來告。”即令令史某往診。令史某爰書：與牢隸臣某即甲診。男子屍在某室，南首，正偃。某頭左角刃痏一所，背二所，皆縱頭背，袤各四寸，相濡，廣各一寸，皆陷中，類斧。腦、角、頔皆血出，頗污頭、背及地，皆不可爲廣袤。它完。衣布禪帬、襦各一。其襦背直痏者，以刃決二所，應痏。襦背及中衽□污血。男子西有鬃秦綦履一兩，去男子其一奇六步，一十步。以履履男子，利焉。地堅，不可知賊迹。男子丁壯，皙色，長七尺一寸，髮長二尺。其腹有久故瘢二所。男子死所到某亭百步，到某里士伍丙田舍二百步。令甲以布帬剶埋男子某所，待令。以襦、履詣廷。訊甲亭人及丙，知男子何日死，聞號寇者不殹。

白話文
Vernacular Chinese

爰書：某亭求盜甲報告："我的管區内某處有被殺死、梳有髮髻的無名男子一人，我趕來報告。" 當即命令令史某前去檢驗。令史某的爰書："我與牢隸臣某跟隨求盜甲前去檢驗。看到男子的尸體在某屋舍，頭向南，直身仰面。他頭部左額角有鋒刃所造成的創傷一處，後背兩處創傷，都是縱向由頭向背，各長四寸，互相沾染，各寬一寸，都向中間凹陷，像斧頭造成。顱骨、額角、眼眶下部都出血，很大程度上沾染了頭、後背及地面，都不能測量長寬。其他部位完好。穿布質單層的裙、短衣各一件。短衣背面對着創傷的地方，因鋒刃而裂開兩處，與創傷對應。短衣背部及中部衣襟處有血污。男子西側有塗漆的秦形製的帶紋鞋一雙，一鞋距離男子六步稍遠，另一鞋距離男子十步遠。用鞋去給男子試穿，合適。地面堅硬，不能看到盜賊的足迹。死者成年健壯，皮膚白，高七尺一寸，頭髮長二尺。腹部有舊疤兩處。男子死的地方距離某亭一百步，距離某里士伍丙的田舍二百步。命令甲用布裙掩埋男子於某處，等待命令。把短衣、鞋拿到縣廷。訊問甲所在亭内的人員及丙，是否知道男子在哪一天死的，聽到有人號叫賊寇（呼救）與否。"

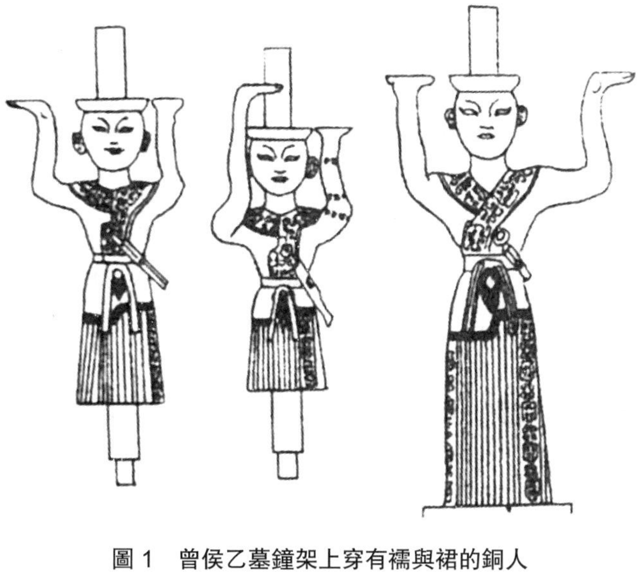

圖 1　曾侯乙墓鐘架上穿有襦與裙的銅人

Figure 1　Bronze figures wearing jackets and skirts on the bell frame unearthed from the tomb of Zēnghóu Yǐ (d. 433 BCE)

（引自黄鳳春:《楚器名物研究》34 頁）

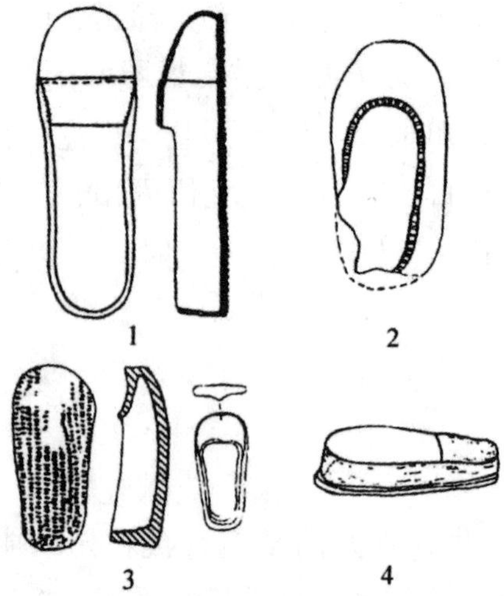

圖 2　戰國秦漢時期的鞋

Figure 2　Shoes of the Warring States Period, Qín and Hàn Dynasties

（引自黃鳳春：《楚器名物研究》40 頁）

英文翻譯
English Translation

Transcript of oral report: Thief Catcher Jiǎ in Guard Station X reported: "In a place under my jurisdiction, there was a murder case of an anonymous male with bound hair. Therefore, I have come here to report." I immediately ordered Prefectural Clerk X to go there and make an examination. The transcript of Prefectural Clerk X's oral report [reads as follows]:

"Prison Bondsman X and I, along with Thief Catcher Jiǎ went to make an examination. The male corpse was situated in a house, the head facing south, lying stretched out straight, face up. There was a blade laceration on the left corner of his head and two lacerations on the back of his body, all vertical, each four inches long, with the blood mixed together, and each one inch wide, all the lacerations were of the axe type. Blood had bled from the cranium, the temples and beneath the eye sockets, stained extensively the head, back and ground, none could be measured as to the width and length. The rest of the body was intact. He wore unlined cloth of a skirt and a jacket made of hemp. There were two places in the back of the jacket that were cut open by a blade corresponding with lacerations [on the body] . The back of the jacket and the middle of the collar were blood stained. There were a pair of lacquered Qín style shoes to the west of the corpse, one was a little more than six paces away from the man, the other one was ten paces away. We put the shoes on the man and they fit him. Because the ground was hard, we could not discern footprints of the assailant. The man was able-bodied, pale of complexion, seven feet one inch tall (about 165 cm), his hair was two feet long. There are two old scars on the belly of the corpse. From the place where the corpse lay to the Guard Station X there was a distance of one hundred paces, and two hundred paces to the house of *Shìwǔ* Bǐng of Village X. I ordered Jiǎ to cover the corpse with the fabric of a skirt and to await orders. We brought the jacket and shoes to the County Court. We also questioned the people in Jiǎ's Guard Station and Bǐng about the date the man died and whether they had heard anyone shouting "[Watch out for the] robber!"

練習
Practice

釋讀圖表 2 中睡虎地秦墓竹簡《封診式》21、22 號簡。
Read slips No.21, 22 in Tableau 2.

第十四組　法律答問
Group 14　Questions and Answers on Laws

簡介
Introduction

《法律答問》，是一種非常特殊的法律文獻。它多採用問答的形式，偶爾也有採用非問答式的情況。內容上主要是對律令中的特定用語進行解釋，或者對律令中的一些規則進行細化，或者對律令未規定的情況進行補充。對於它的性質，存在不同的認識。如有學者認爲是官吏學習法律知識的筆記，也有學者認爲是提供給獄吏的實務參考教科書。目前，《法律答問》在秦簡中僅見於睡虎地秦墓竹簡，共 210 枚簡，簡長 25.5 釐米、寬 0.6 釐米、厚 0.1 釐米。合計共 187 條，所涉及法律規定的年代不一。

Answers to Questions Concerning Qín Statutes (*Fǎlǜ dáwèn* 法律答問) is a very special type of legal document. It is mostly in the form of questions and answers, and occasionally in other forms. It is mainly concerned with explaining specific terms in the statutes or decrees, refining rules in decrees, or supplementing situations not stipulated in decrees. Different scholars may have different understanding of its nature. Some scholars believe that it is a notebook for officials to learn legal knowledge, others believe that it is a practical reference textbook for judiciary or prison officials. To date, *Answers to Questions Concerning Qín Statutes* have only been found among Shuìhǔdì Qín tomb 11 bamboo slips, a total of 210 slips with explanation of 187 terms of laws and regulations from different time periods. The slips are 25.5 cm long, 0.6 cm wide and 0.1 cm thick.

篇目來源
Text Source

第 34 篇　擅殺弟子後（睡虎地秦墓竹簡《法律答問》71）

34. *Unauthorized Murder of Brother's Son* (Shuìhǔdì Qín tomb 11 bamboo slips, *Answers to Questions Concerning Qín Statutes,* No.71)

第 35 篇　毆高大父母何論（睡虎地秦墓竹簡《法律答問》78）

35. *Penalty for Beating Great Grandparents* (Shuìhǔdì Qín tomb 11 bamboo slips, *Answers to Questions Concerning Qín Statutes,* No.78)

第 36 篇　鬬而盡拔人須眉（睡虎地秦墓竹簡《法律答問》81）

36. *Plucking Total Beards and Eyebrows at Brawl* (Shuìhǔdì Qín tomb 11 bamboo slips, *Answers to Questions Concerning Qín Statutes,* No.81)

第 37 篇　何謂梃（睡虎地秦墓竹簡《法律答問》91）

37. *What is Tǐng?*(Shuìhǔdì Qín tomb 11 bamboo slips, *Answers to Questions Concerning Qín Statutes,* No.91)

参考文獻
References

陳偉主編:《秦簡牘合集釋文注釋修訂本（壹）》，武漢大學出版社 2016 年。
程令政:《秦及漢初刑罰制度研究》，吉林大學博士學位論文，2020 年。
睡虎地秦墓竹簡整理小組:《睡虎地秦墓竹簡》，文物出版社 1990 年。
中國政法大學中國法制史基礎史料研讀會:《睡虎地秦簡法律文書集釋（八）：法律答問 61—110 簡》，《中國古代法律文獻研究》第 13 輯，社會科學文獻出版社 2019 年。

照片、隸定本
Photo, Transcription

圖表 1　睡虎地秦墓竹簡《法律答問》71, 78, 81, 91
Tableau 1: Shuìhǔdì Qín tomb 11 bamboo slips, *Answers to Questions Concerning Qín Statutes,* No.71, 78, 81, 91

圖表 1　Tableau 1

睡虎地《法律答問》91		睡虎地《法律答問》81		睡虎地《法律答問》78		睡虎地《法律答問》71	
隸定	照片	隸定	照片	隸定	照片	隸定	照片
以梃賊傷人可謂梃木可以伐者爲梃		或與人鬬縛而盡拔其須麇論可毆當完城旦		毆大父母黥爲城旦舂今毆高大父母可論比大父母		士五甲毋子其弟子以爲後與同居而擅殺之當棄市	

三十四、擅殺弟子後
34. Unauthorized Murder of Brother's Son

原文
Bamboo Script

士五（伍）甲毋（無）子，其弟子①以爲後②，與同居而擅③殺之，當棄市④。

注釋
Annotation

① 弟子：弟弟的兒子。
② 後：繼承人。
③ 擅：擅自。
④ 棄市：死刑的一種，斬首後置於市示衆。

1. 弟子 *dì zǐ*: brother's son.
2. 後 *hòu*: heir at law.
3. 擅 *shàn*: unauthorized; doing something at will.
4. 棄市 *qì shì*: lit. "beheading and casting someone away in the market place," a form of public capital punishment.

寬式隸定
Loose Transcription

士伍甲無子，其弟子以爲後，與同居而擅殺之，當棄市。

白話文
Vernacular Chinese

士伍甲没有兒子，以他的弟弟的兒子作爲繼承人，與他一起居住而擅自將他殺害，應判決棄市之刑。

英文翻譯
English Translation

As a commoner (*Shìwŭ*: an ordinary person without titles of nobility) Jiă had no son, [he adopted] his brother's son as his heir. They lived together, but [he] killed this son without authorization. [He] should be punished with *qìshì* [that is, beheading and casting someone away in the market place] .

三十五、毆高大父母何論
35. Penalty for Beating Great Grandparents

原文
Bamboo Script

毆大父母①，黥爲城旦舂②。今毆高大父母③，可（何）論？比④大父母。

注釋
Annotation

① 大父母：祖父母。
② 黥爲城旦舂：黥是肉刑的一種，在臉上刻字。城旦舂是勞役刑中最重的一種。
③ 高大父母：曾祖父母。
④ 比：比照。

1. 大父母 *dà fù mǔ*: grandparents.
2. 黥爲城旦舂 *qíng wéi chéng dàn chōng*: *qíng* 黥，to tatoo [a criminal offender] on the forehead or cheekbone, a type of corporal punishment; *chéngdàn* 城旦 (male builders of walls) and *chōng* 舂 (female pounders of rice) are the most severe forms of hard labor as wall building convicts and grain pounding convicts, respectively.
3. 高大父母 *gāo dà fù mǔ*: great grandparents.
4. 比 *bǐ*: confer, to treat analogous to existing cases or precedents.

寬式隸定
Loose Transcription

毆大父母，黥爲城旦舂。今毆高大父母，何論？比大父母。

白話文
Vernacular Chinese

毆打祖父母，處以黥刑的肉刑及城旦舂的勞役刑。現毆打曾祖父母，如何判決？比照祖父母。

英文翻譯
English Translation

For beating grandparents, [one] was sentenced to the corporal punishment of being tattooed on the forehead and being punished to be male builders of walls or female pounders of rice. How should beating of one's great grandparents be judged? Treat this analogous to the case for grandparents.

三十六、鬬而盡拔人須眉
36. Plucking Total Beards and Eyebrows at Brawl

原文
Bamboo Script

或與人鬬，縛而盡拔其須麋（眉）①，論可（何）殹？當完城旦②。

注釋
Annotation

① 麋：通“眉”。
② 當完城旦：完，刑罰的一種，與肉刑相對，或認爲保持身體、頭髮、鬍鬚的完整，或認爲僅保持身體的完整。城旦，勞役刑的一種。對比漢律，拔光鬍鬚、眉毛相比骨折等傷人情況判罰更重，可能與古人對於鬚眉更爲看重有關，體現了古人的身體觀。

1. 麋 *mí*: equivalent to eyebrows.
2. 當完城旦 *dāng wán chéng dàn*: *wán* 完, “without mutilation”, a form of punishment which in contrast to corporal punishments such as tattooing leaves the body intact; *chéngdàn* 城旦, “male builders of walls”, a form of hard labor. Compared with Hàn law, plucking beards and eyebrows is punished more severely than fractures and other injuries. It may be related to the fact that the ancients paid more attention to beard and eyebrows, reflecting the ancients’ view of the body.

寬式隸定
Loose Transcription

或與人鬬，縛而盡拔其須眉，論何殹？當完城旦。

白話文
Vernacular Chinese

有人與人鬬毆，捆綁該人並完全拔掉該人的鬍鬚與眉毛，判決什麼罪？判處完城旦的刑罰。

英文翻譯
English Translation

If someone fights another person, then binds that person and completely plucks that person's beard and eyebrows, what sentence should he be given? He should be sentenced to be "male builders of walls" but be spared mutilation.

三十七、何謂梃
37. What is Tǐng?

原文
Bamboo Script

以梃①賊②傷人。可（何）謂“梃”？木可以伐③者爲“梃”。

注釋
Annotation

① 梃：可以用來敲打人的木棍。
② 賊：故意。
③ 伐：敲，打。

1. 梃 *tǐng*: a stick, club or cudgel that can be used to beat people.
2. 賊 *zéi*: here used as a legal term, deliberately and with malice.
3. 伐 *fá*: to beat, to hit.

寬式隸定
Loose Transcription

以梃賊傷人。何謂“梃”？木可以伐者爲“梃”。

白話文
Vernacular Chinese

用梃蓄意傷人。什麽叫作“梃”？可以用來敲打人的木棍叫作“梃”。

英文翻譯
English Translation

Intentionally wounding [someone] with *tǐng*. What is a *tǐng*? Wood club [or wooden stick] that can be used to attack people are called *tǐng*.

練習
Practice

釋讀圖表 2 中的睡虎地秦墓竹簡《法律答問》簡。

Read slips in Tableau 2.

圖表 2　Tableau 2

《法律答問》209	《法律答問》187	《法律答問》180	《法律答問》172	《法律答問》150

第十五組　户籍等其他行政文書
Group 15　Household Registration and Other Administrative Documents

簡介
Introduction

秦簡中有大量的各種類型的行政文書，前文已經介紹了一些政府機構的往來文書，此外，還有録、志、課、簿籍、符券、檢、楬、里程書等很多類型。這些文書，往往有着特殊的形製、行文習慣、常用術語，也有着特定的功用。文書的内容關涉秦國以及秦代經濟、政治、軍事、民俗、地理等方方面面，是了解秦國、秦代歷史的重要窗口。行政文書以里耶秦簡所見最爲豐富、集中，這裏選取户籍等五種不同類型的文書，供讀者參考。

第一種是户籍。所選“南陽户籍”出自里耶古城護城壕，由斷裂的三塊拼綴而成，故有三個整理編號。木牘所記爲南陽里某户的户籍，由墨線分隔爲五欄，每一欄所記内容有所區别，分别是户主、妻、兒子、女兒、户主職務。

第二種是伐閱。用來記載官吏的功勞經歷。

第三種是券。在中國古代的買賣借貸、取予授受等活動中，往往需要一種憑證，即券。券或有刻齒，對應券上文字所記的物質數量，或無刻齒。里耶秦簡所見多爲校券，即記録錢、糧食、物品進出的券。校券爲細長條形，一般長 36.5—37.2 釐米，寬 0.8—2.1 釐米，其標準長度應爲 37 釐米，秦制 1 尺 6 寸。製作者製作一式兩份的校券時，先將木材加工爲具有一定厚度的契券，通常厚 1.1—1.2 釐米，再將其正反兩面切割開，但下端不切割到底，最後在記録完成並刻上刻齒後，再切開下端剩下的部分。製作“三辨券”即一式三份的券時，首先將木材加工成可以切割成三片的、具有足夠厚度的木條，然後將其切割爲正面、中間、反面三片，但下端不切割到底，之後將正面和背面的記録完成並刻入刻齒，再將剩餘部分切割到底，最後將中間的一片一面削平，謄寫好簡文。所選爲一枚出糧券。

第四種是檢。有學者認爲此類簡牘應該被稱爲“署”，暫依舊説。檢大多下端被削尖，長 8—23 釐米，有的簡首被塗黑。檢用來覆蓋在文書之上，寫有收件、發件等要素，起着指示傳遞的作用。題寫内容可能包括下列要素中的 1—4 點：（1）收件地點；（2）傳遞方式；（3）開啟者；（4）關於文書緊急程度的描述。

第五種是楬。掛在承裝實物的器皿上標示承載物類别和數量等的標籤，被稱爲楬。所選“卅四年遷陵課笥楬”是一枚木牘。該木牘通長 13.2 釐米，底部寬 9.4 釐米，上端圓弧，正面頂部塗黑，塗黑部分高 3.2 釐米，下鑽二孔，兩孔中心相距 2.65 釐米。

There is a large number of various types of administrative documents in the excavated corpus of Qín slips. We have already introduced some government agencies' correspondence documents in the previous section. In addition, there are many types such as proofreading records (*lù* 録), records (*zhì* 志), evaluations (*kè* 課), account books (*bùjí* 簿籍), tallies (*fúquàn* 符券), checks (*jiǎn* 檢), tags (*jié* 楬), and mileage books (*lǐchéng shū* 里程書). These documents often have special forms, writing styles, special terms, jargons and serve very specific functions. The content of the document touches on all aspects of the Qín state, including economy, politics, military affairs, folk customs, geography, and much more. It is an important window for us to understand the Qín state and its predynastic and dynastic history. Lǐyē Qín slips represent the most abundant and concentrated cache of administrative documents. In this section, we select five different types of documents from Lǐyē Qín slips.

The first document type is called *hùjí* 户籍， household registers. The selected *Household Register of Nányáng* (*Nányáng hùjí* 南陽户籍) was recovered from the moat of the ancient city of Lǐyē and consists of three broken pieces, hence the three sorting numbers K1/K25/K50. The wooden slips record the household registration of a certain household in Nányáng. The text is divided into five segments, each marked by a separate ink line drawn across the wooden slip. The contents recorded in each segment are different, namely, information on the household head, wife, son, daughter and position of the household head.

The second document type is called *fáyuè* 伐閱 or curriculum vitae recording the meritorious experience of officials.

The third document type is called *quàn* 券 or coupons. In ancient China, when buying, selling, lending, taking, granting or accepting something, a certificate or voucher is often needed. The coupons may or may not have engraved teeth, with the corresponding quantity of items written on the coupons. Most coupons in Lǐyē Qín slips belong to the subtype of checking tallies, that is, coupons that record the entry and exit of money, food or commercial items. Checking tallies in Lǐyē Qín slips are slender slips, generally 36.5-37.2 cm long and 0.8-2.1 cm wide. The standard length of tallies was supposed to be 37 cm or 1 *chǐ* 尺 and 6 *cùn* 寸 in Qín measurements. To make duplicate coupons, the wood was processed to a certain thickness, usually 1.1-1.2 cm thick, and then cut in front and back, but the lower part was not cut all the way to the end. After recording, the engraving teeth were made and the remaining part of the lower end was cut. When making *sānbiàn quàn* 三辨券， that is, coupons in triplicate, the wood was first processed into wooden slips with sufficient thickness that could be cut into three pieces, and then cut into three pieces of front, middle and back, but the lower end was not cut. In the end, after finishing recording on the front and back, the engraving teeth was made, then the remaining part was cut to the end, and finally the middle piece was flattened on one side, and the recording text was copied. Here, we have selected a piece called *chūliáng quàn* 出糧券 (voncher for food delivery).

The fourth document type is called type is called *jiǎn* 檢， lit. "inspection or check." Some scholars believe that such slips should be called *shǔ* 署 . For now, we will still call them *jiǎn*. Most of the lower ends of the *jiǎn* were sharpened, with a length ranging from 8 cm to 23 cm, and some of them were painted black at the top. The *jiǎn,* with the information of delivery method, was attached at the cover of the document. The information generally includes several of the following elements: (1)the place of receipt; (2)the method of delivery; (3)the person who issued it; and (4)a description of the urgency of the document.

The fifth document type is the *jié* 楬 or tag, a label that is hung on the container that carries an object to indicate the type and quantity of the object. The selected document *A Tag Hung on a Vessel with Evaluations of Qiānlíng County during the Thirty-fourth Regnal Year* (*Sàsìnián Qiānlíng Kèsìjié* 卅四年遷陵課笥楬) is a wooden slip, 13.2 cm long and 9.4 cm wide at the bottom, with an arc at the upper end, and the top of the front is painted black. The black part is 3.2 cm high, with two holes, the centers of which are 2.65 cm apart.

篇目來源
Text Source

第 38 篇　南陽户籍（里耶秦簡 K1/25/50）

38. *Household Register of Nányáng* (Lǐyē Qín slips, No.K1/25/50)

第 39 篇　令史釦伐閱（里耶秦簡 8-269）

39. *Curriculum Vitae of a Lìngshǐ Named Kòu* (Lǐyē Qín slips, No.8-269)

第 40 篇　出糧券（里耶秦簡 8-763）

40. *Voucher of Food Delivery* (Lǐyē Qín slips, No.8-763)

第 41 篇　檢（里耶秦簡 9-24）

41. *Sealing Tag* (Lǐyē Qín slips, No.9-24)

第 42 篇　卅四年遷陵課笥楬（里耶秦簡 8-906）

42. *A Tag Hung on Vessel with Evaluations of Qiānlíng County during the Thirty-fourth Regnal Year* (Lǐyē Qín slips, No.8-906)

參考文獻
References

陳偉主編:《里耶秦簡牘校釋（第一卷）》，武漢大學出版社 2012 年。

陳偉主編:《秦簡牘校讀及所見制度考察》，武漢大學出版社 2017 年。

陳偉主編:《里耶秦簡牘校釋（第二卷）》，武漢大學出版社 2018 年。

湖南省文物考古研究所:《里耶秦簡（壹）》，文物出版社 2012 年。

湖南省文物考古研究所:《里耶秦簡（貳）》，文物出版社 2017 年。

里耶秦簡博物館、出土文獻與中國古代文明研究協同創新中心中國人民大學中心編著:《里耶秦簡博物館藏秦簡》，中西書局 2016 年。

汪桂海:《考古資料所見簡帛時代書籍裝具》，《文獻》2021 年第 1 期。

張春龍、[日]大川俊隆、[日]籾山明:《里耶秦簡刻齒簡研究——兼論嶽麓秦簡〈數〉中的未解讀簡》,《文物》2015年第3期。
張今:《里耶秦簡中的楬》, 簡帛網, http://www.bsm.org.cn/show_article.php?id=2609, 2016年8月21日。

照片、隸定本
Photo, Transcription

圖表 1　里耶秦簡 K1/25/50

Tableau 1: Lǐyē Qín slips, No.K1/25/50

圖表 2　里耶秦簡 8-269, 8-763, 9-24

Tableau 2: Lǐyē Qín slips, No.8-269, 8-763, 9-24

圖表 3　里耶秦簡 8-906

Tableau 3: Lǐyē Qín slips, No.8-906

圖表 1　Tableau 1

里耶秦簡 K1/25/50 下半部		里耶秦簡 K1/25/50 上半部		里耶秦簡 K1/25/50
隸定	照片	隸定	照片	完整照片
子小女虖 子小女移 子小女平 五長	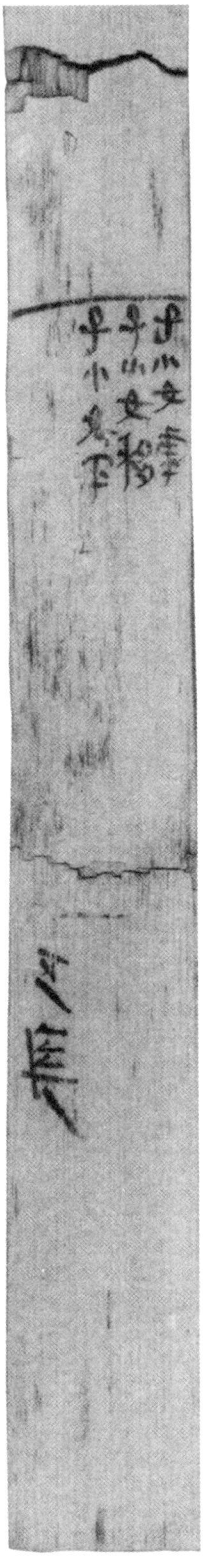	南陽户人荊不更□得 妻曰嗛 子小上造台 子小上造甯 子小上造定	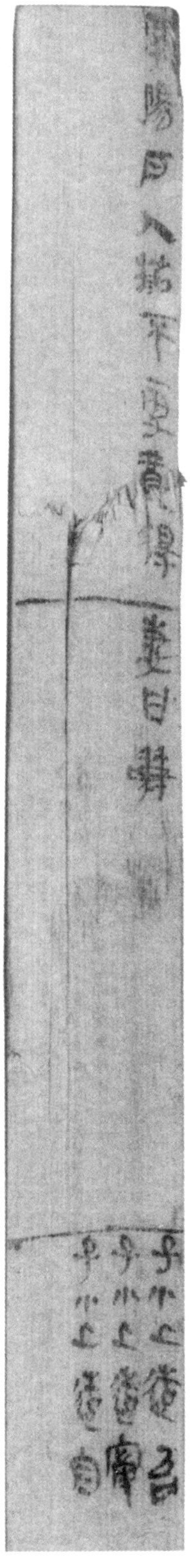	

圖表 2　Tableau 2

里耶秦簡 9-24		里耶秦簡 8-763		里耶秦簡 8-269	
隸定	照片	隸定	照片	隸定	照片
遷陵以郵 行洞庭		粟=一石二斗半斗卅一年三月癸丑倉守武史感稟人援出稟大隸妾并 令史犴視平　感手	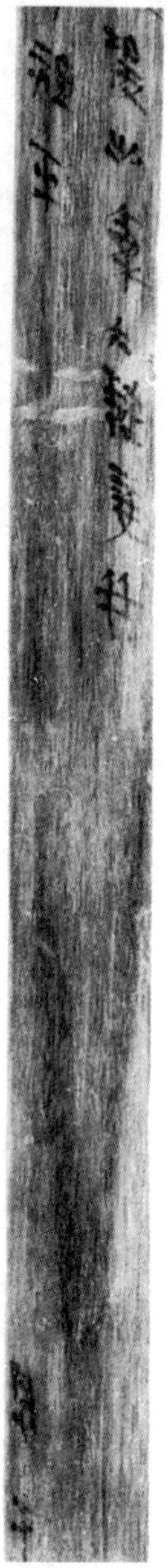 	資中令史陽里釦伐閱 十一年九月隃爲史　□計　户計 爲鄉史九歲一日　年卅六 爲田部史四歲三月十一日　可直司空曹 爲令史二月	

圖表 3　Tableau 3

里耶秦簡 8-906	
隸定	照片
卅四年 遷陵課 笥	

三十八、南陽户籍
38. Household Register of Nányáng

原文
Bamboo Script

南陽户人①荆不更②□得。A
妻曰嗛。B
子小上造③台，CI 子小上造簾，CII 子小上造定。CIII
子小女④虖，DI 子小女移，DII 子小女平。DIII
五（伍）長⑤。E

注釋
Annotation

① 户人：户主。
② 荆不更：荆，標記爵位的地域爲楚地，是爲了與秦的爵位相區别。不更，爵位等級。
③ 小上造：小爵的一種。
④ 小女：指未成年女子，與大女相對。
⑤ 五長：五，通“伍”。秦實行編伍連坐制度，五户編爲一伍，設有伍長。

1. 户人 *hù rén*: head of the household.
2. 荆不更 *jīng bù gēng*: Jīng 荆 refers to the area of the former state of Chǔ 楚 ; *Bùgēng* 不更，a level of meritorious status.
3. 小上造 *xiǎo shàng zào*: lit. “Small Sovereign’s Accomplished,” a level of meritorious status for juveniles.
4. 小女 *xiǎo nǚ*: lit. “little girl,” underage girls, as opposed to *dànǚ* 大女 (lit. “big girl”), older adult girls.
5. 五長 *wǔ zhǎng*: lit. “Squad Leader.” The Qín state implemented the so-called *biānwǔ liánzuò* 編伍連坐 system: five households are organized into a squad (*wǔ* 伍), headed by a chief called Squad Leader (*wǔzhǎng* 伍長).

寬式隸定
Loose Transcription

南陽户人荆不更□得。

妻曰嗛。
子小上造台，子小上造甯，子小上造定。
子小女虖，子小女移，子小女平。
伍長。

白話文
Vernacular Chinese

南陽里户主名爲某得，爵位爲荆不更。妻子名爲嗛。兒子小上造台，兒子小上造甯，兒子小上造定。女兒小女虖，女兒小女移，女兒小女平。某得擔任伍長。

英文翻譯
English Translation

Nányáng Village, household head, X Dé, with merit rank of *Bùgēng* in Jīng. Wife called Xián. Child, with *Xiǎoshàngzào* rank, [called] Tái; *Child,* with *Xiǎoshàngzào* rank, [called] Níng; Child, with *Xiǎoshàngzào* rank, [called] Dìng. Child, minor female, Hū; Child, minor female, Yí; Child, minor female, Píng. [X Dé serves as] Squad Leader.

三十九、令史釦伐閲
39. Curriculum Vitae of a Lìngshǐ Named Kòu

原文
Bamboo Script

資中①令史陽里②釦伐閲③。AI 十一年九月隃爲史。AII 爲鄉史九歲一日。AIII 爲田部④史四歲三月十一日。AIV 爲令史二月。AV □計。BI 年卅六。BII 户計⑤。C 可直⑥司空曹⑦。D

注釋
Annotation

① 資中：縣名，治所在今四川資陽市。
② 陽里：里名。
③ 伐閲：功勞及爲官經歷（是統計功勞的重要依據）情況。
④ 田部：主管與田作有關事務的官署，主官爲田嗇夫。
⑤ 計：統計記録。
⑥ 直：值守，主持。
⑦ 司空曹：縣廷内部設置的主管與司空有關事務的曹。

1. 資中 *zī zhōng*: county name, the county government is located in Zīyáng City, Sìchuān Province.
2. 陽里 *yáng lǐ*: name of a village (lǐ, composed of about 25 households).
3. 伐閲 *fá yuè*: credit, merit and official experience, similar to official curriculum vitae, a basis for evaluating human resource statistics.
4. 田部 *tián bù*: office that handles matters of agriculture and land. The chief officer is called Bailiff of Farmland (*Tián sèfū* 田嗇夫).
5. 計 *jì*: statistical records, accounting.
6. 直 *zhí*: to be in charge; on duty.
7. 司空曹 *sī kōng cáo*: Bureau in charge of affairs related to Convict Labor.

寬式隸定
Loose Transcription

資中令史陽里釦伐閲。十一年九月隃爲史。爲鄉史九歲一日。爲田部史四歲三月十一日。爲令史二月。□計。年卅六。户計。可直司空曹。

白話文
Vernacular Chinese

資中縣陽里令史釦的功勞經歷：秦王政十一年九月選拔爲史。做鄉史九年一天。做田部史四年三月十一天。做令史二月。某計。三十六歲。户計。可主持司空曹。

英文翻譯
English Translation

Merit and days of service of a Prefectural Clerk named Kòu from Yáng Village, Zīzhōng County: Selected to be a Scribe in the ninth month, eleventh year [of King Zhèng of Qín (236 BCE)] ; [served] as the Scribe of the Township for nine years and one day; [served as] the Scribe of the Department of Agriculture for four years, three months and eleven days; [served as] Prefectural Clerk for two months. [Illegible character] account. [Age] thirty-six, Household Department registered. Qualifies to be in charge of Bureau of Convict Labor.

四十、出糧券
40. Voucher of Food Delivery

原文
Bamboo Script

粟₌（粟米）一石二斗半斗①。卅一年三月癸丑，倉守武、史感、稟人②援出稟大隸妾③并。Ⅰ

令史犴視平④。感手。Ⅱ

注釋
Annotation

① 一石二斗半斗：是成年女性刑徒一個月的供食數量。
② 稟人：具體負責發放糧食者，一般由隸妾充當。
③ 大隸妾：隸妾，女性刑徒的一種。大隸妾，指成年隸妾。
④ 視平：監督。

1. 一石二斗半斗 *yī dàn èr dǒu bàn dǒu*: amount of crops provided to a female adult prisoner over one month.
2. 稟人 *bǐng rén*: the person responsible for distributing food, usually done by bondwomen.
3. 大隸妾 *dà lì qiè*: *dà* 大 , refers to adult; *lìqiè* 隸妾 , bondwomen, a kind of female prisoners.
4. 視平 *shì píng*: lit. "to oversee the fairness," to supervise.

寬式隸定
Loose Transcription

粟米一石二斗半斗。卅一年三月癸丑，倉守武、史感、稟人援出稟大隸妾并。

令史犴視平。感手。

白話文
Vernacular Chinese

粟米一石二又二分之一斗。始皇三十一年三月癸丑日，代理倉嗇夫武、史感、稟人援拿出發放給名爲并的大隸妾。

令史犴督看。感手寫。

英文翻譯
English Translation

One *dàn* and two and a half *dǒu* of [untreated] grain. On the *guǐchǒu* day of the third month in the thirty-first regnal year of the First Emperor of Qín. Acting Bailiff of the Granary Wǔ, Scribe Gǎn and Disburser Yuán took out an amount of one *dàn* and two and half *dǒu* of grain to give to the adult bondwoman Bìng. Supervised by Prefectural Clerk Yú. Handwritten by Gǎn.

四十一、檢
41. Sealing Tag

原文
Bamboo Script

遷陵①。以郵行②。洞庭③。

注釋
Annotation

① 遷陵：縣名。
② 以郵行：表明傳遞方式。郵，秦時在主要的道路上每隔一定距離設置一個郵，用於文書傳遞、來往官吏休息等。
③ 洞庭：郡名。這裏標明遷陵縣的歸屬。

1. 遷陵 *qiān líng*: county name.
2. 以郵行 *yǐ yóu xíng*: by way of post, indicating the delivery method is via postal dispatch. In the Qín Dynasty, posts stations were set up throughout the county at certain distances on the main roads for document delivery. They provided places where officials could rest.
3. 洞庭 *dòng tíng*: name of a commandery. Qiānlíng County was under the administration of Dòngtíng Commandery.

寬式隸定
Loose Transcription

遷陵。以郵行。洞庭。

白話文
Vernacular Chinese

目的地爲遷陵縣。用郵傳遞。洞庭郡。

英文翻譯
English Translation

[Destination:] Qiānlíng [County] . Delivered by post. Dòngtíng [Commandery] .

四十二、卅四年遷陵課笥楬
42. A Tag Hung on Vessel with Evaluations of Qiānlíng County during the Thirty-fourth Regnal Year

原文
Bamboo Script

卅四年遷陵課①笥②。

注釋
Annotation

① 課：文書名稱，考課的記録。
② 笥：一種器皿名稱，常用竹子編成，往往有蓋，可用來盛裝文書、絲織物、飯食等。

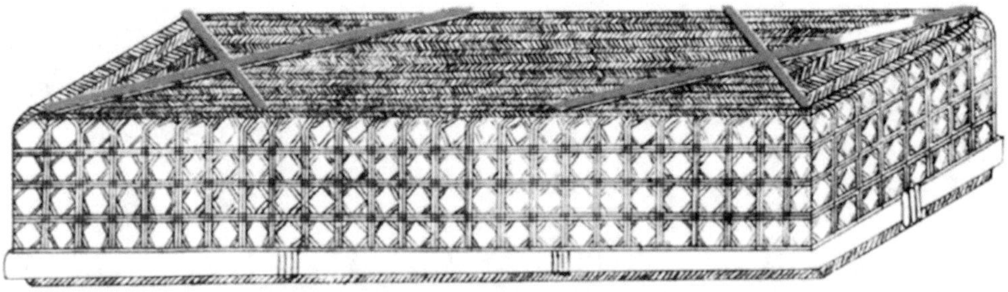

圖 1　長沙子彈庫楚帛書竹笥線描圖
Figure 1　Line drawing of the bamboo *sì* vessel holding Chǔ silk scriptures unearthed from Zǐdànkù, Chángshā
（引自汪桂海：《考古資料所見簡帛時代書籍裝具》）

圖 2　荊州胡家草場西漢墓出土竹笥
Figure 2　Bamboo *sì* vessel unearthed from the Western Hàn tomb at Hújiācǎochǎng, Jīngzhōu
（引自汪桂海：《考古資料所見簡帛時代書籍裝具》）

1. 課 *kè*: a type of official documents that deals with the performance of officials and evaluates how well they fulfill their official duties.
2. 笥 *sì*: a vessel or container made of bamboo, often with a lid, which can be used to hold documents, silk fabrics, meals, etc.

寬式隸定
Loose Transcription

卅四年遷陵課笥。

白話文
Vernacular Chinese

始皇三十四年（裝有）遷陵縣考課文書的竹笥。

英文翻譯
English Translation

Bamboo vessel [containing] records of official performance evaluations of [officials in] Qiānlíng County during the thirty-fourth regnal year of the First Emperor of Qín.

練習
Practice

釋讀圖表 4 中的 4 枚簡牘。
Read the 4 slips in Tableau 4.

圖表 4　Tableau 4

里耶秦簡 8-94	里耶秦簡 8-762	里耶秦簡 12-853	里耶秦簡 K49
			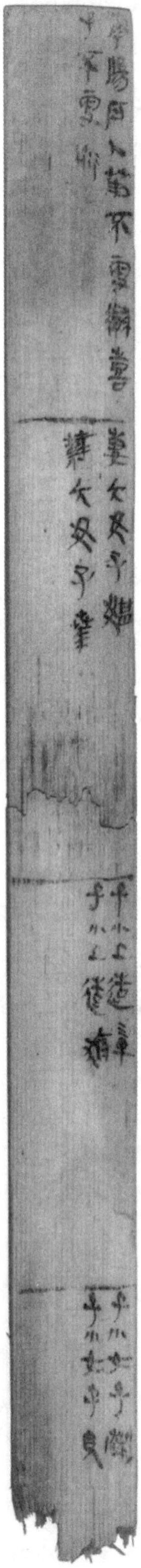

第十六組　其他文獻
Group 16　Other Documents

簡介
Introduction

秦簡中有一些文獻性質比較特殊，不能歸入上述類型，但也具有重要的價值。這裏選擇兩種介紹。

北京大學藏秦簡牘中有一篇名爲《泰原有死者》的文獻，内容包含兩部分，前一部分用一句話介紹了一個死而復生者，後一部分借死而復生者之口介紹喪葬及祭祀死者的宜忌，體現了當時人的死生觀念及信仰習俗。放馬灘秦簡《丹》(也有人稱爲《墓主記》《志怪故事》等)與《泰原有死者》性質較爲類似。從此類文獻見於不同墓葬，可知此類故事是廣爲流傳的，可能對於當時百姓的生活有特定的意義。

里耶秦簡中有一枚更名方，記録了秦代用字、用詞方面的一些改變，對於瞭解秦代語言文字面貌具有重要意義。關於其性質，有人認爲是私人擁有的供提示書寫的材料，有人則認爲是官方文書。不管是哪一種，它記録的應該是秦時官方推行的用字、用詞政策，與歷史上著名的秦代“書同文”有關。相關記載如《史記・秦始皇本紀》:“一法度衡石丈尺，車同軌，書同文字。”北京大學藏漢簡《趙正書》:“斯且死，故上書曰:‘……更㓨(刻)畫斗甬(桶)度量，壹文章，布之天下，以樹秦之名者，……’”所謂“書同文字”，以往一般認爲指用秦系文字代替東方六國文字，而更名方公佈後，一些學者提出“書同文字”不僅是文字層面的，還有語言層面的内容，即還包括“正用語”(包括避諱)。

Some documents on Qín bamboo slips are of special nature and cannot be classified into the above categories, but they also have important value. We have chosen two additional document types to introduce them here.

The piece *A Dead Person at Tàiyuán* (*Tàiyuán yǒu sǐzhě* 泰原有死者) is selected from the Peking University corpus of Qín wood boards. This piece first introduces in one sentence the Dead who returned to life and came to the capital city of Xiányáng. The rest of the piece introduces proper burial practices and funeral rituals of offering sacrifices, including taboos, dos and don'ts, through the voice of the Dead. This piece vividly reflects the popular view of life and death, commoners' beliefs and customs in the state of Qín. *A Dead Person at Tàiyuán* is quite similar to another piece entitled "*Dān*" 丹 in the Fàngmǎtān Qín bamboo slips. This piece is also known as *The Tomb Occupant* (*Mùzhǔ jì* 墓主記) or *Story of Strange Things* (*Zhìguài gùshì* 志怪故事). The discovery of similar narratives from different tombs at different sites indicates that this kind of stories circulated widely in the state of Qín and may have had a special meaning to the people at that time.

A slip entitled *Name-changing Formula* (*Gēngmíng fāng* 更名方) stands out in the Lǐyē Qín slips in that it lists about fifty words and terms and their suggested replacements under the newly established Qín Dynasty. This slip is significant in that it provides an authentic glimpse on how the Qín unification impacted language. The Qín sought to unify and standardize the language, script, measures and laws as an expedient means of consolidating and maintaining centralized control over its own territories, as well as the new territories recently acquired via conquest. In addition to orthography or standardization of paticular graphs, the slip provides evidence that the Qín rulers also exerted control at the level of language use, including the establishment of taboo characters and avoiding taboos (*bìhuì* 避諱). For example, the graph *zhēng*/*zhèng* 正 was replaced by *duān* 端 (beginning) since the First Emperor's given name was *zhèng* 政 . This explains the switch from *zhēngyuè* 正月 to *duānyuè* 端月 and from *lǐzhèng* 里正 (Village Chief) to *lǐdiǎn* 里典 in the Qín texts, just to name two examples.

篇目來源
Text Source

第 43 篇　泰原有死者（北京大學藏秦木牘）
43. *A Dead Person at Tàiyuán* (Peking University corpus of Qín wood board)
第 44 篇　更名方（里耶秦簡 8-461 號簡）
44. *Name-Changing Formula* (Lǐyē Qín slips, No.8-461)

參考文獻
References

北京大學出土文獻研究所:《北京大学藏秦簡牍概述》,《文物》2012 年第 6 期。
陳劍:《據出土文獻説"懸諸日月而不刊"及相關問題》,《嶺南學報》第 10 輯。
陳偉:《北大藏秦簡〈泰原有死者〉識小》, 簡帛網, 2012 年 7 月 14 日。
蔣文:《"黃豆瓜子"何以支付"地下賦"》,《簡帛》第 20 輯, 上海古籍出版社 2020 年。
李零:《北大秦牘〈泰原有死者〉簡介》,《文物》2012 年第 6 期。
姜守誠:《北大秦牘〈泰原有死者〉考釋》,《中華文史論叢》2014 年第 3 期。
劉國勝:《北大藏秦簡讀後記》,《簡帛》第 8 輯, 上海古籍出版社 2013 年。
尚宇昌:《北大秦牍〈泰原有死者〉"勿束缚"新解》,《咸陽師範學院學報》2017 年第 3 期。
雍淑鳳:《北大藏秦牘〈泰原有死者〉斷句、語譯、闡釋商榷》,《古籍研究》2017 年第 1 期。
張春龍、龍京沙:《湘西里耶 8-455 號》,《簡帛》第 4 輯, 上海古籍出版社 2009 年。
胡平生:《里耶秦簡 8-455 號木方性質芻議》,《簡帛》第 4 輯, 上海古籍出版社 2009 年。
陳偉:《里耶秦簡牘校釋(第一卷)》, 武漢大學出版社 2012 年。
游逸飛:《里耶 8-461 號"秦更名方"選釋》,《古代長江中游社會研究》, 上海古籍出版社

2013 年。
陳侃理:《里耶秦方與書同文字》,《文物》2014 年第 9 期。
郭永秉:《讀里耶 8:461 號木方札記》,《古文字與出土文獻論集續編》,上海古籍出版社 2015 年。
田煒:《論秦始皇"書同文字"政策的内涵及影響:兼論判斷出土秦文獻文本年代的重要標尺》,《中央研究院歷史語言研究所集刊》第 89 本第 1 分,"中央研究院"歷史語言研究所 2018 年。
張惟捷、覃怡:《里耶秦簡"更名方"考釋與字體相關問題淺析:兼論秦"書同文字"政策》,《厦大中文學報》2019 年第 6 期。

照片、隸定本
Photo, Transcription

圖表 1　北京大學藏秦木牘(《泰原有死者》)

Tableau 1: Peking University corpus of Qín wooden board, *A Dead Person at Tàiyuán*

圖表 2　里耶秦簡 8-461 號簡

Tableau 2: Lǐyē Qín slips, slip No.8-461

圖表 1 Tableau 1

北京大學藏秦木牘《泰原有死者》	
隸定	照片
泰原有死者三歲而復產獻之咸陽言曰死人之所惡解 予死人衣必令產見之弗產見鬼輒奪而入之少內死 人所貴黃〃圈〃以當金黍粟以當錢白菅以當繇女子死三 歲而復嫁後有死者勿并其冢祭死人之冢勿哭須其已食 乃哭之不須其已食而哭之鬼輒奪而入之廚祠毋以酒與 羹沃祭而沃祭前收死人勿束縛毋決其履毋毀其器 令如其產之卧殹令其魖不得若思黃圈者大叔 殹毄去其皮置於土中以爲黃金之勉	

圖表 2　Tableau 2

里耶秦簡 8-461 號簡

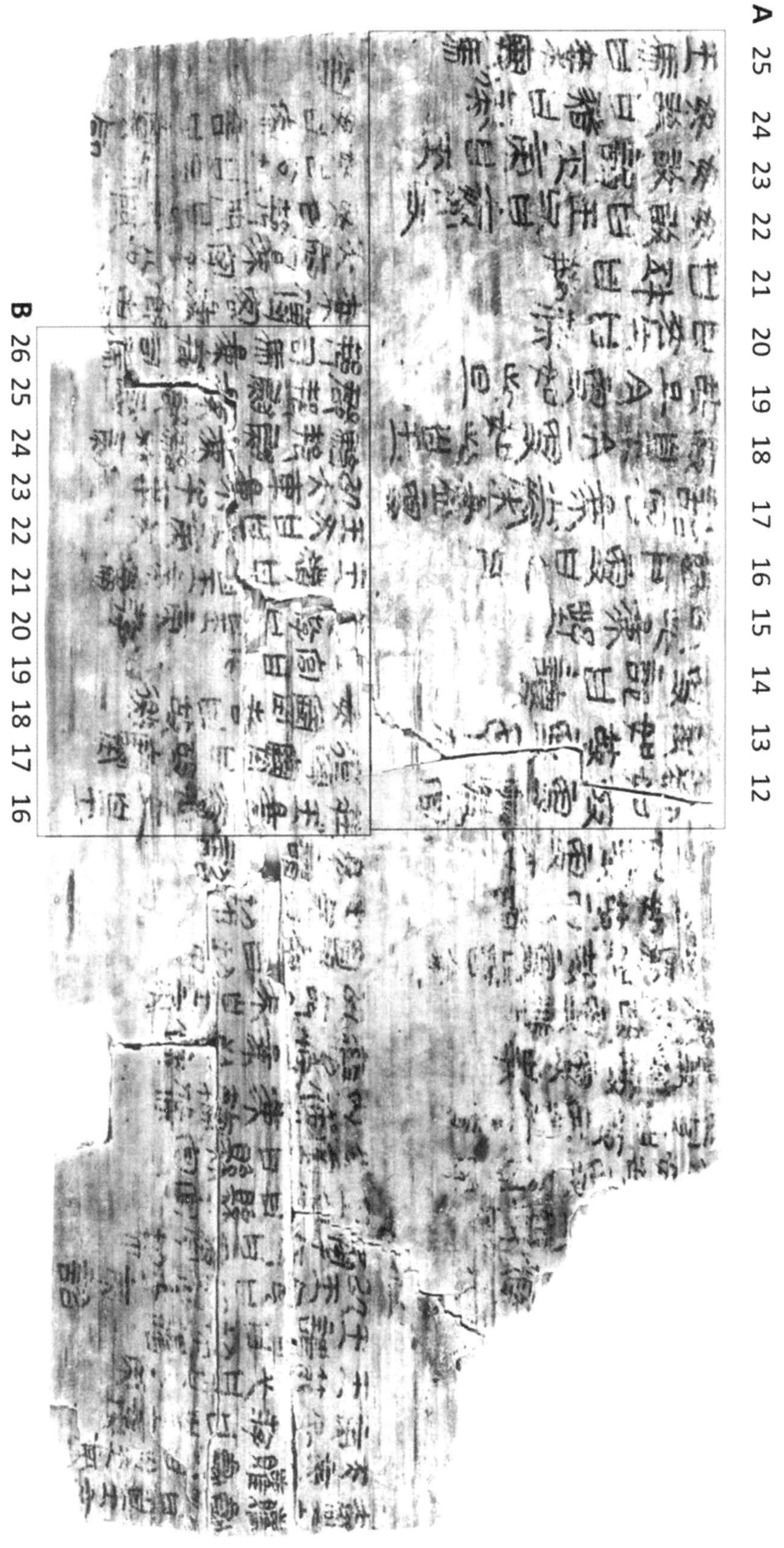

四十三、泰原有死者
43. A Dead Person at Tàiyuán

原文
Bamboo Script

泰原有死者，三歲而復産，獻之咸陽，言曰：死人之所惡，解予死人衣①。必令産見之，弗産見，鬼輒奪而入之少内②。死人所貴黄₌圈₌（黄圈③。黄圈）以當金，黍粟以當錢，白菅④以當繇〈縣（繇）〉⑤。女子死三歲而復嫁⑥，後有死者，勿并其冢。祭死人之冢，勿哭。須其已食乃哭之，不須其已食而哭之，鬼輒奪而入之廚⑦。祠，毋以酒與羹沃祭⑧，而沃祭前。收死人，勿束縛⑨。毋決其履⑩，毋毀其器。令如其産之卧殹，令其魆（魄）⑪不得若思⑫。黄圈者，大叔⑬（菽）殹（也），剺（剺）⑭，去其皮，置於土中，以爲黄金之勉⑮。

注釋
Annotation

① 解予死人衣：脱掉死者舊衣，給他穿上新的葬衣。

② 少内：秦漢時縣政府設有此官署機構，主管錢財。這裹的少内應是虚構的地下世界的少内。

③ 黄圈：《神農本草經》有“大豆黄卷”，一般認爲是豆芽。本文最後一句指出黄圈是大豆。

④ 白菅：白茅。

⑤ 繇：“縣”的訛字，通“繇”。或認爲通“徭”，徭役。或認爲通“紬”，絲綢。

⑥ 女子死三歲而復嫁：女子死三年後就會在陰間再嫁。或認爲復指復活，認爲是復活的女子再嫁。

⑦ 廚：虚構的地下世界主管餐食的機構。

⑧ 沃祭：沃指澆灌，是祭祀的方式，放馬灘秦墓竹簡中載“毋以羹沃腏上，鬼弗食殹”，所述大致相同。

⑨ 束縛：這裹指一種下葬時捆縛人的胳膊與腿部的行爲風俗。

⑩ 決其履：指撕裂死者的鞋子。或認爲指弄斷連接兩隻鞋的帶子而使兩足分開。

⑪ 魆：即“魄”，魂魄。

⑫ 若思：若，至，到。以往多將“若”誤釋爲“苔”，故解説多誤讀。思，通“斯”，此。或認爲是語氣詞。

⑬ 大叔：叔，通“菽”，大菽即大豆。

⑭ 剺：即“熬”，乾炒，乾煎。

⑮ 勉：意義不明。

1. 解予 *jiě yǔ*: to remove the deceased's old clothes and put on graveclothes.
2. 少内 *shào nèi*: an institution of Qín state in charge of finance. Here it most likely refers to a similar institution operating in the Underworld.
3. 黄圈 *huáng quān*: lit. "yellow circle," this term is equivalent to *huángjuǎn* 黄卷（"yellow rolls or curls"）, mentioned in *Shénnóng's Materia Medica* (*Shénnóng běncǎo jīng* 神農本草經), both refer to the soy bean. At the end of the text, it is clearly indicated that *huángquān* is equated with the soy bean.
4. 白菅 *bái jiān*: cogongrass (Imperata cylindrica), it has a distinctive silver-white seedhead that resembles a silk cocoon.
5. 繇 *yáo*: a scribal mistake for the word *xiàn* 縣，equivalent to *mián* 緜，"silk wadding." Some scholars suggest that it is equivalent to *yáo* 徭，meaning "corvee." Yet other scholars suggest that it is equivalent to *chóu* 紬，meaning silk or silk fabric.
6. 女子死三歲而復嫁 *nǚ zǐ sǐ sān suì ér fù jià*: "a girl dead for three years then being re-married." In this reading of the sentence, *fùjià* 復嫁 is understood to mean "being re-married［in the Underworld］" and refers to the practice of spirit marriage (*mínghūn* 冥婚). In the *Rites of Zhōu* (*Zhōulǐ* 周禮), where this practice is called "to give the deceased into matrimony" (*jiàshāng* 嫁殤), there is a prohibition against shifting burial site and spirit marriages. Another interpretation considers the word *fù* 復 in *fùjià* as *fùhuó* 復活, meaning "resurrection" or "resurrected." Hence according to this interpretation, the sentence reads as follows: "A woman resurrected three years after her death and then being re-married."
7. 廚 *chú*: kitchen. Here it refers to the Kitchen Facilities in the Underworld.
8. 沃祭 *wò jì*: a kind of libation, referring to the sprinkling of liquid on top of sacrificial food; *wò* 沃 refers to the action of sprinkling, spraying.
9. 束縛 *shù fù*: to restrain or to restrict, or to bind. Here it refers to the burial custom of binding the four limbs of the corpse.
10. 決其履 *jué qí lǚ*: literally the term means "to break the shoes." The shoes that the corpse wears are tied together and are not supposed to be separated apart for fear that otherwise the deceased may walk away.
11. 魄 *pò*: equivalent to *pò* 魄，meaning "spirit."
12. 若思 *ruò sī*: *ruò* 若 means "to arrive, to come." *Sī* 思 is equivalent to *sī* 斯，meaning "this" or "here." Some scholars suggest that *sī* is used as a modal particle here. Many mistakenly surmise that the word *ruò* is equivalent to *luò* 笿，meaning "to restrain."
13. 大叔 *dà shū*: soybean; the character *shū* 叔 is equivalent to *shū* 菽.
14. 骜 *áo*: the character *áo* 骜 is equivalent to *áo* 熬，meaning "to fry."
15. 勉 *miǎn*: the meaning is unclear, we tentatively translate it as "to apply" in accordance with the context.

寬式隸定
Loose Transcription

泰原有死者，三歲而復産，獻之咸陽，言曰：死人之所惡，解予死人衣。必令産見之，弗産見，鬼輒奪而入之少內。死人所貴黄圈。黄圈以當金，黍粟以當錢，白菅以當緜。女子死三歲而復嫁，後有死者，勿并其冢。祭死人之冢，勿哭。須其已食乃哭之，不須其已食而哭之，鬼輒奪而入之廚。祠，毋以酒與羮沃祭，而沃祭前。收死人，勿束縛。毋決其履，毋毀其器。令如其産之卧殹，令其魄不得若思。黄圈者，大菽也，熬，去其皮，置於土中，以爲黄金之勉。

白話文
Vernacular Chinese

泰原有死去的人，三年後再生，被獻到咸陽。他對人説：死者所厭惡的是：在死後才爲死者脱去舊衣換上壽服。換壽衣一定要在人活着時做，可以親眼看到，否則鬼吏就會奪走這些衣物收納入冥府的少內官署。死人以大豆爲貴。用大豆當金子，用黍與粟當銀子，用白茅充當絲綿。女子死了三年可以冥婚再嫁，但是如果原來的丈夫死後，就不要合葬在一起。在墳墓祭祀死人時先不要哭，等死者已經享用祭品完畢，才爲死者哭泣。如果不等死者享用完祭品就哭祭，鬼吏就會奪走祭品收入冥府廚官。祭奠時，不要用酒和羹澆祭品，而澆在祭品之前。收殮屍體時，不要綑綁死者的手腳。不要撕裂死者的鞋子，不要毁壞隨葬的器物。讓死者如活着時那様躺卧，使他的魂魄不再回來。黄圈就是大豆，乾炒後，去掉它的皮，放置於土中，可以當作黄金來使用。

英文翻譯
English Translation

There was a person who died in Tàiyuán, and after three years he was reborn. He was presented at Xiányáng, and he said: What the dead dislike: having their clothes changed after their demise; [the living] must let the to-be-dead see the clothes before they die. Otherwise, the Underground Official would immediately take the clothes and put them into the Underground Storehouse. What the dead value: dried soybeans, which take the place of gold; millets which takes the place of coins; cogongrass which takes the place of silk wadding. If a female has been dead for three years, she is allowed to go through underworld marriage. In such case, her original husband should not be buried with her together in the same lot after his death. When sacrificing at the burial mound of the dead, do not cry. Wait until the dead have finished eating and only then cry over them. If you don't wait until they have finished eating, then demons will immediately take the food and put it away in the Underworld Kitchen. When making offerings to the family, do not pour wine or broth on the sacrificial offerings to moisten them, pour them in front of the offerings. Place the deceased [in the coffin] without binding [their limbs] . Do not separate shoes, do not destroy their vessels. Arrange [the body of the dead] in a lying position as if it were still alive, so that their souls will not come back. Yellow circles (*huángquān*) are also known as soybeans; remove their skin by pan frying and place them underground; in this way they can be used [by the dead] as gold.

四十四、更名方
44. Name-Changing Formula

原文
Bamboo Script

……

A12 灋如故，更廢官①。
A13 鼠如故，更予人。
A14 更詑曰謾②。
A15 以此爲野。
A16 歸户更曰乏户③。
A17 諸官爲秦盡更。
A18 故皇今更如此皇。
A19 故旦今更如此旦。
A20 曰産，曰族④。
A21 曰荓，曰荆⑤。
A22 毋敢曰王父⑥，曰泰父。
A23 毋敢曰巫帝，曰巫。
A24 毋敢曰豬，曰彘。
A25 王馬曰乘輿⑦馬。
……
B16 莊王⑧爲泰上皇。
B17 邊塞⑨曰故塞。
B18 毋塞者曰故徼。
B19 王宫曰皇帝宫。
B20 王遊⑩曰皇帝遊。
B21 王獵⑪曰皇帝獵。
B22 王犬曰皇帝犬。
B23 以大車爲牛車。
B24 騎邦尉爲騎校尉⑫。
B25 郡邦尉爲郡尉⑬。
B26 邦司馬爲郡司馬⑭。
……

注釋
Annotation

① 某如故，更某：該句式指根據不同的詞義，區分用字。
② 詑，謾：欺騙。
③ 歸户，乏户：意義不明。
④ 曰產，曰族：用“產”不用“生”，用“族”不用通“姓”的“生”。
⑤ 曰荆：義爲改稱楚爲荆。
⑥ 王父，泰父：祖父。
⑦ 乘輿：古代特指天子和諸侯乘坐的車子。
⑧ 莊王：秦莊王，名子楚。
⑨ 塞：多指邊界上可以據險固守的要塞。
⑩ 遊：巡行。
⑪ 獵：打獵。
⑫ 騎邦尉，騎校尉：主管一郡騎兵的官員。
⑬ 郡邦尉，郡尉：主管一郡士兵的官員。
⑭ 邦司馬，郡司馬：郡裏的軍事官員之一，官名取義於主管馬匹。

1. 某如故，更某 *mǒu rú gù, gēng mǒu*: a standard format meaning: the word/character X (i.e., *mǒu* 某) remains to be used as before, but in a particular context word X should be replaced by word/character Y.
2. 詑，謾 *tuó, mán*: both words mean “cheating.”
3. 歸户，乏户 *guī hù, fá hù*: the meaning is unclear.
4. 曰產，曰族 *yuē chǎn, yuē zú* : lit. “say *chǎn* 產 and say *zú* 族 .” For the meaning of giving birth to a child or living, use the character *chǎn* instead of *shēng* 生； for the meaning of family name, use the character *zú* instead of *shēng* (equivalent to *xìng* 姓， surname).
5. 曰荆 *yuē jīng*: lit. “say Jīng 荆 .” Jīng is a place name, also known as Chǔ 楚 .
6. 王父，泰父 *wáng fù, tài fù:* lit. “grandfather.” Here, it means that the term *wángfù* 王父 should be replaced by the term *tàifù* 泰父 .
7. 乘輿 *chéng yú*: lit. “ride cart.” Here, it specifically refers to the emperor’s cart.
8. 莊王 *zhuāng wáng*: King Zhuāng 莊 of Qín.
9. 塞 *sài*: garrison station at the border.
10. 遊 *yóu*: procession, expedition.
11. 獵 *liè*: hunting.
12. 騎邦尉，騎校尉 *qí bāng wèi, qí xiào wèi*: the officer in charge of the cavalry of a commandery.
13. 郡邦尉，郡尉 *jùn bāng wèi, jùn wèi*: Commandant in charge of soldiers in a commandery.
14. 邦司馬，郡司馬 *bāng sī mǎ, jùn sī mǎ*: one of the military officials in a commandery. The

official name is derived from his charge of horses.

寬式隸定
Loose Transcription

A12　瀘如故，更廢官。
A13　鼠如故，更予人。
A14　更詑曰謾。
A15　以此爲野。
A16　歸户更曰乏户。
A17　諸官爲秦盡更。
A18　故皇今更如此皇。
A19　故旦今更如此旦。
A20　曰産，曰族。
A21　曰荈，曰荊。
A22　毋敢曰王父，曰泰父。
A23　毋敢曰巫帝，曰巫。
A24　毋敢曰豬，曰彘。
A25　王馬曰乘輿馬。
……
B16　莊王爲泰上皇。
B17　邊塞曰故塞。
B18　毋塞者曰故徼。
B19　王宫曰皇帝宫。
B20　王遊曰皇帝遊。
B21　王獵曰皇帝獵。
B22　王犬曰皇帝犬。
B23　以大車爲牛車。
B24　騎邦尉爲騎校尉。
B25　郡邦尉爲郡尉。
B26　邦司馬爲郡司馬。

白話文
Vernacular Chinese

A12　“瀘”字同以前一樣不必改動，更改“廢官”(廢除官職)的用字爲“廢”。
A13　“鼠”字同以前一樣不必改動，更改“予人”(給予人)的用字爲“予”。

A14　更改欺騙義的用字“訑”爲“謾”。
A15　用這種寫法的“野”字（從田從土予聲）作爲野字的正體。
A16　“歸户”更名作“乏户”。
A17　諸官署名爲“秦”的人都改掉（名字）。
A18　以前的“皇”字現在改爲這樣的寫法（）。
A19　以前的“旦”字現在改爲這樣的寫法（）。
A20　“生”説作“産”，“姓”説作“族”。
A21　“楚”説作“⿰王疋”與“荆”。
A22　不要稱“王父”，改稱“泰父”。
A23　不要稱“巫帝”，改稱“巫”。
A24　不稱豬爲“豬”，改稱“彘”。
A25　“王馬”改稱爲“乘輿馬”。
……
B16　改稱“莊王”爲“太上皇”。
B17　改稱“邊塞”爲“故塞”。
B18　没有邊塞的改稱“故徼”。
B19　改稱“王宫”爲“皇帝宫”（義爲皇帝的宫殿）。
B20　改稱“王遊”（義爲王巡遊）爲“皇帝遊”。
B21　改稱“王獵”（義爲王狩獵）爲“皇帝獵”。
B22　改稱“王犬”（義爲王的狗）爲“皇帝犬”。
B23　改稱“大車”爲“牛車”。
B24　改稱“騎邦尉”爲“騎校尉”。
B25　改稱“郡邦尉”爲“郡尉”。
B26　改稱“邦司馬”爲“郡司馬”。

英文翻譯
English Translation

A12 The character *fǎ* 灋 stays in use. The character *fèi* 廢 (to abolish) will be used in terms such as *fèiguān* 廢官 (to dismiss an official).

A13 The character *shǔ* 鼠 stays in use. The character *yǔ* 予 (to give) will be used in terms such as *yǔrén* 予人 (to give to somebody).

A14 For the word cheating use the character *mán* 謾 instead of *tuó* 訑 .

A15 The character *yě* 壄 should be written in this way (composed of *tián* 田 , *tǔ* 土 , *yǔ* 予).

A16 Change the term *guīhù* 歸户 to *fáhù* 乏户 .

A17 Any office worker whose name contains the character *qín* 秦 should change his name.

A18 The character *huáng* 皇 previously written as the first form in picture, should now be written like the second form in picture.

A19 The character *dàn* 旦 previously written as the first style in picture, should now be written like the second style in picture.

A20 [*Shēng* 生] should be expressed as *chǎn* 產 , [*shēng*] should be expressed as *zú* 族 to refer to surname.

A21 [Chǔ 楚] should be expressed as *wǔ* 荊 . [Chǔ] should be expressed as Jīng 荆 .

A22 Do not use *wángfù* 王父 to refer to grandfather, instead use *tàifù* 泰父 .

A23 Do not say shamanistic emperor (*wūdì* 巫帝), instead say shaman (*wū* 巫).

A24 Do not use *zhū* 豬 to refer to a pig, instead use *zhì* 彘 .

A25 Change king's horses (*wángmǎ* 王馬) to emperor's horses (*chéngyú mǎ* 乘輿馬).

B16 Change the title of King Zhuāng (*Zhuāngwáng* 莊王) to Supreme Emperor Emeritus (*Tàishànghuáng* 太上皇).

B17 Change the name frontier garrison station (*biānsài* 邊塞) to old garrison station (*gùsài* 故塞).

B18 If there is no garrison station, call it old border (*gùjiào* 故徼).

B19 Change palace of the king (*wánggōng* 王宮) to palace of the emperor (*huángdì gōng* 皇帝宮).

B20 Change royal procession (*wángyóu* 王遊) to imperial procession (*huángdì yóu* 皇帝遊).

B21 Change royal hunt (*wángliè* 王獵) to imperial hunt (*huángdì liè* 皇帝獵).

B22 Change royal hounds (*wángquǎn* 王犬) to imperial hounds (*huángdì quǎn* 皇帝犬).

B23 Change big cart (*dàchē* 大車) to ox cart (*niúchē* 牛車).

B24 Change the title Cavalry State Commandant (*qíbāngwèi* 騎邦尉) to Cavalry Commandant (*qíxiàowèi* 騎校尉).

B25 Change the title Commandery State Commandant (*jùnbāngwèi* 郡邦尉) to Commandery Commandant (*jùnwèi* 郡尉).

B26 Change the title State Major (*bāngsīmǎ* 邦司馬) to Commandery Major (*jùnsīmǎ* 郡司馬).

附録一　秦制術語輯録
Appendix 1　Qín Terminology

一、干支紀日表（Table of *Gānzhī* Dating）

甲子 *jiǎzǐ* 1	乙丑 *yǐchǒu* 2	丙寅 *bǐngyín* 3	丁卯 *dīnmǎo* 4	戊辰 *wùchén* 5	己巳 *jǐsì* 6	庚午 *gēngwǔ* 7	辛未 *xīnwèi* 8	壬申 *rénshēn* 9	癸酉 *guǐyǒu* 10
甲戌 *jiǎxū* 11	乙亥 *yǐhài* 12	丙子 *bǐngzǐ* 13	丁丑 *dīngchǒu* 14	戊寅 *wùyín* 15	己卯 *jǐmǎo* 16	庚辰 *gēngchén* 17	辛巳 *xīnsì* 18	壬午 *rénwǔ* 19	癸未 *guǐwèi* 20
甲申 *jiǎshēn* 21	乙酉 *yǐyǒu* 22	丙戌 *bǐngxū* 23	丁亥 *dīnghài* 24	戊子 *wùzǐ* 25	己丑 *jǐchǒu* 26	庚寅 *gēngyín* 27	辛卯 *xīnmǎo* 28	壬辰 *rénchén* 29	癸巳 *guǐsì* 30
甲午 *jiǎwǔ* 31	乙未 *yǐwèi* 32	丙申 *bǐngshēn* 33	丁酉 *dīngyǒu* 34	戊戌 *wùxū* 35	己亥 *jǐhài* 36	庚子 *gēngzǐ* 37	辛丑 *xīnchǒu* 38	壬寅 *rényín* 39	癸卯 *guǐmǎo* 40
甲辰 *jiǎchén* 41	乙巳 *yǐsì* 42	丙午 *bǐngwǔ* 43	丁未 *dīngwèi* 44	戊申 *wùshēn* 45	己酉 *jǐyǒu* 46	庚戌 *gēngxū* 47	辛亥 *xīnhài* 48	壬子 *rénzǐ* 49	癸丑 *guǐchǒu* 50
甲寅 *jiǎyín* 51	乙卯 *yǐmǎo* 52	丙辰 *bǐngchén* 53	丁巳 *dīngsì* 54	戊午 *wùwǔ* 55	己未 *jǐwèi* 56	庚申 *gēngshēn* 57	辛酉 *xīnyǒu* 58	壬戌 *rénxū* 59	癸亥 *guǐhài* 60

二、秦爵位名稱表（Qín Orders of Ranks and Titles）

等級 （Rank Number）	爵位名（Title）
20	徹侯（列侯）Chèhóu（or Lièhóu, Penetrating Lord）
19	關内侯（倫侯）Guānnèi Hóu（or Lúnhóu, Lord within the Passes）
18	大庶長 Dà Shùzhǎng（Great Leader of the Masses）
17	駟車庶長 Sìchē Shùzhǎng（Leader of the Masses Riding Quadrigae）
16	大良造 Dà Liángzào（Greater Leader of the Sovereign's Accomplished）
15	少上造 Shào Shàngzào（Lesser Leader of the Sovereign's Accomplished）
14	右更 Yòugēng（Marshal of the Conscripts of the Right）
13	中更 Zhōnggēng（Marshal of the Conscripts of the Center）
12	左更 Zuǒgēng（Marshal of the Conscripts of the Left）

（續表）

等級（Rank Number）	爵位名（Title）
11	右庶長 Yòu Shùzhǎng（Leader of the Masses of the Right）
10	左庶長 Zuǒ Shùzhǎng（Leader of the Masses of the Left）
9	五大夫 Wǔ dàfū（Fifth Grandee）
8	公乘 Gōngshèng（Royal Conveyance）
7	公大夫 Gōng dàfū（Grandee of the Realm）
6	官大夫 Guān dàfū（Grandee of the Bureaucracy）
5	大夫 Dàfū（Grandee）
4	不更 Bùgēng（Service-Rotation Exempt）
3	走馬（簪裊）Zǒumǎ（or Zānniǎo, Embellished Horse）
2	上造 Shàngzào（Sovereign's Accomplished）
1	公士 Gōngshì（Knight of the Realm）

三、秦行政層級列表（Qín Administrative Level）

等級 (Rank Number)	行政機構名稱 (Name of Administrative Agency)	下設官署 (Office under the Adminstrative Agency)
4	内史 Nèishǐ (capital area)，郡 Jùn (commandery/prefecture)	
3	縣 Xiàn (county)，道 Dào (county established in minority region)	尉官 Wèiguān (Commandant Office)；倉 Cāng (Granary Office)；司空 Sīkōng (Convict Labor Office)；田官 Tiánguān (Fields Office)；少内 Shàonèi (Storehouse)；庫 Kù (Armory Office)；亭 Tíng (Guard Station/ Police Station)
2	鄉 Xiāng (township/district)	
1	里 Lǐ (village/ward)	

四、秦度量衡列表（Qín Units of Measurement）

類別（Type）	名稱（Name）	換算（Conversion）	
容量單位 Volume	石 *dàn*/shí	1 石 =10 斗 1 石≈今 20 升	1 *dàn*=10 *dǒu* 1 *dàn* ≈ Now 20 L
	斗 *dǒu*	1 斗 =10 升 1 斗≈今 2 升	1 *dǒu*=10 *shēng* 1 *dǒu* ≈ Now 2 L
	升 *shēng*	1 升≈今 200 毫升	1 *shēng* ≈ Now 200 mL
	龠 *yuè*	1 升 =20 龠 1 龠≈今 10 毫升	1 *shēng*=20 *yuè* 1 *yuè* ≈ Now 10 mL

（續表）

類別（Type）	名稱（Name）	換算（Conversion）	
長度 Length	則　zé	1 則 =30 步 =180 尺 1 則 =41.58 米	1 *zé*=30 *bù*=180 *chǐ* 1 *zé*=41.58 m
	步　*bù*	1 步 =6 尺 1 步 =1.386 米	1 *bù*=6 *chǐ* 1 *bù*=1.386 m
	尺　*chǐ*	1 尺 =23.1 釐米	1 *chǐ*=23.1 cm
	寸　*cùn*	1 尺 =10 寸 1 寸 =2.31 釐米	1 *chǐ*=10 *cùn* 1 *cùn*=2.31 cm
面積單位 Area	頃　*qǐng*	1 頃 =100 畝 =4.61 公頃 1 *qǐng*=100 *mǔ*=4.61 hectares	
	畝　*mǔ*	1 畝 =240 平方步 =461 平方米 1 *mǔ*=240 sq. *bù*=461 sq. meters	
重量單位 Weight	石　*dàn*	1 石 =4 鈞 =120 斤 1 石≈ 30 千克	1 *dàn*=4 *jūn*=120 *jīn* 1 *dàn* ≈ 30 kg
	鈞　*jūn*	1 鈞 =30 斤 1 鈞≈ 7.5 千克	1 *jūn*=30 *jīn* 1 *jūn* ≈ 7.5 kg
	斤　*jīn*	1 斤 =248 ± 2 克	1 *jīn*=248 ± 2 g
	兩　*liǎng*	1 斤 =16 兩 1 兩≈ 15.5 克	1 *jīn*=16 *liǎng* 1 *liǎng* ≈ 15.5 *g*
	垂　*chuí*	1 垂 =8 銖 1 垂≈ 5.2 克	1 *chuí*=8 *zhū* 1 *chuí* ≈ 5.2 *g*
	銖　*zhū*	1 兩 =24 銖 1 銖≈ 0.65 克	1 *liǎng*=24 *zhū* 1 *zhū* ≈ *0.65 g*

五、官吏身份名稱列表（Title of Officials and Staff）

序號	名稱（Name）	序號	名稱（Name）
1	史 Shǐ（Scribe）	9	田嗇夫 Tián Sèfū（Bailiff of Farmland）
2	令史 Lìngshǐ （Prefectural Clerk/Scribe Director）	10	田官嗇夫 Tiánguān Sèfū（Bailiff of Fields）
3	獄史 Yùshǐ（Judiciary Scribe）	11	司空嗇夫 Sīkōng Sèfū （Bailiff of Convict Labor）
4	卒史 Zúshǐ（Accessory Scribe）	12	少内嗇夫 Shàonèi Sèfū（Bailiff of Revenue）
5	佐 Zuǒ（Assistant）	13	倉嗇夫 Cāng Sèfū （Bailiff of the Granary）
6	求盜 Qiúdào（Thief Catcher）	14	庫嗇夫 Kù Sèfū（Bailiff of the Armory）
7	校長 Xiàozhǎng（Constable）	15	鄉嗇夫 Xiāng Sèfū（Bailiff of Township）
8	官嗇夫 Guān Sèfū（Bailiff of the Office）	16	發弩嗇夫 Fānǔ Sèfū （Bailiff of the Crossbowmen）

（續表）

序號	名稱（Name）	序號	名稱（Name）
17	尉 Wèi（Commandant）	22	丞 Chéng （Assistant Magistrate/Vice Magistrate）
18	郡尉 Jùnwèi （Commandery Commandant）/ 郡邦尉 Jùn Bāngwèi （Commandery State Commandant）	23	令 Lìng（Magistrate）
19	騎校尉 Qí Xiàowèi （Cavalry Commandant）/ 騎邦尉 Qí Bāngwèi （Cavalry State Commandery）	24	太守 Tàishǒu（Commandery Governor）
20	司馬 Sīmǎ（Major）	25	御史 Yùshǐ （Imperial Counselor/Royal Scribe）
21	邦司馬 Bāng Sīmǎ（State Major）/ 郡司馬 Jùn Sīmǎ（Commandery Major）	26	丞相 Chéngxiàng （Chief Minister/Prime Minister）

六、秦刑罰名稱表 (Table of Qín Penalties)

死刑 （death penalty）	肉刑（corporal）/ 恥辱刑（humiliating punishment）	勞役刑（servitude punishment）	其他處罰 （others）
磔 *Zhé* （to carve into pieces）	腐 *Fǔ*/ 宮 *Gōng*（to castrate）	城旦 *Chéngdàn*/ 舂 *Chōng* （wall-builder/grain-pounder）	笞 *Chī* （to cane）
棄市 *Qìshì* （to cast away in the marketplace）	斬左趾 *Zhǎnzuǒzhǐ*（to sever the left foot）/ 斬右趾 *Zhǎnyòuzhǐ*（to sever the right foot）	鬼薪 *Guǐxīn*/ 白粲 *Báicàn* （to gather firewood for the spirits/ to sift white rice）	遷 *Qiān* （to banish）
	劓 *Yì*（to sever nose）	隸臣 *Lìchén*（bondsman）/ 隸妾 *Lìqiè*（bondwoman）	贖 *Shú* （to redeem）
	黥 *Qíng*（to tatoo signs on the forehead or cheekbone）	司寇 *Sīkòu*（robber-guard）	貲 *Zī*（to fine）
	髡 *Kūn*（to shave one's hair）	候 *Hòu*（watchman）	
	耐 *Nài*（to shave one's beard）		

附録二　練習答案
Appendix 2　Answers to All Practice Problems

第一組

廿三年。（23 壹）
卅二年，攻啟封。（32 壹）
卅三年，攻蔡、中陽。（33 壹）
卌五年，攻大壄（野）王。十二月甲午雞鳴時，喜産。（45 壹）
十六年，七月丁巳，公終。自占年。（23 貳）
廿五年。（32 貳）
廿六年。（33 貳）

第二組

簡號	第 1 欄	第 2 欄	第 3 欄	第 4 欄	第 5 欄	第 6 欄
51	己丑	己丑宿迣離涌西	丁亥治競（竟）陵	丙戌	乙酉	乙酉
52	庚寅	庚寅宿迣□□郵北	戊子	丁亥	丙戌	丙戌
55	癸巳	癸巳宿區邑	辛卯	庚寅	己丑	己丑
56	甲午	甲午宿競（竟）陵	壬辰	辛卯	庚寅	庚寅

第三組

南山有鳥，北山直（置）羅，念思公子，毋柰（奈）遠道何。安得良馬從公子，委纍□ 3
妻牽未嘗敢得罪，不中公子所也。公子從軍，牽送公子錢五百，謂公子自以買 6
牽非愛此也，直欲出牽之所者（著），以傅公子身也。公子從軍，牽送公子，回二百 8

第四組

死之。其吉日，戊寅、戊辰、戊戌、戊申。（189 貳）
凡癸爲屏圂，必富。（190 貳）
辰不可以哭、穿肄（肂），且有二喪，不可卜筭、爲屋。（191 貳）
辛卯壬午不可寧人，人反寧之。（192 貳）

凡【酉、午】、巳、寅、辛亥、辛卯問病者，代之。(193 貳)
月旬七日毀垣，其室日減。☐(195 貳)

第五組

夢繩外刖（劓）爲外憂，内刖（劓）爲中憂。夢見豆，不出三日家☐ 33
女子而夢以亓（其）帬被邦門及游渡江河，其占大貴人。夢見棗，得君子好言。34
夢伐鼓聲，必長衆有司，必知邦端。36

第六組

取車前草實，以三指竄（撮），入酒若鬻（粥）中，歙（飲）之，下氣。312
去黑子方　取稾（藁）本小弱者，齊（劑），約大如小指。取東〈柬〉灰一升，漬之。染稾（藁）本東〈柬〉315 灰中，以靡（摩）之，令血欲出。因多食葱，令汗出。極（恒）多取櫌（杻）桑木，燔以爲 316 炭火，而取牛肉剥之，小大如黑子，而炙之炭火，令温勿令焦，即 317 以傅黑子，寒輒更之。318

第七組

十六兩一斤。卅斤一鈞。四鈞一石。80
四萬六千八十朱（銖）一石。千九百廿兩一石。百廿斤一石。81

第八組

	第 1 欄	第 2 欄	第 3 欄
27	言毋作色	毋非（誹）旁（謗）人	吏有五善
28	☐富毋驕	安樂之所必戒	一曰忠信敬上
29	☐智必問	好言塞責	二曰精廉无旁（謗）
30	【毋】傷官事	上交不勝樂	三曰舉吏審當
31	多傷多患	下交不勝憂	四曰喜爲善行
32	毋多貰貣	安徐審祭（察）之	五曰龔（恭）敬多讓

第九組

敢再拜問……毋（無）恙?
爲報
……得毋（無）恙?

第十組

制曰：吏上請、對、奏者，皆傳牒牘數。節（即）不具而卻，復上者，令其牒牍毋與前同數。以爲恒。廷卒乙（嶽麓伍 185）
昭襄王命曰：置酒節（即）徵錢金及它物以賜人，令獻（讞），丞請出；丞獻（讞），令請出，以爲恒。●三（嶽麓肆 344）復用。（嶽麓肆 345）

第十一組

卅三年二月壬寅朔₌（朔朔）日，遷陵守丞都敢言之：令曰恒以Ⅰ朔日上所買徒隸數。問之，毋當令者。敢言之。Ⅱ 8-154
二月壬寅水十一刻₌（刻刻）下二，郵人得行。圂手。8-154 背

第十二組

一甲；卒歲，責之。有爲故秦人出，削籍，上造以上爲鬼薪，公士以下刑爲城旦。游士律。（《秦律雜抄》5）
當除弟子籍不得，置任不審，皆耐爲侯（候）。使其弟子贏律，及治（笞）之，貲一甲；決革，二甲。（《秦律雜抄》6）
廿六年正月丙申以來，新地爲官未盈六歲節（即）有反盜，若有敬（警），其吏自佐史以上去繇（徭）使私謁之（嶽麓伍 30）它郡縣官，事已行，皆以彼（避）陳（陣）去敵律論之。吏遣許者，與同辠。以反盜敬（警）事故，繇（徭）使不用（嶽麓伍 31）此令。十八（嶽麓伍 32）

第十三組

盜馬　爰書：市南街亭求盜才（在）某里曰甲縛詣男子丙，及馬一匹，騅牝右剽；緹復（複）衣，（《封診式》21）帛裏莽緣領褎（袖），及履，告曰："丙盜此馬、衣，今日見亭旁，而捕來詣。"（《封診式》22）

第十四組

實官户扇不致，禾稼能出，廷行事貲一甲。（《法律答問》150）
同母異父相與奸，可（何）論？棄市。（《法律答問》172）
"使者（諸）候（侯）、外臣邦，其邦徒及僞吏（使）不來，弗坐。"可（何）謂"邦徒""僞吏（使）"？徒、吏與偕使而弗爲私舍人，是謂"邦徒""僞使"。（《法律答問》180）
可（何）謂"宫均人"？宫中主循者殹。（《法律答問》187）

可（何）如爲“大誤”？人户、馬牛及者（諸）貨材（財）直（值）過六百六十錢爲“大誤”，其它爲小。（《法律答問》209）

第十五組

南陽户人荊不更蠻喜 A Ⅰ
子不更衍 A Ⅱ
妻大女子媐 B Ⅰ
隸大女子華 B Ⅱ
子小上造章 C Ⅰ
子小上造𤜱 C Ⅱ
子小女子趙 D Ⅰ☐
子小女子見 D Ⅱ☐　K49
私進令史相柏。12-853
徑廥粟＝（粟米）一石二斗半斗。卅一年十二月戊戌，倉妃、史感、稟人援出稟大隸妾援。
Ⅰ令史朝視平。Ⅱ 8-762
群志Ⅰ式具此Ⅱ中。巳（已）。Ⅲ 8-94

附録三　西方學者秦簡研究論著目録

Appendix 3　Western Scholarship on Excavated Texts of the Pre-Dynastic and Dynastic Qín State

This bibliography includes monographs, book chapters, journal articles, and a small number of unpublished conference papers documenting the achievements of Western scholarship on excavated texts of the pre-dynastic and dynastic Qín state. In addition, the bibliography also contains a few publications that focus on broader methodological issues related to editorial practices and uses of excavated material in general (see for example the articles by William Boltz, Imre Galambos, Enno Giele, Martin Kern, Rens Krijgsman, Mathias Richter, Thies Staack, and Xing Wen). For a comprehensive bibliography on early Chinese excavated texts, please see Paul R. Goldin's "Ancient Chinese Manuscripts: Bibliography of Materials in Western Languages," last updated on October 18, 2022.

To keep current on Western scholarship on early Chinese manuscripts, the reader is advised to refer to Goldin's bibliography, which is continuously updated, as well as the following journals that regularly publish articles on this topic:

- *Bamboo and Silk* (Vol.1, Issue 1, 2018-　)
- *Early China* (Vol.1, Issue 1, Fall 1975-　)
- *Journal of Chinese History* (Vol.1, Issue 1, 2016-　)
- *Asia Major* (Third Series, Vol.1, Part 1, 1988-　)

The best source for information on Ph.D. dissertations completed at North American universities on early excavated manuscripts is the ProQuest Dissertations & Theses Global database available at https://www.proquest.com/pqdtglobal.

Anicotte, Rémi. "Bidimensional Expressions of Fractions in Chinese." *Cahiers de linguistique Asie Orientale* 44.1 (2015), pp.36-56.

Barbieri-Low, Anthony J. *The Many Lives of the First Emperor of China.* Seattle: University of Washington Press, 2022.

Barbieri-Low, Anthony J. *Ancient Egypt and Early China: State, Society, and Culture.* Seattle: University of Washington Press, 2021.

Barbieri-Low, Anthony J. "Coerced Migration and Resettlement in the Qin Imperial Expansion." *Journal of Chinese History* 5.2 (2021), pp.181-202.

Barbieri-Low, Anthony J. "Copyists, Compilers, and Commentators: Constructing the Statutes and Ordinances of the Second Year and the Book of Submitted Doubtful Cases." *Asia Major* (3rd Series) 32.2 (2019), pp.33-56.

Barbieri-Low, Anthony J. "Intransigent and Corrupt Officials in Early Imperial China." In *Behaving Badly in Early and Medieval China.* Ed. N. Harry Rothschild and Leslie V. Wallace.

Honolulu: University of Hawai'i Press, 2017, pp.70-87.

Barbieri-Low, Anthony J., and Robin D.S. Yates. *Law, State, and Society in Early Imperial China: A Study with Critical Edition and Translation of the Legal Texts from Zhangjiashan Tomb No.247*. Leiden; Boston: Brill, 2015.

Barbieri-Low, Anthony. "Model Legal and Administrative Forms from the Qin, Han, and Tang and Their Role in the Facilitation of Bureaucracy and Literacy." In *Oriens Extremus* 50 (2011), pp.125-156.

Barbieri-Low, Anthony J. *Artisans in Early Imperial China*. Seattle: University of Washington Press, 2007.

Barbard, Noel. "The Nature of the Ch'in 'Reform of the Script' as Reflected in Archaeological Documents Excavated under Conditions of Control." In *Ancient China: Studies in Early Chinese Civilization*. Ed. David T. Roy and Tsuen-hsuin Tsien. Hong Kong: Chinese University Press, 1978, pp.181-213.

Behnke Kinney, Anne. "Husbands and Wives in Qin and Han-Dynasty Bamboo Legal Texts." *Journal of Chinese History* 6 (2022), pp.225-245.

Boltz, William G. "Textual Criticism and Early Chinese Manuscripts." In *Exploring Written Artefacts: Objects, Methods, and Concepts*. Ed. Jörg B. Quenzer. Berlin; Boston: De Gruyter, 2021, pp.845-864.

Boltz, William G. "Reading Early Chinese Manuscripts." *Journal of Chinese Studies* 47 (2017), pp.459-480.

Boltz, William G. "Why so Many Laozi-s?" In *Studies in Chinese Manuscripts: From the Warring States Period to the 20th Century*. Ed. Imre Galambos. Budapest: Institute of East Asian Studies, Eötvös Loránd University, 2013, pp.1-31.

Boltz, William G. "The Composite Nature of Early Chinese Texts." In *Text and Ritual in Early China*. Ed. Martin Kern. Seattle: University of Washington Press, 2005, pp.50-78.

Bréard, Andrea, and Constance A. Cook. "Cracking Bones and Numbers: Solving the Enigma of Numerical Sequences on Ancient Chinese Artifacts." *Archive for History of Exact Sciences* 74.4 (2020), pp.313-343.

Brown, Miranda, and Charles Sanft. "Categories and Legal Reasoning in Early Imperial China: The Meaning of *fa* in Recovered Texts." *Oriens Extremus* 50 (2011), pp.283-306.

Bujard, Marianne. "Daybooks in Qin and Han Religion." In *Books of Fate and Popular Culture in Early China: The Daybook Manuscripts of the Warring States, Qin, and Han*. Ed. Donald Harper and Marc Kalinowski. Leiden; Boston: Brill, 2017, pp.305-335. (Handbuch der Orientalistik IV, Volume: 33)

Caldwell, Ernest. *Writing Chinese Laws: The Form and Function of Legal Statutes Found in the Qin Shuihudi Corpus*. London; New York: Routledge, 2018.

Caldwell, Ernest. "Writing Chinese Laws: The Form and Function of Statutes in Qin Legal

Culture." Ph.D. thesis, University of Chicago, 2014. Advisor: Edward L.Shaughnessy.

Caldwell, Ernest. "Social Change and Written Law in Early Chinese Legal Thought." *Law and History Review* 32.1 (2014), pp.1-30.

Cao, Feng. "Value and Limitations: Significance and Value of Excavated Texts for Intellectual History." Tr. Jeffrey Keller. *Contemporary Chinese Thought* 44.4 (2013), pp.10-45.

Chapman, Jesse James. "The Rhetoric and Ritual of Celestial Signs in Early Imperial China." Ph.D. thesis, University of California, Berkeley, 2015. Advisors: Mark Csikszentmihalyi, Robert Ashmore, Michael Nylan.

Chemla, Karine. "How Do Excavated Manuscripts and Transmitted Canons and Commentaries Shed Light on Each Other? An Outlook from Mathematics." *Early China* 45 (2022), pp.269-301.

Chemla, Karine. "Numerical Tables in Chinese Writings Devoted to Mathematics: From Early Imperial Manuscripts to Printed Song-Yuan Books." *East Asian Science, Technology, and Medicine* 44 (2016), pp.69-121.

Chen, Kanli. "Time Notation and Methods for Timekeeping in the Liye Qin Strips." *Bamboo and Silk* 3 (2020), pp.74-96.

Chen, Songchang. "Reconsidering the Slip Order and Reading of the Yuelu Academy Qin *Wei li zhi guan ji qianshou* 爲吏治官及黔首 Manuscript." *Bamboo and Silk* 6 (2023), pp.61-77.

Chen, Songchang. "Two Ordinances Issued During the Reign of the Second Emperor of the Qin Dynasty in the Yuelu Academy Collection of Qin Slips." Tr. Christopher J. Foster. *Chinese Cultural Relics* 3.1-2 (2016), pp.288-297.

Chen, Wei. "'Event Calendars' in the Early Imperial Era: A Re-Assessment." *Bamboo and Silk* 1 (2018), pp.446-468.

Chen, Wei, and Cai Dan. "Yue Ren, Luli, and Anlu: the Tomb Occupant of Yunmeng Shuihudi Han Tomb No.77 and the Village Where He Resided." *Bamboo and Silk* 3 (2020), pp.232-274.

Chen, Wei. "A Few Issues Regarding the *Statutes on Corvée Labor* in the Yuelu Academy Qin Dynasty Bamboo Slip Manuscripts." Tr. Christopher J. Foster. *Chinese Cultural Relics* 2.1-2 (2015), pp.275-282.

Cheng, Shaoxuan. "Additional Notes on the Arrangement of the Qin Bamboo Manuscripts Rishu 日書 and *Saliu nian ri* 卅六年日 from Zhoujiatai 周家臺." *Bamboo and Silk* 3 (2020), pp.130-148.

Cook, Constance. "Divination in BCE China According to Newly-Recovered and Excavated Texts: An Overview." In *Handbook of Divination and Prognostication in China.* Part One: *Introduction to the Field.* Ed. Michael Lackner and Lu Zhao. Leiden; Boston: Brill, 2022, pp.61-122. (Handbuch der Orientalistik IV. 37)

Cullen, Christopher. "Calendars and Calendar Making in Qin and Han Times." In *Books of*

Fate and Popular Culture in Early China: The Daybook Manuscripts of the Warring States, Qin and Han. Ed. Donald Harper and Marc Kalinowski. Leiden; Boston: Brill, 2017, pp.278-304.

Cullen, Christopher. *The* Suànshùshū 筭數書 *"Writings on Reckoning": A Translation of a Chinese Mathematical Collection of the Second Century BC, with Explanatory Commentary.* Cambridge: Needham Research Institute, 2004. (Needham Research Institute Working Papers 1)

Elman, Benjamin A., and Martin Kern, ed. *Statecraft and Classical Learning: The Rituals of Zhou in East Asian History.* Leiden; Boston: Brill, 2010.

Emmerich, Reinhard. "Die Autorität eines chinesischen Dynastiegründers: Das Beispiel des Ersten Kaisers." In *Macht und Herrschaft transkulturell: Vormoderne Konfigurationen und Perspektiven der Forschung.* Ed. Matthias Becher, Stephan Conermann, and Linda Dohmen. Bonn: Bonn University Press, 2018, pp.225-268.

Emmerich, Reinhard. "Chinas Zweiter Kaiser in neuem Lichte?" In *Über den Alltag hinaus: Festschrift für Thomas O. Höllmann zum 65. Geburtstag.* Ed. Shing Müller and Armin Selbitschka. Wiesbaden: Harrassowitz, 2017, pp.53-87.

Fan, Guodong, and Luo Yunbing. "The *Sui* Chapter of the Zhoujiazhai *Daybook*." Tr. Shih-han Wang. *Bamboo and Silk* 4.2 (2021), pp.271-290.

Fodde-Reguer, Anna-Alexandra. "Divining Bureaucracy: Divination Manuals as Technology and the Standardization of Efficacy in Early China." Ph.D. thesis, University of Michigan, 2014. Advisor: Miranda D. Brown.

Fölster, Max Jakob and Thies Staack. "Collation in Early Imperial China: From Administrative Procedure to Philological Tool". In *Exploring Written Artefacts: Objects, Methods, and Concepts.* Ed. Jörg B. Quenzer. Berlin; Boston: De Gruyter, 2021, pp.889-912.

Fölster, Max Jakob. "The Imperial Collection of the Former Han and the Origins of Philology in China. A Study of the *Bielu, Qilüe* and *Hanshu Yiwenzhi*." Ph.D. thesis, Universität Hamburg, 2016.

Foster, Christopher J. "Introduction to the Peking University Han Bamboo Strips: On the Authentication and Study of Purchased Manuscripts." *Early China* 40 (2017), pp.167-239.

Foster, Christopher J. "Study of the *Cang Jie pian*: Past and Present." Ph.D. thesis, Harvard University, 2017. Advisor: Michael Puett.

Fuminori, Tsuchiguchi. "A Preliminary Study of 'Other Post Slips' from Liye Site J1." *Bamboo and Silk* 5 (2022), pp.132-158.

Galambos, Imre. "Chinese Character Variants in Medieval Dictionaries and Manuscripts." In *Exploring Written Artefacts: Objects, Methods, and Concepts.* Ed. Jörg B. Quenzer. Berlin; Boston: De Gruyter, 2021, pp.491-511.

Galambos, Imre. "The Myth of the Qin Unification of Writing in Han Sources." *Acta Orientalia Academiae Scientiarum Hungaricae* 57.2 (2004), pp.181-203.

Galambos, Imre. "The Evolution of Chinese Writing: Evidence from Newly Excavated Texts

(490-221 BCE)." Ph.D. thesis, University of California, Berkeley, 2002. Advisor: Jeffrey K. Riegel.

Gentz, Joachim. "Zur Deutung früher Grabbefunde: Das *Renzi pian* aus Shuihudi." In *Han-Zeit: Festschrift für Hans Stumpfeldt aus Anlaß seines 65. Geburtstages.* Ed. Michael Friedrich, unter Mitwirkung von Reinhard Emmerich und Hans Ess. Wiesbaden: Harrassowitz, 2006, pp.535-553. (Lun Wen: Studien zur Geistesgeschichte und Literatur in China 8)

Giele, Enno. "Materialität antiker Handschriften: Beispiele aus China." In *China and the World—the World and China: Essays in Honor of Rudolf Wagner.* Vol. 1: *Transcultural Perspectives on Pre-Modern East Asia.* Ed. Joachim Gentz. Gossenberg: Ostasien Verlag, 2019, pp.25-36. (Deutsche Ostasienstudien 37)

Giele, Enno. *Imperial Decision-Making and Communication in Early China. A Study of Cai Yong's Duduan.* Wiesbaden: Harrassowitz, 2006. (Opera Sinologica, 20)

Giele, Enno. "Signatures of 'Scribes' in Early Imperial China." *Asiatische Studien/Études Asiatiques* 59.1 (2005), pp.353-387.

Giele, Enno. "Using Early Chinese Manuscripts as Historical Source Materials." *Monumenta Serica* 51 (2003), pp.409-438.

Giele, Enno. "Early Chinese Manuscripts: Including Addenda and Corrigenda to 'New Sources of Early Chinese History: An Introduction to the Reading of Inscriptions and Manuscripts'."*Early China* 23/24 (1998-1999), pp.247-337.

Habberstad, Luke. "Notes on the 'Note' *(ji 記)* in Early Administrative Texts." *Early China* 45 (2022), pp.135-165.

Hafner, Arnd Helmut. "The State of Research in Early Chinese Legal History: A Review of Two Important Recent Annotated Translations in English." *Bamboo and Silk* 6 (2023), pp.103-157.

Harkness, Ethan Richard. "Good Days and Bad Days: Echoes of the Third-Century BCE Qin Conquest in Early Chinese Hemerology." *Journal of the American Oriental Society* 139.3 (2019), pp.545-568.

Harkness, Ethan. "A Parallel Universe: The Transmission of Astronomical Terminology in Early Chinese Almanacs." In *The Circulation of Astronomical Knowledge in the Ancient World.* Ed. John M. Steele. Leiden; Boston: Brill, 2016, pp.396-415. (Time, Astronomy, and Calendars 6)

Harkness, Ethan Richard. "Cosmology and the Quotidian: Day Books in Early China." Ph.D. thesis, University of Chicago, 2011. Advisor: Donald Harper.

Harper, Donald, and Marc Kalinowski, ed. *Books of Fate and Popular Culture in Early China: The Daybook Manuscripts of the Warring States, Qin and Han.* Leiden; Boston: Brill, 2017.

Harper, Donald. "Daybooks in the Context of Manuscript Culture and Popular Culture Studies." In *Books of Fate and Popular Culture in Early China: The Daybook Manuscripts of the Warring States, Qin and Han.* Ed. Donald Harper and Marc Kalinowski. Leiden; Boston: Brill,

2017, pp.91-137.

Harper, Donald. "The Zhoujiatai Occult Manuscripts." *Bamboo and Silk* 1 (2018), pp.53-70.

Harper, Donald. "Warring States Natural Philosophy and Occult Thought." In *The Cambridge History of Ancient China*. Ed. Micheal Loewe and Edward L. Shaugh nessy. Cambridge: Cambridge University Press, 1999, pp.813-884.

He, Youzu. "An Ancient Medical Formula on the Liye Qin Slips and the Detoxification Recipe of *dijiangshui* 地漿水 ('Earth Elixir') from the Later Ages." Tr. Georgijs Dunajevs. *Bamboo and Silk* 3.2 (2020), pp.275-293.

Herzog, Alexander. "Rechtsvorschriften und deren Ausführung in der Qin-Dynastie am Beispiel der Liye-Holztäfelchen." *Bochumer Jahrbuch zur Ostasienforschung* 42 (2019), pp.5-35.

Hsing, I-tien. "Qin-Han Census and Tax and Corvée Administration: Notes on Newly Discovered Materials." Tr. Hsieh Mei-yu and William G. Crowell. In *Birth of an Empire: The State of Qin Revisited*. Ed. Yuri Pines, Gideon Shelach, Lothar von Falkenhausen, and Robin S. Yates. Berkeley: University of California Press, 2014, pp.155-186.

Hsu, Mei-ling. "The Qin Maps: A Clue to Later Chinese Cartographic Development." *Imago Mundi* 45 (1993), pp.90-100.

Huang, Haijing, and Xing Wen. "'Graph-Book' and Layout Design in Ancient China." In *The History and Cultural Heritage of Chinese Calligraphy, Printing and Library Work*. Ed. Susan M. Allen, Lin Zuzao, Cheng Xiaolan, and Jan Bos. Berlin; New York: K. G. Saur, 2010, pp.135-146.

Hulsewé, A.F.P. "The Legalists and the Laws of Ch'in." In *Leyden Studies in Sinology*. Ed. W.L. Idema. Leiden; Boston: Brill, 1981, pp.1-22.

Hulsewé, A.F.P. *Remnants of Ch'in Law. An Annotated Translation of the Ch'in Legal and Administrative Rules of the 3rd Century B.C. Discovered in Yün-meng Prefecture, Hu-pei Province, in 1975*. Leiden; Boston: Brill, 1985. (Sinica Leidensia, 17)

Hulsewé, A.F.P. "The Wide Scope of *tao* Theft in Ch'in-Han Law." *Early China* 13 (1988), pp.166-200.

Hulsewé, A.F.P. "Weights and Measures in Ch'in Law." In *State and Law in East Asia: Festschrift Karl Bünger*. Ed. Dieter Eikemeier and Herbert Franke. Wiesbaden: Harrassowitz,1981, pp.25-39.

Jiang, Wen. "To Turn Soybeans into Gold: A Case Study of Mortuary Documents from Ancient China." *Bamboo and Silk* 2.1 (2019), pp.32-51.

Kalinowski, Marc. "The Understanding and Uses of the 'Day Court Diagram' in Qin-Han Hemerology and Calendrical Astrology." *Bamboo and Silk* 3 (2020), pp.294-343.

Kalinowski, Marc. "Hemerology and Prediction in the Daybooks: Ideas and Practices." In *Books of Fate and Popular Culture in Early China: The Daybook Manuscripts of the Warring States, Qin, and Han*. Ed. Donald Harper and Marc Kalinowski. Leiden; Boston: Brill, 2017, pp.138-206. (Handbook of Oriental Studies. Section 4 China, Volume: 33)

Kalinowski, Marc. "The Notion of 'Shi' 式 and Some Related Term in Qin-Han Calendrical Astrology." *Early China* 35 (2014), pp.331-360.

Kalinowski, Marc. "Divination and Astrology: Received Texts and Excavated Manuscripts." In *China's Early Empires: A Re-appraisal.* Ed. Michael Nylan and Michael Loewe. Cambridge: Cambridge University Press, 2010, pp.339-366.

Kalinowski, Marc. "Diviners and Astrologers under the Eastern Zhou: Transmitted Texts and Recent Archaeological Discoveries." In *Early Chinese Religion, Part One: Shang through Han (1250 BC-220 AD).* Ed. John Lagerwey and Marc Kalinowski. Leiden, Boston: Brill, 2009, Vol.1, pp.341-396. (*Handbook of Oriental Studies,* 4, 1)

Kalinowski, Marc. "Les livres des jours (rishu) des Qin et des Han: la logique éditoriale du recueil A de Shuihudi (217 avant notre ère)." *T'oung-Pao* 94.1-3 (2008), pp.1-48.

Kalinowski, Marc, and Phyllis Brooke. "The Xingde 刑德 Texts from Mawangdui." *Early China* 23/24 (1998-1999), pp.125-202.

Kalinowski, Marc. "Les traités de Shuihudi et l'hémérologie chinoise à la fin des Royaumes-Combattants." *T'oung Pao* 72/4-5 (1986), pp.175-228.

Kern, Martin. "Early Chinese Divination and Its Rhetoric." In *Coping with the Future: Theories and Practices of Divination in East Asia.* Ed. Michael Lackner. Leiden; Boston: Brill, 2018, pp.255-288.

Kern, Martin. "'Xi shuai' 蟋蟀［"Cricket"］and Its Consequences: Issues in Early Chinese Poetry and Textual Studies." *Early China* 42 (2019), pp.39-74.

Kern, Martin. "Methodological Reflections on the Analysis of Textual Variants and the Modes of Manuscript Production in Early China." *Journal of East Asian Archeology* 4.1-4 (2002), pp.143-181. Chinese translation: "方法論反思：早期中國文本異文之分析和寫本文獻之産生模式." In 尹佩霞、姚平、陳致編，當代西方漢學研究集萃，上古史卷. 上海：上海古籍出版社，2012, pp.349-385.

Kim, Kyung-ho, and Ming-chiu Lai. "An Overview of the Qin-Han Legal System from the Perspective of Recently Unearthed Documents." In *Routledge Handbook of Early Chinese History.* Ed. Paul Goldin. London; New York: Routledge, 2018, pp.386-404.

Kim, Moonsil Lee. "Food Distribution for the People: Welfare, Food, and Feasts in Qin/Han China and in Rome." In *Rulers and Ruled in Ancient Greece, Rome, and China.* Ed. Hans Beck and Griet Vankeerberghen. Cambridge: Cambridge University Press, 2021, pp.225-265.

Khayutina, Maria, ed. *Qin: The Eternal Emperor and His Terracotta Warriors.* Zürich: Neue Zürcher Zeitung Publishing, 2013.

Kim, Moonsil Lee. "Food Redistribution during China's Qin and Han Periods: Accordance and Discordance Among Ideologies, Policies, and Their Implementation." Ph.D. thesis, UC Santa Barbara, 2014. Advisor: Anthony J. Barbieri-Low.

Kim, Moonsil Lee. "Discrepancy Between Laws and Their Implementation: An Analysis of

Granaries, Statutes, and Rations during China's Qin and Han Periods." *Journal of the Economic and Social History of the Orient* 59 (2016), pp.555-589.

Kinney, Anne Behnke. "Husbands and Wives in Qin and Han-Dynasty Bamboo Legal Texts." *Journal of Chinese History* 6.2 (2022), pp.225-245.

Korolkov, Maxim. *The Imperial Network in Ancient China: The Foundation of Sinitic Empire in Southern East Asia.* Abingdon and New York: Routledge, 2022. (Routledge Studies in the Early History of Asia)

Korolkov, Maxim. "Arguing about Law: Interrogation Procedure under the Qin and Former Han Dynasties." *Études chinoises* 30 (2011), pp.37-71.

Korolkov, Maxim. "Calculating Crime and Punishment: Unofficial Law Enforcement, Quantification, and Legitimacy in Early Imperial China." *Critical Analysis of Law* 3.1 (2016), pp.70-86.

Korolkov, Maxim. "Legal Process Unearthed: A New Source of Legal History of Early Imperial China." *Journal of the American Oriental Society* 137.2 (2017), pp.383-391.

Krijgsman, Rens. "A Preliminary Analysis of Rhymed Passages in the Daybook Manuscripts." *Bamboo and Silk* 4 (2021), pp.291-335.

Krijgsman, Rens. "A Self-Reflexive Praxis: Changing Attitudes Towards Manuscript and Text in Early China." *Early* China 42 (2019), pp.75-110.

Kroll, J.L. "Notes on Ch'in and Han Law." In *Thought and Law in Qin and Han China: Studies Dedicated to Anthony Hulsewé on the Occasion of His Eightieth Birthday.* Ed. W.L. Idema and E. Zürcher. Leiden; Boston: Brill, 1990. pp.63-78. (Sinica Leidensia 24)

Kudo Motoo. "The Ch'in Bamboo Strip *Book of Divination* (*Jih-shu*) and Ch'in Legalism." *Acta Asiatica* 58 (1990), pp.24-37.

Kudo, Motoo. "Trends in Research on Qin Bamboo Strips in Japan (2011-2013)." *Bamboo and Silk* 1.1 (2018), pp.250-261.

Lackner, Michael, ed. *Coping with the Future: Theories and Practices of Divination in East Asia.* Leiden; Boston: Brill, 2018.

Lau, Ulrich, and Thies Staack. *Legal Practice in the Formative Stages of the Chinese Empire: An Annotated Translation of the Exemplary Qin Criminal Cases from the Yuelu Academy Collection.* Leiden; Boston: Brill, 2016.

Lau, Ulrich. "Qin Criminal Case Records of the Collection *Wei yu deng zhuang.*" *Oriens Extremus* 53 (2014), pp.139-192.

Lau, Ulrich, and Michael Lüdke. *Exemplarische Rechtsfälle vom Beginn der Han-Dynastie: Eine Kommentierte Übersetzung des* Zouyanshu *aus Zhangjiashan/Provinz Hubei.* Tokyo: Research Institute for Languages and Cultures of Asia and Africa (ILCAA), Tokyo University of Foreign Studies, 2012. (Study of Languages and Cultures of Asia and Africa Monograph Series 50)

Lau, Ulrich. "The Scope of Private Jurisdiction in Early Imperial China: The Evidence of Newly Excavated Legal Documents." *Asiatische Studien/Études Asiatiques* 59.1 (2005), pp.333-352.

Lau, Ulrich. "Die Rekonstruktion des Strafprozesses und die Prinzipien der Strafzumessung zu Beginn der Han-Zeit im Lichte des *Zouyanshu*." In *Und folge nun dem, was mein Herz begehrt: Festschrift für Ulrich Unger zum 70. Geburtstag.* Ed. Reinhard Emmerich and Hans Stumpfeldt. Hamburg: Hamburger Sinologische Gesellschaft, 2002, pp.343-395. (Hamburger Sinologische Schriften 8)

Lau, Ulrich. "Han-zeitliche Rechtsentscheidungen als Auskunftsquellen zur Stellung der Frau." In *Frauenleben im traditionellen China: Grenzen und Möglichkeiten einer Rekonstruktion.* Ed. Monika Übelhör. Marburg: Philipps-Universität Marburg, 1999, pp.37-59. (Schriften der Universitätsbibliothek Marburg 94)

Li, Jingrong. "The Nature and Function of the *Ernian lüling* Manuscript Unearthed from Zhangjiashan Han Tomb No.247." *Bulletin of the School of Oriental and African Studies* 82.1 (2019), pp.143-158.

Li, Jingrong. "The Governance of New Territories during the Qin Unification." *T'oung Pao* 108.1-2 (2022), pp.1-35.

Li, Jingrong, and Chen Songchang. "The Promulgation of Law in Qin and Western Han China." *Early China* 44 (2021), pp.393-418.

Li, Jingrong. "The *Ernian lüling* Manuscript." Ph.D. thesis, Universität Hamburg, 2014 Advisors: Michael Friedrich; Ulrich Lau.

Li, Kin Sum (Sammy). "Attaining Accuracy and Precision of Measuring Containers during the Qin Dynasty." *Journal of Chinese History* 6 (2022), pp.1-22.

Li, Kin Sum (Sammy). "To Rule by Manufacture: Measurement Regulation and Metal Weight Production in the Qin Empire." *T'oung Pao* 103.1-3 (2017), pp.1-32.

Li, Xueqin, and Wen Xing. "New Light on the Early-Han Code: A Reappraisal of the Zhangjiashan Bamboo-slip Legal Texts." *Asia Major* (3rd Series) 14.1 (2001), pp.125-146.

Liu Guosheng. "Some Remarks on the 'Five Conquerors' Passage of the Han Daybook from Kongjiapo." Tr. Ethan Harkness. *Bamboo and Silk* 3.1 (2020), pp.149-159.

Liu, Lexian. "Daybooks: A Type of Popular Hemerological Manual of the Warring States, Qin, and Han." In *Books of Fate and Popular Culture in Early China: The Daybook Manuscripts of the Warring States, Qin, and Han.* Ed. Donald Harper and Marc Kalinowski. Leiden; Boston: Brill, 2017, pp.57-90. (Handbook of Oriental Studies. Section 4 China, Volume: 33)

Liu, Lexian. "Comparison of the Chu and Qin Art of Selection: A Study Based on Excavated Documents." Tr. Xiaobing Wang-Riese and Hannah Rehle. In *Time and Ritual in Early China.* Ed. Xiaobing Wang-Riese and Thomas O. Höllmann. Wiesbaden: Harrassowitz, 2009, pp.153-168. (Asiatische Forschungen 153)

Liu, Tseng-kuei. "Taboos: An Aspect of Belief in the Qin and Han." Tr. John Lagerwey. In

Early Chinese Religion, Part One: Shang through Han (1250 BC-220 AD). Ed. John Lagerwey and Marc Kalinowski. Leiden; Boston: Brill, 2009, vol. II, pp.881-948. (*Handbook of Oriental Studies* , Section 4 China, Volume: 21/1)

Liu, Xinfang. "A Comparative Reading of the Shuihudi Qin Daybook 'Stars' Text and Ancient Theories on Astrological Divination." Tr. Roland Borsos. *Bamboo and Silk* 3.1 (2020), pp.97-129.

Liu, Yongping. *Origins of Chinese Law: Penal and Administrative Law in Its Early Development*. Hong Kong; New York: Oxford University Press, 1998.

Lo, Vivienne, and Gu Man. "Re-Envisioning Chinese Medicine: The View from Archaeology." In *Routledge Handbook of Chinese Medicine*. Ed. Vivienne Lo, Michael Stanley-Baker and Dolly Yang. London; New York: Routledge, 2022, pp.51-71.

Loewe, Michael. *The Men Who Governed Han China: Companion to a Biographical Dictionary of the Qin, Former Han and Xin Periods*. Leiden; Boston: Brill, 2004. (Handbuch der Orientalistik IV.17)

Loewe, Michael. *The Government of the Qin and Han Empires: 221 BCE-220 CE* Indianapolis and Cambridge, Mass.: Hackett, 2006.

Lu, Jialiang and Li Jing. "Summary of Research Published in 2015 on Bamboo and Wood Manuscripts from the Qin through Jin Dynasties." Tr. David J. Lebovitz. *Bamboo and Silk* 2.1 (2019), pp.104-140.

Lüdke, Michael. "Professional Practice: Law in Qin and Han China." Ph.D. thesis, Ruprecht-Karls-Universität Heidelberg, 2016. Advisors: Ulrich Lau, Rudolf Wagner.

Ma, Tsang Wing. "Categorizing Laborers: Glimpses of Qin Management of Human Resources from an Administrative Document from Liye, Hunan Province." *Early China* 44 (2021), pp.351-391.

Ma, Tsang Wing. "12.B Excavated Texts." In *Handbook of Ancient Afro-Eurasian Economies: Volume 1: Contexts*. Ed. Sitta Reden. Berlin; Boston: De Gruyter Oldenbourg, 2019, pp.529-556.

Ma, Tsang Wing. "Scribes in Early Imperial China." Ph.D. thesis, University of California, Santa Barbara, 2017. Advisor: Anthony J. Barbieri-Low.

Meyer, Dirk. *Philosophy on Bamboo: Text and the Production of Meaning in Early China*. Leiden; Boston: Brill, 2012.

Milburn, Olivia. "*Gai Lu*: A Translation and Commentary on a Yin-Yang Military Text Excavated from Tomb M 247, Zhangjiashan." *Early China* 33-34 (2010-2011), pp.101-140.

Milburn, Olivia. "Envisaging the Empire: Administrative Nomenclature and the Bureaucratic Worldview in Early Imperial China." *Omnes* 5.1 (2014), pp.76-113.

Mittag, Achim. "The Qin Bamboo Annals of Shuihudi: A Random Note from the Perspective of Chinese Historiography." *Monumenta Serica* 51 (2003), pp.543-570.

Miyake, Kiyoshi. "The Military History of Qin and the Composition of Its Expeditionary Forces." *Bamboo and Silk* 1.1 (2018), pp.121-151.

Miyake, Kiyoshi. "The Withdrawal of the Qin Army from Qianling Prefecture: From the End of Conquest to the Beginning of Occupation." Tr. Benjamin Daniels. *Bamboo and Silk* 5.1 (2022), pp.73-105.

Morgan, Daniel Patrick, and Karine Chemla. "Writing in Turns. An Analysis of Scribal Hands in the Bamboo Manuscript Suan shu shu 算數書 (Writings on Mathematical Procedures) from Zhangjiashan Tomb No.247." *Bamboo and Silk* 1 (2018), pp.152-190.

Nylan, Michael. "Notes on a Case of Illicit Sex from Zhangjiashan: A Translation and Commentary." *Early China* 30 (2005-2006), pp.25-45.

Park, Haeree. *The Writing System of Scribe Zhou: Evidence from Late Pre-imperial Chinese Manuscripts and Inscriptions* (*5th-3rd Centuries BCE*). Berlin; Boston: De Gruyter, 2016.

Pham, Lee-moi, and Kuan-yun Huang. "Newly Excavated Texts in the Digital Age: Reflections on New Resources." *Early China* 37 (2014), pp.551-565.

Pines, Yuri, Paul Goldin, and Martin Kern, ed. *Ideology of Power and Power of Ideology in Early China.* Leiden; Boston: Brill, 2015. (Sinica Leidensia 124)

Pines, Yuri, Gideon Shelach, Lothar von Falkenhausen, and Robin D.S. Yates, ed. *Birth of an Empire: The State of Qin Revisited.* Berkeley: University of California Press, 2014.

Poo, Mu-chou. "How to Steer Through Life: Negotiating Fate in the Daybook." In *The Magnitude of ming: Command, Allotment, and Fate in Chinese Culture.* Ed. Christopher Lupke. Honolulu: University of Hawai'i Press, 2005, pp.107-125.

Richter, Matthias L. "Manuscript Formats and Textual Structure in Early China." In *Confucius and the* Analects *Revisited: New Perspectives on Composition, Dating, and Authorship.* Ed. Michael Hunter, and Martin Kern. Leiden; Boston: Brill, 2018, pp.187-217. (Studies in the History of Chinese Texts 11)

Richter, Mathias. "Towards a Profile of Graphic Variation: On the Distribution of Graphic Variants within the Mawangdui Laozi Manuscripts." *Asiatische Studien/Études Asiatiques* 59.1 (2005), pp.169-207.

Sabattini, Elisa Levi, and Christian Schwermann. *Between Command and Market: Economic Thought and Practice in Early China*. Leiden; Boston: Brill, 2022.

Sanft, Charles. "Interacting with Text in Early China and Beyond." *Fragments* 8 (2019), pp.54-73.

Sanft, Charles. "Evaluating Swords: Introduction and Translation of a How-to Guide from the Han-Xin Period." *Early China* 39 (2016), pp.231-253.

Sanft, Charles. "Population Records from Liye: Ideology in Practice." In *Ideology of Power and Power of Ideology in Early China.* Ed. Yuri Pines, Paul Goldin, and Martin Kern. Leiden; Boston: Brill, 2015, pp.249-269.

Sanft, Charles. *Communication and Cooperation in Early Imperial China: Publicizing the Qin Dynasty.* Albany: State University of New York Press, 2014. (SUNY Series in Chinese

Philosophy and Culture)

Sanft, Charles. "Palaeographic Evidence of Qin Religious Practice from Liye and Zhoujiatai." *Early China* 37 (2014), pp.327-358.

Sanft, Charles. "Debating the Route of the Qin Direct Road (*zhidao*): Text and Excavation." *Frontiers of History in China* 6.3 (2011), pp.323-346.

Sanft, Charles. "Law and Communication in Qin and Western Han China." *Journal of the Economic and Social History of the Orient* 53/5 (2010), pp.679-711.

Sanft, Charles. "Environment and Law in Early Imperial China (Third Century BCE-First Century CE): Qin and Han Statutes Concerning Natural Resources." *Environmental History* 15.4 (2010), pp.701-721.

Sanft, Charles. "Notes on Penal Ritual and Subjective Truth under the Qin." *Asia Major* (3rd Series) 21.2 (2008), pp.35-57.

Sanft, Charles. "Edict of Monthly Ordinances for the Four Seasons in Fifty Articles from 5 C.E.: Introduction to the Wall Inscription Discovered at Xuanquanzhi, with Annotated Translation." *Early China* 32 (2008-2009), pp.125-208.

Selbitschka, Armin. "'I Write Therefore I Am': Scribes, Literacy, and Identity in Early China." Harvard Journal of Asiatic Studies 78.2 (2018), pp.413-476.

Selbitschka, Armin. "Sacrifice vs. Sustenance: Food as a Burial Good in Late Pre-imperial and Early Imperial Chinese Tombs and Its Relation[to] Funerary Rites." *Early China* 41 (2018), pp.179-243.

Shaughnessy, Edward L. "The Wangjiatai *Gui Cang*: An Alternative to *Yi jing* Divination." In *Facets of Tibetan Religious Tradition and Contacts with Neighbouring Cultural Areas.* Ed. Alfredo Cadonna and Ester Bianchi. Florence: Olschki, 2002, pp.95-126. (Orientalia Venetiana 12)

Shaughnessy, Edward L. *Chinese Annals in the Western Observatory: An Outline of Western Studies of Chinese Unearthed Documents*. Berlin; Boston: De Gruyter Mouton, 2019.

Smith, Adam D. "Early Chinese Manuscript Writings for the Name of the Sage Emperor Shun 舜, and the Legacy of Warring States-Period Orthographic Variation in Early Chinese Received Texts." *Early China* 40 (2017), pp.63-88.

Smith, Adam. "Writing at Anyang: The Role of the Divination Record in the Emergence of Chinese Literacy." Ph.D. thesis, University of California, Los Angeles, 2008. (Advisor: Lotharvon Falkenhausen; David Schaberg.)

Song, Jie. "The Master of Works (*sikong*) in the Armies of the Qin and Han Dynaties." Tr. Kai Filipiak and Eugenia Werzner. In *Civil-Military Relations in Chinese History: From Ancient China to the Communist Takeover.* Ed. Kai Filipiak. London and New York: Routledge, 2015, pp.47-62. (Asian States and Empires 7)

Song, Yunwoo. "The Emergence of the Notion of Predetermined Fate in Early China." *Dao* 18.4 (2019), pp.509-529.

Sou, Daniel Sungbin. "Crossing Borders: Control of Geographical Mobility in Early China." *T'oung-Pao* 103.3-4 (2018), pp.217-250.

Sou, Daniel S., Suh Sungbin, and Xu Chengbin. "Shaping Qin Local Officials: Exploring the System of Values and Responsibilities Presented in the Excavated Qin Tomb Bamboo Strips." *Monumenta Serica* 61 (2013), pp.1-34.

Sou, Daniel Sungbin. "In the Government's Service: A Study of the Role and Practice of Early China's Officials Based on Excavated Manuscripts." Ph.D. thesis, University of Pennsylvania, 2013. Advisor: Paul R. Goldin.

Staack, Thies. "'Drafting,' 'Copying,' and 'Adding Notes': On the Semantic Field of 'Writing' as Reflected by Qin and Early Han Legal and Administrative Documents." *Bamboo and Silk* 2 (2019), pp.290-318.

Staack, Thies. "Single- and Multi-Piece Manuscripts in Early Imperial China: On the Background and Significance of a Terminological Distinction." *Early China* 41 (2018), pp.245-295.

Staack, Thies. "Could the Peking University Laozi 老子 Really be a Forgery? Some Skeptical Remarks." Unpublished ms, 2017.

Staack, Thies. "The Neglected 'Backyard' of Early Chinese Manuscripts: How an Analysis of the Verso of Bamboo Slips can Enable the Reconstruction of a Manuscript Roll." Unpublished ms, 2017.

Staack, Thies. "Reconstruction of Early Chinese Bamboo and Wood Manuscripts: A Review (1900-2010)." CSMC Occasional Paper, No.5 (2016).

Sun, Wenbo. "Bureaus and Offices in Qin County-Level Administration: In Light of an Excerpt from the Lost *Hongfan wuxing zhuan* (*Great Plan Five Phases Commentary*)." *Bamboo and Silk* 1.1 (2018), pp.71-120.

Sun, Wenbo. "Shang Yang's Promotion of the County System and the County-Canton Relations: An Analysis Based on Official Titles, Salary Grades and the Size of the Employed Personnel." Tr. Yuri Pines. *Bamboo and Silk* 3.2 (2020), pp.344-388.

Sypniewski, Bernard Paul. "The Use of Variables in the *Remnants of Qin Law.*" *Monumenta Serica* 52 (2004), pp.345-361.

Thierry, François. *La ruine du Qin: Ascension, triomphe et mort du premier empereur de Chine.* Paris: Vuibert, 2013.

Thote, Alain. "Daybooks in Archaeological Context." In *Books of Fate and Popular Culture in Early China: The Daybook Manuscripts of the Warring States, Qin and Han.* Ed. Donald Harper, and Marc Kalinowski. Leiden; Boston: Brill, 2017, pp.11-56.

Tian, Tian. "From 'Clothing Strips' to Clothing Lists: Tomb Inventories and Western Han Funerary Ritual." Tr. David Sena. *Bamboo and Silk* 2.1 (2019), pp.52-86.

Tian, Tian. "Rethinking the Ancestral Shrines in the Early Empires." Tr. Zhou Wen. *Early China* 45 (2022), pp.167-201.

Tong, Chun Fung. "The Construction of Territories in the Qin Empire." *T'oung Pao* 107.5-6 (2021), pp.509-554.

Tong, Chun Fung. "Framing the Qin Collapse: Redaction and Authorship of the *Shiji* 史記 ." *Asiatische Studien/Études Asiatiques* 75.4 (2021), pp.901-946.

Tsuchiguchi, Fuminori. "A Preliminary Study of 'Other Post Slips' from Liye Site J1." *Bamboo and Silk* 5.1 (2022), pp.132-158.

Turner, Karen Gottschang. "Laws, Bureaucrats, and Imperial Women in China's Early Empires." In *Law and Empire Ideas, Practices, Actors.* Ed. Jeroen Duindam et al. Leiden; Boston: Brill, 2013, pp.63-85. (Rulers & Elites, Volume 3)

Valmisa, Mercedes. *Adapting: A Chinese Philosophy of Action.* New York; Oxford: Oxford University Press, 2021.

Venture, Olivier. "Recently Excavated Inscriptions and Manuscripts (2008-2018)." *Early China* 44 (2021), pp.493-546.

Venture, Olivier. "The Usage of *yu* 于 and *yu* 於 in Warring States Period and Han Dynasty and the Transmission and Writing Habit of Classical Texts." Tr. Leung Yuet Ngo. *Bamboo and Silk* 3.2 (2020), pp.206-231.

Venture, Olivier, and Marc Kalinowski. "A Review of Scholarship in Western Languages on Qin Bamboo and Wooden Documents." *Bamboo and Silk* 2 (2019), pp.160-192.

Wang, Haicheng. *Writing and the Ancient State: Early China in Comparative Perspective.* Cambridge: Cambridge University Press, 2014.

Waring, Luke. "Writing and Materiality in the Three Han Dynasty Tombs at Mawangdui." Ph.D. thesis, Princeton University, 2019. Advisor: Martin Kern.

Watson, Jesse David. "Paperwork Before Paper: Law and Materiality in Early Imperial China." Ph.D. thesis, University of California, Berkeley, 2019. Advisors: Michael Nylan, Nicolas Tackett, Mark Csikszentmihalyi.

Wu, Hu-Mei. "Reading Early Manuscripts with Transmitted Counterparts: Methodological Problems and Consequences for Textual History." Ph.D. thesis, University of Colorado, 2009. Advisor: Matthias L. Richter.

Xiao, Yunxiao. "Restoring Bamboo Scrolls: Observations on the Materiality of Warring States Bamboo Manuscripts." Tr. Carissa Fletcher. *Chinese Studies in History* 50.3 (2017), pp.235-254.

Xing, Wen. "Towards a Transparent Transcription." *Asiatische Studien/Études Asiatiques* 59.1 (2005), pp.51-60.

Xing, Wen. "Paleographic, Historical, and Intellectual History Approaches to Warring States Manuscripts Written on Bamboo Slips: A Review Article." *Early China* 33-34 (2010-2011), pp.233-262.

Yang, Soon-ja. "The Reconciliation of Filial Piety and Political Authority in Early China." *Dao* 16.2 (2017), pp.187-203.

Yang, Zhenhong. "The Statute Regarding the Remarriage of Women in the Qin Bamboo Slips in the Collection of Yuelu Academy (Vol.5) and the Scandal of Lao'ai." *Bamboo and Silk* 5 (2022), pp.106-131.

Yates, Robin D.S. "Dated Legislation in the Late-Qin State and Early Empire." *Asia Major* (3rd series), 35.1, pp.121-163.

Yates, Robin D.S. "The Fate of the Defeated: Qin's Treatment of Their Enemies." *Bamboo and Silk* 5 (2022), pp.1-72.

Yates, Robin D.S. "Female Commoners and the Law in Early Imperial China: Evidence from Recently Recovered Documents with Some Comparisons with Classical Rome." In *Rulers and Ruled in Ancient Greece, Rome, and China.* Ed. Griet Vankeerberghen and Hans Beck. Cambridge: Cambridge University Press, 2021, pp.156-192.

Yates, Robin D.S. "Evidence for Qin Law in the Qianling County Archive: A Preliminary Survey." *Bamboo and Silk* 1.2 (2018), pp.403-445.

Yates, Robin D.S. "The Changing Status of Slaves in the Qin-Han Transition." In *The Birth of Empire: The State of Qin Revisited.* Ed. Yuri Pines, Gideon Shelach, Lothar von Falkenhausen, and Robin D.S. Yates. Berkeley: University of California Press, 2013, pp.206-223.

Yates, Robin D.S. "Chinese Law, History of Eastern Zhou, Warring States (464-221 BCE), and Qin State and Empire (c.350-206 BCE)." In *The Oxford International Encyclopedia of Legal History.* Ed. Stanley N. Katz. Oxford: Oxford University Press, 2009, Vol.1, pp.406-412.

Yates, Robin D.S. "Law and the Military in Early China." In *Military Culture in Imperial China.* Ed. Nicola Di Cosmo. Cambridge: Harvard University Press, 2009, pp.23-44; 341-343.

Yates, Robin D.S. "Slavery in Early China: A Socio-cultural Perspective." *Journal of East Asian Archaeology* 3.1-2 (2002), pp.283-331.

Yates, Robin D.S. "Social Status in the Ch'in: Evidence from the Yün-meng Legal Documents. Part One: Commoners." *Harvard Journal of Asiatic Studies* 47.1 (1987), pp.197-236.

Yates, Robin D.S. "Notes on Ch'in Law." *Early China* 11-12 (1985-1987), pp.243-275.

Yates, Robin D.S., and Katrina C.D. McLeod. "Forms of Ch'in Law: An Annotated Translation of the *Feng-chen shih*." *Harvard Journal of Asiatic Studies* 41.1 (1981), pp.111-163.

Zhang, Chunlong, Toshitaka Okawa, and Akira Momiyama. "A Study of the Notched Slips of the Qin Dynasty Unearthed from Liye Town." Tr. Christopher J. Foster. *Chinese Cultural Relics* 2.3-4 (2015), pp.279-307.

Zhang, Zhaoyang. *A History of Civil Law in Early China: Cases, Statutes, Concepts and Beyond.* Leiden; Boston: Brill, 2022. (Legal History Library, Volume: 60)

Zhang, Zhaoyang. "Civil Laws and Civil Justice in Early China." Ph.D. thesis, University of California, Berkeley, 2010. Advisor: Michael Nylan.

Zou, Dahai. "Shuihudi Bamboo Strips of the Qin Dynasty and Mathematics in Pre-Qin Period." *Frontiers of History in China* 2.4 (2007), pp.632-654.

后 記

本書的編寫歷經整整三年。2019 年 11 月，本書編著者之一趙岩到美國羅格斯大學訪學，合作方爲羅格斯大學的陳光宇教授。陳教授曾與中國社會科學院歷史研究所的宋镇豪、劉源兩位先生編寫過《商代甲骨中英讀本》。該書面向國内外讀者，頗獲好評，已有法文、韓文等譯本。有鑒於此，陳教授提出了合作編寫一本《秦簡中英讀本》的想法，並在次年邀請了詹富國博士（Dietrich Tschanz）的加入，形成了本書的編寫團隊，開展了初步的編寫工作。2020 年 7 月，趙岩因疫情提前回到中國，編寫團隊在中美兩地開展工作，多次召開網絡視頻會議，到書稿形成時，收發電子郵件有一百多封。2022 年 11 月，本書完全定稿。三年裏，本書編寫團隊克服了很多困難，付出了很多心血。看到這本書稿現在的模樣，我們禁不住感慨編寫工作的不易。

本書的編寫過程，是我們反復閲讀秦簡材料的過程。我們始終保持對材料的敬畏，反復推敲字詞、語句的意義，努力體會秦簡創作者的本意，盡可能科學地呈現材料的内容並解讀。在盡可能引用學術界前沿考釋成果的同時，本書也不乏一些我們自己的思考。當然，限於材料自身的局限性及我們的認知能力，本書大概也不乏誤讀之處，還請方家批評指正。

我們要特别感謝本書的參考文獻的作者們。這些學者的整理、研究工作，推動了秦簡整理、研究的進步，本書的編寫離不開他們的著述的支持。本書附録部分羅列的一些西方學者及他們的著作，將秦簡及相關文獻介紹給中國以外的世界其他角落，使秦簡成爲人類共同的文化財富，要特别感謝他們爲中華文明的傳播作出的貢獻。他們的研究，也是我們完成本書英文部分編寫的動力和保障。還要感謝張世超教授和白軍鵬、袁開惠副教授等提供材料及指出初稿中的錯誤。還要感謝東北師範大學，提供了本書的出版經費，保證了本書的順利出版。還要感謝上海人民出版社的編輯們，本書的校稿工作頗爲複雜，涉及古文字、繁體字、英文等，編輯們的高效工作保證了本書的出版質量。

Postscript

In November 2019, Zhao Yan, a scholar on Qín bamboo slips and one of the authors of this book, went to Rutgers-The State University of New Jersey, United States, as a visiting scholar, with Professor Kuang Yu Chen as the faculty host. Professor Chen has previously published a book entitled *Reading of Shāng Inscriptions* (商代甲骨中英讀本) jointly with Song Zhenhao and Liu Yuan from the Institute of History of the Chinese Academy of Social Sciences. The book aims at introducing reading materials selected from inscriptions on excavated oracle bones and shells of late Shāng Dynasty (c.1300-1146 BCE). The book is bi-lingual, but the English-only version is also available. Since its publication, the book has been translated into French and Korean, and the Spanish translation is on-going. So, with that experience, Professors Zhao and Chen started to collaborate on the current book *Reading of Qín Bamboo Slips* (秦簡中英讀本). In a similar spirit, this book aims at introducing reading materials, selected from excavated bamboo and wood slips of pre-dynastic and dynastic Qín state (c.310-207 BCE). The book is bi-lingual and suited for readers whose primary language is either Chinese or English. Zhao left Rutgers in July, 2020, earlier than planned because of the COVID-19 pandemic. Before his departure, the collaboration was strengthened with a new member joining the team, Dr. Dietrich Tschanz, a scholar of classic Chinese and an avid reader of Qín history. After hundreds of emails and many zoom meetings, we are truly happy that we are able to bring this project to completion.

Tremendous progress has been made on the research of Qín bamboo slips during the past several decades. The work of so many scholars in the field has pushed our understanding in every aspect of Qín society and culture. Our thanks go to all scholars whose work is being cited directly or indirectly in this book. Without them, this book would not exist. Some western scholars and their works are listed separately in the appendix of this book, as they have been invaluable in our translation work. We would also like to thank Professor Zhang Shichao, Associate Professors Bai Junpeng, and Yuan Kaihui for providing materials and pointing out some errors in the initial draft of this book. We greatly appreciate the Northeast Normal University for providing the publishing funds of this book ensuring the smooth publication of this book. We would also like to thank the editors of Shanghai People's Publishing House. The proofreading work of this book has been quite complicated, involving ancient characters, traditional Chinese characters, English, translations, etc. The efficient work of the editors, particular Ms. Huang Yuting, ensures the quality of the publication of this book.

圖書在版編目(CIP)數據

秦簡中英讀本/趙岩,(美)陳光宇,(美)詹富國
編著.—上海:上海人民出版社,2024
ISBN 978-7-208-18284-4

Ⅰ.①秦… Ⅱ.①趙… ②陳… ③詹… Ⅲ.①簡(考
古)-介紹-中國-秦代-漢、英 Ⅳ.①K877.5

中國國家版本館 CIP 數據核字(2023)第 114278 號

責任編輯 黄玉婷 黄好彦
封面設計 陳緑競

秦簡中英讀本
趙 岩 [美]陳光宇 [美]詹富國 編著

出 版 上海人民出版社
(201101 上海市閔行區號景路 159 弄 C 座)
發 行 上海人民出版社發行中心
印 刷 上海盛通時代印刷有限公司
開 本 889×1194 1/16
印 張 17.25
插 頁 5
字 數 386,000
版 次 2024 年 1 月第 1 版
印 次 2024 年 1 月第 1 次印刷
ISBN 978-7-208-18284-4/K·3286
定 價 178.00 圓